Craig A. Everett, PhD
Editor

Child Custody: Legal Decisions and Family Outcomes

Child Custody: Legal Decisions and Family Outcomes has been co-published simultaneously as *Journal of Divorce & Remarriage*, Volume 28, Numbers 1/2 1997.

Pre-publication
REVIEWS,
COMMENTARIES,
EVALUATIONS . . .

"**T**his book . . . is a library MUST for all family therapists, attorneys and judges who work with families impacted by divorce. It contains up to the minute research on the wide range of issues surrounding the complex problems of divorce . . . , offering the clinician new insight or at least a reminder of what their clients are experiencing and the long range impact of the process.

This interesting and scholarly book will help professionals working in the field of divorce put some theory behind their interventions!"

Madge Homes, PhD
Psychology Coordinator,
Chapman University, Monterey

Child Custody: Legal Decisions and Family Outcomes

Child Custody: Legal Decisions and Family Outcomes has been co-published simultaneously as *Journal of Divorce & Remarriage,* Volume 28, Numbers 1/2 1997.

The *Journal of Divorce & Remarriage* Monographs/"Separates"
(formerly the *Journal of Divorce* series)*

Impact of Divorce on the Extended Family, edited by Esther Oshiver
Fisher*

Therapists, Lawyers, and Divorcing Spouses, edited by Esther Oshiver
Fisher and Mitchell Salem Fisher*

Divorce Mediation: Perspectives on the Field, edited by Craig A. Everett*

The Divorce Process: A Handbook for Clinicians, edited by Craig A.
Everett*

Minority and Ethnic Issues in the Divorce Process, edited by Craig A.
Everett*

Children of Divorce: Developmental and Clinical Issues, edited by Craig
A. Everett*

*Women and Divorce/Men and Divorce: Gender Differences in Separa-
tion, Divorce, and Remarriage,* edited by Sandra S. Volgy

*Marital Instability and Divorce Outcomes: Issues for Therapists and Edu-
cators,* edited by Craig A. Everett

*The Consequences of Divorce: Economic and Custodial Impact on Chil-
dren and Adults,* edited by Craig A. Everett

*Divorce and the Next Generation: Effects on Young Adults' Patterns of
Intimacy and Expectations for Marriage,* edited by Craig A. Everett

The Stepfamily Puzzle: Intergenerational Influences, edited by Craig A.
Everett

The Economics of Divorce: The Effects on Parents and Children, edited
by Craig A. Everett

Understanding Stepfamilies: Their Structure and Dynamics, edited by
Craig A. Everett

Divorce and Remarriage: International Studies, edited by Craig A. Everett

Child Custody: Legal Decisions and Family Outcomes, edited by Craig
A. Everett

These books were published simultaneously as special thematic issues of
the *Journal of Divorce & Remarriage* and are available bound separately.
Visit Haworth's website at http://www.haworth.com to search our online
catalog for complete tables of contents and ordering information for these
and other publications. Or call 1-800-HAWORTH (outside US/Canada:
607-722-5857), Fax: 1-800-895-0582 (outside US/Canada: 607-771-0012),
or e-mail getinfo@haworth.com

Child Custody: Legal Decisions and Family Outcomes

Craig A. Everett, PhD
Editor

Child Custody: Legal Decisions and Family Outcomes has been co-published simultaneously as *Journal of Divorce & Remarriage*, Volume 28, Numbers 1/2 1997.

The Haworth Press, Inc.
New York•London

Child Custody: Legal Decisions and Family Outcomes has been co-published simultaneously as *Journal of Divorce & Remarriage*, Volume 28, Numbers 1/2 1997.

The development, preparation, and publication of this work has been undertaken with great care. However, the publisher, employees, editors, and agents of The Haworth Press and all imprints of The Haworth Press, Inc., including The Haworth Medical Press and The Pharmaceutical Products Press, are not responsible for any errors contained herein or for consequences that may ensue from use of materials or information contained in this work. Opinions expressed by the author(s) are not necessarily those of The Haworth Press, Inc.

The Haworth Press, Inc., 10 Alice Street, Binghamton, NY 13904-1580 USA

Cover design by Thomas J. Mayshock Jr.

Library of Congress Cataloging-in-Publication Data

Child custody: legal decisions and family outcomes / Craig A. Everett, editor.
     p. cm.
     Published also as v. 28, no. 1/2, 1997 of the Journal of divorce & remarriage.
     Includes bibliographical references and index.
     ISBN 0-7890-0387-2 (alk. paper)
     1. Children of divorced parents–United States. 2. Children of divorced parents–United States–Family relationships. 3. Custody of children–United States. I. Everett, Craig A. II. Journal of divorce & remarriage.

HQ777.5.C424 1997
306.89–dc21

97-45974
CIP

INDEXING & ABSTRACTING

Contributions to this publication are selectively indexed or abstracted in print, electronic, online, or CD-ROM version(s) of the reference tools and information services listed below. This list is current as of the copyright date of this publication. See the end of this section for additional notes.

- *Abstracts of Research in Pastoral Care & Counseling*, Loyola College, 7135 Minstrel Way, Suite 101, Columbia, MD 21045
- *Applied Social Sciences Index & Abstracts (ASSIA) (Online: ASSI via Data-Star) (CD-Rom: ASSIA Plus)*, Bowker-Saur Limited, Maypole House, Maypole Road, East Grinstead, West Sussex RH19 1HH, England
- *CNPIEC Reference Guide: Chinese National Directory of Foreign Periodicals*, P.O. Box 88, Beijing, People's Republic of China
- *Current Contents . . . . see: Institute for Scientific Information*
- *Expanded Academic Index*, Information Access Company, 362 Lakeside Drive, Forest City, CA 94404
- *Family Studies Database (online and CD/ROM)*, National Information Services Corporation, 306 East Baltimore Pike, 2nd Floor, Media, PA 19063
- *Gay & Lesbian Abstracts*, National Information Services Corporation, 306 East Baltimore Pike, 2nd Floor, Media, PA 19063
- *Guide to Social Science & Religion in Periodical Literature*, National Periodical Library, P.O. Box 3278, Clearwater, FL 33767
- *Index to Periodical Articles Related to Law*, University of Texas, 727 East 26th Street, Austin TX 78705
- *Institute for Scientific Information*, 3501 Market Street, Philadelphia, Pennsylvania 19104. Coverage in:
    a) Social Science Citation Index (SSCI): print, online, CD-ROM
    b) Research Alerts (current awareness service)
    c) Social SciSearch (magnetic tape)
    d) Current Contents/Social & Behavioral Sciences (weekly current awareness service)
- *INTERNET ACCESS (& additional networks) Bulletin Board for Libraries ("BUBL"), coverage of information resources on INTERNET, JANET, and other networks.*
    - <URL:http://bubl.ac.uk/>
    - The new locations will be found under <URL:http://bubl.ac. uk/link/>.
    - Any existing BUBL users who have problems finding information on the new service should contact the BUBL help line by sending e-mail to <bubl@bubl.ac.uk>.
    The Andersonian Library, Curran Building, 101 St. James Road, Glasgow G4 0NS, Scotland

(continued)

- *MasterFILE*: updated database from EBSCO Publishing, 83 Pine Street, Peabody, MA 01960

- *Mental Health Abstracts (online through DIALOG)*, IFI/Plenum Data Company, 3202 Kirkwood Highway, Wilmington, DE 19808

- *Periodical Abstracts, Research II* (broad coverage indexing & abstracting database from University Microfilms International (UMI), 300 North Zeeb Road, P.O. Box 1346, Ann Arbor, MI 48106-1346), UMI Data Courier, P.O. Box 32770, Louisville, KY 40232-2770

- *Periodical Abstracts Select* (abstracting & indexing service covering most frequently requested journals in general reference, plus journals requested in libraries serving undergraduate programs, available from University Microfilms International (UMI), 300 North Zeeb Road, P.O. Box 1346, Ann Arbor, MI 48106-1346), UMI Data Courier, Attn: Library Services, Box 34660, Louisville, KY 40232

- *Population Index,* Princeton University Office Population, 21 Prospect Avenue, Princeton, NJ 08544-2091

- *Psychological Abstracts (PsycINFO)*, American Psychological Association, P.O. Box 91600, Washington, DC 20090-1600

- *Published International Literature On Traumatic Stress (The PILOTS Database)*, National Center for Post-Traumatic Stress Disorder (116D), VA Medical Center, White River Junction, VT 05009

- *Sage Family Studies Abstracts (SFSA)*, Sage Publications, Inc., 2455 Teller Road, Newbury Park, CA 91320

- *Social Planning/Policy & Development Abstracts (SOPODA)*, Sociological Abstracts, Inc., P.O. Box 22206, San Diego, CA 92192-0206

- *Social Science Citation Index. . . . see: Institute for Scientific Information*

- *Social Work Abstracts*, National Association of Social Workers, 750 First Street NW, 8th Floor, Washington, DC 20002

- *Sociological Abstracts (SA)*, Sociological Abstracts, Inc., P.O. Box 22206, San Diego, CA 92192-0206

- *Studies on Women Abstracts*, Carfax Publishing Company, P.O. Box 25, Abingdon, Oxon OX14 3UE, United Kingdom

- *Violence and Abuse Abstracts: A Review of Current Literature on Interpersonal Violence (VAA),* Sage Publications, Inc., 2455 Teller Road, Newbury Park, CA 91320

(continued)

SPECIAL BIBLIOGRAPHIC NOTES

related to special journal issues (separates)
and indexing/abstracting

❏ indexing/abstracting services in this list will also cover material in any "separate" that is co-published simultaneously with Haworth's special thematic journal issue or DocuSerial. Indexing/abstracting usually covers material at the article/chapter level.

❏ monographic co-editions are intended for either non-subscribers or libraries which intend to purchase a second copy for their circulating collections.

❏ monographic co-editions are reported to all jobbers/wholesalers/approval plans. The source journal is listed as the "series" to assist the prevention of duplicate purchasing in the same manner utilized for books-in-series.

❏ to facilitate user/access services all indexing/abstracting services are encouraged to utilize the co-indexing entry note indicated at the bottom of the first page of each article/chapter/contribution.

❏ this is intended to assist a library user of any reference tool (whether print, electronic, online, or CD-ROM) to locate the monographic version if the library has purchased this version but not a subscription to the source journal.

❏ individual articles/chapters in any Haworth publication are also available through the Haworth Document Delivery Service (HDDS).

Child Custody:
Legal Decisions
and Family Outcomes

CONTENTS

Introduction 1
    Craig A. Everett

LEGAL AND LEGISLATIVE ISSUES

Judges' Beliefs Dealing with Child Custody Decisions 3
    Leighton E. Stamps
    Seth Kunen
    Anita Rock-Faucheux

Evolution of Residential Custody Arrangements
    in Separated Families: A Longitudinal Study 17
    Richard Cloutier
    Christian Jacques

The Impact of an Educational Seminar for Divorcing Parents:
    Results from a National Survey of Family Court Judges 35
    Robert L. Fischer

Children Denied Two Parents: An Analysis of Access Denial 49
    Lynda Fox Fields
    Beverly W. Mussetter
    Gerald T. Powers

An Evaluation of the New Hampshire Child Support
    Guidelines: Using Social Science Research to Shape
    Child Support Policy 63
    Walter L. Ellis

CUSTODIAL ISSUES FOR FATHERS, MOTHERS AND GRANDPARENTS

Noncustodial Fatherhood: Research Trends and Issues   77
    Kris Kissman

Why Do Fathers Become Disengaged from Their Children's
Lives? Maternal and Paternal Accounts of Divorce
in Greece   89
    Charlie Lewis
    Zoe Maka
    Amalia Papacosta

Post-Divorce Father Custody: Are Mothers the True Predictors
of Adult Relationship Satisfaction?   119
    Steven T. Olivas
    Cal D. Stoltenberg

Stigma, Identity Dissonance, and the Nonresidential Mother   139
    Ginna M. Babcock

The Relation of State-Anger to Self-Esteem, Perceptions
of Family Structure and Attributions of Responsibility
for Divorce of Custodial Mothers in the Stabilization
Phase of the Divorce Process   157
    Solly Dreman
    Charles Spielberger
    Orly Darzi

Tendency to Stigmatize Lesbian Mothers in Custody Cases   171
    Kelly A. Causey
    Candan Duran-Aydintug

Young People's Attitudes Toward Living in a Lesbian Family:
A Longitudinal Study of Children Raised by Post-Divorce
Lesbian Mothers   183
    Fiona Tasker
    Susan Golombok

Grandparent Involvement Following Divorce: A Comparison
  in Single-Mother and Single-Father Families   203
          Jeanne M. Hilton
          Daniel P. Macari

Index   225

ABOUT THE EDITOR

Craig A. Everett, PhD, is a marriage and family therapist in private practice in Tucson, Arizona, and Director of the Arizona Institute of Family Therapy. In addition to his 20 years of experience in clinical practice, he was formerly President of the American Association for Marriage and Family Therapy. Dr. Everett's previous positions include Director of Family Therapy Training and Associate Professor at both Florida State University and Auburn University. He has been the editor of the *Journal of Divorce & Remarriage* since 1983 and is an editorial board member of six other professional journals.

Introduction

This volume has evolved into a unique collection of studies addressing both child custody decisions and the resultant outcomes for the children and their families. The majority of literature in the field of divorce and remarriage, published both in this book and elsewhere, has focused traditionally on aspects of personal divorce adjustment during and after the divorce. Here, the reader can begin to see the inextricable interactions between the legal and legislative systems and the resultant outcome patterns and dilemmas for families. For those of us who have worked many years with both systems, this volume only begins to touch the surface of these inherent struggles and the intrinsic flaws that continue to exist. However, it is hoped that these studies will focus and contribute to further ongoing research and clinical efforts.

The volume is divided into two sections. The first is a collection of papers which uniquely address aspects of the legal decision-making process as well as legislative guidelines that affect custody and post-divorce issues. Access to judges for research is rare and there are two papers here reporting judges' attitudes and another that follows residential custody patterns over two years. The legislative role is addressed in two studies which evaluate the evolution and enforcement of child support guidelines.

The second section of this volume focuses on a variety of post-divorce family patterns for fathers, mothers and grandparents. These studies identify issues both of custodial and non-custodial roles for fathers and mothers. Two papers address the role of lesbian mothers in post-divorce families and the final paper focuses on the post-divorce involvement of grandparents.

Craig A. Everett, PhD
Editor

[Haworth co-indexing entry note]: "Introduction." Everett, Craig A. Co-published simultaneously in *Journal of Divorce & Remarriage* (The Haworth Press, Inc.) Vol. 28, No. 1/2, 1997, p. 1; and: *Child Custody: Legal Decisions and Family Outcomes* (ed: Craig A. Everett) The Haworth Press, Inc., 1997, p. 1. Single or multiple copies of this article are available for a fee from The Haworth Document Delivery Service [1-800-342-9678, 9:00 a.m. - 5:00 p.m. (EST). E-mail address: getinfo@haworth.com].

Judges' Beliefs
Dealing with Child Custody Decisions

Leighton E. Stamps
Seth Kunen
Anita Rock-Faucheux

SUMMARY. State judges in Louisiana were surveyed with regard to their beliefs dealing with custody issues. These issues dealt with the relationships between custody decisions and maternal preference, maternal employment, remarriage, joint custody, sexual misconduct, and payment of child support. There was significant disagreement among judges regarding the impact of maternal employment and prior sexual misconduct on custody decisions. There was substantial agreement on the remainder of the issues. The judges exhibited a strong maternal preference. The majority chose neutral responses with regard to the impact of remarriage. There was opposition to joint physical custody. The majority of the judges were opposed to tying visitation to the payment of child support. *[Article copies available for a fee from The Haworth Document Delivery Service: 1-800-342-9678. E-mail address: getinfo@haworth.com]*

Leighton E. Stamps, PhD, and Seth Kunen, PhD, are Professors, and Anita Rock-Faucheux, MS, is a doctoral student in the Department of Psychology, University of New Orleans, New Orleans, LA 70148.

[Haworth co-indexing entry note]: "Judges' Beliefs Dealing with Child Custody Decisions." Stamps, Leighton E., Seth Kunen, and Anita Rock-Faucheux. Co-published simultaneously in *Journal of Divorce & Remarriage* (The Haworth Press, Inc.) Vol. 28, No. 1/2, 1997, pp. 3-16; and: *Child Custody: Legal Decisions and Family Outcomes* (ed: Craig A. Everett) The Haworth Press, Inc., 1997, pp. 3-16. Single or multiple copies of this article are available for a fee from The Haworth Document Delivery Service [1-800-342-9678, 9:00 a.m. - 5:00 p.m. (EST). E-mail address: getinfo@haworth.com].

JUDGES' BELIEFS DEALING WITH CUSTODY ISSUES

Over the last 30-40 years, sweeping changes have occurred in societal attitudes toward divorce. These changes have been reflected in the laws governing divorce and child custody as well as the increasing rate of divorce in the United States. Just as divorce laws have changed, making the divorce process much less difficult, there have also been dramatic changes in custody and visitation regulations. From the mid-1800s until the 1960s maternal preference was the general rule in the large majority of judicial custody decisions. During this period, the mother's "natural ability" to nurture the child was considered as a primary factor in custody decisions. This attitude was especially prominent with regard to younger children or children of the "tender years" (McCahey, Kaufman, Kraut, Gaffmer, Silverman, & Zett, 1986). This "tender years doctrine" developed in some jurisdictions through legislation and in others through judicial opinion (Derdeyn, 1978). Reference was frequently made in judicial opinions to the mother's "natural superiority" in caring for children. There was little public controversy regarding this attitude since it seemed to reflect current societal values (Jacob, 1988). Thus, from the second half of the nineteenth century until the 1960s, legal norms dictated that custody of the children belonged with the mother unless she was incapable of providing appropriate care, usually due to mental illness or moral depravity as evidenced by adultery (Folberg & Graham, 1979). A finding of inability to care for the children was usually related to a finding of fault in the divorce proceedings (Deleury & Cloutier, 1988).

In the 1950s and 1960s, there was a subtle shift in the tender years doctrine. Less emphasis was being placed on the mother's natural superiority in judicial opinions. The courts began to emphasize the "best interests of the child," giving more discretion to judges to consider other factors in custody decisions. In many jurisdictions, however, "the best interests of the child" standard was simply another name for the "tender years doctrine," since most courts held that maternal custody was usually in the best interests of the child. This shift in legal thought, however, did open the door for the consideration of other factors. This situation resulted in slightly more frequent assignment of custody to fathers although this shift was far from substantial (Jacob, 1988).

In the 1970s, social attitudes were again shifting. The preference for maternal custody was being questioned on several fronts. More and more women were entering the work force as both part-time and full-time employees. Thus, differences between men and women were being reduced with regard to their roles in the family. In addition, the feminist movement was questioning the assumption that only women could do housework and raise children. As a result, fathers were becoming more involved in the parenting process at the same time that divorce was becoming more frequent. During this period, two opposing positions were often considered by the courts when determining the best interests of the child with regard to custody decisions. According to the traditional viewpoint, children need a stable home life and therefore, should not be shuttled back and forth from parent to parent on a regular basis. The parent with whom the child lives should have almost exclusive responsibility for raising the child, with only occasional visitation with the non-custodial parent. This position, which had been used for many years, was supported by many mental health professionals at the time and was reflected in the book entitled *Beyond the Best Interests of the Child* by Goldstein, Freud, and Solnit (1979). Goldstein et al. also held that there should be no court ordered visitation and that visitation with the non-custodial parent should be solely at the discretion of the custodial parent. This publication was frequently cited in judicial decisions as well as in the legal literature (Jacob, 1988).

The alternative viewpoint, which was emerging in the 1970s, reflected parental desires for joint custody or a more equal sharing of time with, and responsibility for, the children following divorce. This position reflected changing middle class lifestyles as well as demands from fathers' groups for more active participation in the parenting process (Jacob, 1988). As a result of pressure from parents' groups, joint custody legislation was passed rather quickly, and with little public opposition, in the late 1970s and early 1980s. At this time, however, there was a great deal of opposition to joint custody in the legal and, to a lesser extent, the mental health communities. As indicated above, this approach ran counter to the opinions of some in the mental health community. There was also a great deal of resistance from both attorneys and judges since joint custody represented a dramatic change in the traditional approach to this situation. At the present time, all states have provisions for joint custody arrangements.

Since maternal custody is no longer automatic, and distinctions between maternal and paternal roles have been blurred over the past 30 years, judges must now consider a number of issues that were not relevant in the past. Since custody laws in all states are now gender neutral, maternal preference is no longer legally sanctioned. There has been a great deal of speculation in the legal literature, however, that many judges still have a preference for maternal custody (Jacob, 1988; Kelly, 1993). Judges are now expected to assess the potential impact of a number of factors on the child's post-divorce adjustment, such as maternal employment and remarriage. The judge must evaluate various aspects of parent-child relationships, such as whether children adjust better when living with the same sex parent or whether children are more obedient to mothers or fathers. The judge must determine whether prior sexual misconduct by a parent is relevant in custody determinations. The judge also tries to assure adequate financial support to meet the child's needs.

In approximately 90% of divorces involving minor children, the parents reach agreement on custody and visitation arrangements. This agreement is then approved by the court. In the remaining 10% of the cases, custody is contested and the decision must be made by the court. Judges are expected to make their decisions in the best interests of the child. This standard, however, gives judges a tremendous amount of discretion in making these decisions. Clearly, every judge has his or her own set of opinions and presumptions regarding custody issues which affect rulings. A number of authors have suggested that judges are frequently free to impose their own personal values due to the indeterminacy of the substantive standards that apply in custody decisions (Levy, 1985; Payne & Edwards, 1991; Schwarz, 1996). These conclusions are based primarily on case law. Case law itself, however, is not necessarily representative of judicial attitudes in general since published cases represent only a small minority of actual decisions. Several studies have attempted to assess judges' assumptions regarding some aspects of these situations through the use of judicial surveys. Stamps, Kunen, and Lawyer (1996) examined Louisiana judges' preferences for various custody and visitation arrangements, as well as some of the factors considered in these decisions. Stamps and Kunen (1996) completed a similar study of Quebec Superior Court judges.

The purpose of the present study was to further assess judicial assumptions regarding custody decisions. The assumptions that have been evaluated in the present research were reported in various legal publications as having been applied in certain custody decisions. The following assumptions were examined:

1. Maternal preference and the "tender years doctrine." Payne (1986), Weitzman (1985), and Santilli and Roberts (1990) have all suggested that maternal preference may still be the rule in many courts, with children of most ages, but especially when children of the "tender years" (young children) are involved, in spite of gender neutral custody laws in most jurisdictions. This type of presumption could be justified if the judge assumes that mothers are superior to fathers as parents, especially with younger children. Thus, given this assumption, it would be in the child's best interests to be placed in the custody of the mother.

2. Maternal employment may place a mother at a disadvantage in a custody proceeding. It has been suggested that some judges may feel that mothers who work outside of the home may not be able to provide a home life that is as stable as would a mother who is not employed (Nugent, 1994; Schwarz, 1996; Weitzman, 1985).

3. A remarried parent can provide a more stable home life than can a single parent. Weitzman (1985) indicated that many judges prefer to award custody to remarried parents rather than single parents, since a two parent home is more "normal."

4. Joint physical custody is usually not in the best interests of the child. According to this assumption, a near equal sharing of physical custody is too stressful on the child, since it forces the child to frequently move back and forth from home to home (Irving & Benjamin, 1991; Payne, 1986; Ryan, 1986).

5. Sexual misconduct prior to the divorce may be used in evaluating an individual's fitness as a parent. Although this factor has been eliminated from most legal standards for custody decisions, several authors believe that many judges still take it into consideration (Weitzman, 1985; Wexler, 1985).

6. Visitation by the non-custodial parent should be tied to the payment of child support. Although this is a very controversial proposal, it has been suggested by a number of authors as a method to increase compliance with child support orders (Hetherington, 1989).

METHOD

Subjects

The subjects in this study were state judges in Louisiana, including District Court judges and Family Court judges. The process of assigning custody cases to particular judges varies across jurisdictions in the state. In one jurisdiction, a Family Court exists to deal with all divorce and custody matters. In the remainder of the state these matters are heard in District Courts. In Louisiana, all state judges are elected.

In some of the District Courts, all divorce and custody matters are heard by a single judge or a small group of judges who only deal with family matters. Those judges are often designated according to seniority on the bench, with those having the least seniority assigned to these cases. In other Districts, the judges hearing all family matters rotate from time to time with each judge typically spending 6-18 months handling these types of cases. In still other District Courts, divorce and custody issues are dealt with by all judges in the District, each of whom also hears a variety of other civil and criminal cases. This is usually the situation in smaller, less populous jurisdictions.

Materials

A questionnaire was constructed to measure the judges' beliefs with regard to six issues dealing with custody decisions. These issues were discussed earlier. The judges were asked to respond to each question on a scale of 1-5, with 1 being Definitely Yes and 5 being Definitely No. The questions that were posed to the judges were as follows:

1. Do you believe that young children (six years old or less) adjust better when placed with their mothers than with their fathers ?
2. Do you believe that divorced mothers who do not work can provide a better home for their children than divorced mothers who do work?
3. Do you believe that children adjust better when placed with the same-sex parent (i.e., boys with their father and girls with their mother)?
4. Do you believe that children can adjust better if the custodial parent is remarried than if the custodial parent remains single?
5. Do you believe that boys exhibit more behavioral problems than girls?
6. Do you believe that children are more obedient to their mothers than to their fathers?
7. Do you believe that joint physical custody is in the best interests of the child (i.e., children spending several days per week with each parent)?
8. Do you believe that sexual misconduct by a parent prior to the divorce should be held against the parent in custody decisions?
9. Do you believe that visitation by the non-custodial parent should be tied to the payment of child support?

Questions 1, 3, 5, and 6 relate to various aspects of the maternal preference issue. The remaining questions each address individual issues.

Procedure

Questionnaires were sent to all 175 judges in District Courts and Family Courts where custody cases are heard. In a cover letter, judges were asked to complete the questionnaires if they were currently hearing custody cases or had heard custody cases in the past. The judges were given the option of completing the questionnaires anonymously. Eight weeks after the initial mailing, follow-up letters were sent to encourage additional responses.

Fifty-nine judges returned questionnaires, although not every judge responded to every item. Thirteen judges sent responses indicating that they do not hear custody cases. Three judges sent responses declining to participate, even though they hear custody cases.

Based on the original 175 questionnaires which were sent, the response rate for returned questionnaires was 34%. When the 13 judges who sent responses indicating that they do not hear custody cases were subtracted, the remaining total was 162. Using this total, the response rate was 36%. Of the remaining 64% who did not respond, it is assumed that some of these judges hear custody cases, but chose not to respond, while others do not hear custody cases at all. The 36% return rate is consistent with that reported in a similar study by Stamps, Kunen, and Lawyer (1996) for Louisiana judges and somewhat higher than the rate reported by Stamps and Kunen (1996) for Quebec judges.

RESULTS

The following is a tabulation of the judges' responses showing the number of judges who selected each alternative for each question.

	DEFINITELY YES 1	2	3	4	DEFINITELY NO 5
1.	7	24	24	1	1
2.	8	10	18	11	11
3.	1	3	32	12	10
4.	1	9	30	11	5
5.	1	6	24	16	12
6.	0	2	24	22	11
7.	6	9	12	10	21
8.	5	8	15	14	13
9.	2	11	6	9	30

A chi-square analysis was used to assess the degree of agreement among the judges for each question. Significant results for a given question indicate substantial agreement among judges. The results of these analyses yielded significant findings on seven of the nine questions. Nonsignificant results were found on questions two and eight, indicating a lack of agreement among the judges. Question two is, "Do you believe that divorced mothers who do not work can provide a better home for their children than divorced mothers who do work?" There was a fairly even distribution of responses ranging from Definitely Yes to Definitely No. Question eight is, "Do you believe that sexual misconduct by a parent prior to the divorce should be held against the parent in custody decisions?" Although the majority of responses were four's and five's (NO), there was a substantial number of judges selecting one's and two's (YES). The chi-square results are as follows:

Question

1. $X^2(4) = 48.53, p < .05$
2. $X^2(4) = 4.93$, N.S.
3. $X^2(4) = 52.18, p < .05$
4. $X^2(4) = 44.71, p < .05$
5. $X^2(4) = 26.85, p < .05$
6. $X^2(4) = 41.42, p < .05$
7. $X^2(4) = 11.14, p < .05$
8. $X^2(4) = 6.73$, N.S.
9. $X^2(4) = 40.45, p < .05$

DISCUSSION

The results of the current study indicate that there is substantial agreement among Louisiana judges regarding the majority of the issues covered in this project. In examining the results of this study, we attempted to evaluate the validity of the judges' attitudes by comparing them with the psychological literature. In evaluating individual questions, it can be assumed that a response of 1 or 2 represents an answer of Yes, while a 4 or 5 indicates an answer of No. A response of 3 indicates a neutral opinion on the issue.

The results of the first question indicate that judges continue to show a strong preference for the tender years doctrine. These results occurred in spite of the fact that Louisiana custody laws are gender neutral. A judge could justify this belief if he/she believed that mothers, in general, are better parents than fathers and that awarding custody to the mother is usually in the best interests of the child. Although mothers are the primary custodial parent in 85-90% of all divorces involving children, recent research indicates that children's overall adjustment following divorce does not differ between children living with custodial mothers versus custodial fathers (Hetherington, 1989).

The judges exhibited a great deal of disagreement regarding the issue of maternal employment. Of the 58 judges who responded to this item, 18 gave neutral responses, 18 gave Yes responses, and 22 gave No responses. A Yes response indicated that the judge agreed that divorced, non-working mothers provide a better home for their children than do working mothers. This issue has become highly relevant in recent years since over 40% of mothers of children under the age of six years are employed (U.S. Bureau of Census, 1993). If a mother is employed, especially if she has younger children, the children must be kept in day care or with some type of baby sitter during the mother's working hours. In assessing the impact of maternal employment, a judge must decide whether day care has a positive, negative, or neutral effect on the child.

The large majority of the psychological literature indicates that there are no long-term negative effects of day care for children older than one year of age, especially with high quality day care settings (Farran & Ramey, 1977; Belsky & Steinberg, 1978; Rogers, Langlois, Hubbs-Tate, & Reiser-Danner, 1994). There is even some evidence indicating that children who spend substantial time in day care derive benefits from the situation that are not seen in children without day care experience. For example, Field (1991) reported that the more time a child spent in high quality day care, the more positive were his or her peer interactions. There is also research indicating that low-income children who spend time in day care show better cognitive development than those who do not attend day care (Caughy, DiPietro, & Strobino, 1994). In addition, the literature indicates that there are no differences between home-reared and day care infants with regard to infants' attachment to their mothers (Farran & Ramey, 1977; Etaugh, 1980). A substantial proportion of the current sample of judges appears to believe that children exhibit better development when living with mothers who are not employed and therefore are not in day care. The literature, however, does not appear to support that position.

The third question dealt with the advisability of placing children with the same sex parent. The majority of the judges chose a neutral response to this item. Of the remaining judges, however, twenty-two chose No and only four chose Yes. Although there is limited research dealing with father custody situations, the available literature indicates that boys do adjust better when living with their fathers and girls show more positive adjustment when living with their mothers (Camara & Resnick, 1988; Emery, Hetherington, & DiLalla, 1984; Santrock & Warshak, 1986). In general, boys tend to be more active, assertive, and noncompliant than girls (Feingold, 1994). These behaviors tend to escalate when boys encounter parental conflict and inconsistent discipline, as is often the case prior to, during, and after a divorce (Guidubaldi & Perry, 1985; Hetherington, 1989). Since boys tend to be more compliant to fathers than mothers, fathers are better able to control a son's behavior than are mothers, thus facilitating the post-divorce adjustment for boys (Hetherington, Cox, & Cox, 1982).

The fourth question dealt with the issue of remarriage. The majority of the judges chose the neutral response. When a parent remarries, there is always additional stress and adjustment difficulties for the child. Typically, adjustment to a parent's remarriage will last at least several years or longer (McCombs, Forehand, & Brody, 1987). The type of adjustment problems that the child experiences vary according to the age and sex of the child. Younger children tend to be more flexible and usually adjust more rapidly than older children. Those in the early to mid-adolescent years usually have the most difficulty with a parent's remarriage (Bray & Berger, 1993). When living in mother custody homes, girls tend to have more adjustment difficulties following remarriage than boys. Girls, especially adolescents, often see the stepfather as intruding on the mother-daughter relationship. Daughters living with mothers in single parent homes often play a more powerful and responsible role than do daughters in two parent families. The introduction of a stepfather may put this role in jeopardy (Hetherington, 1989, 1993; Vuchinovich, Hetherington, Vuchinovich, & Clingempeel, 1991). Adolescent boys in single parent homes are often involved in at least somewhat negative, coercive relationships with their mothers (Baldwin & Skinner, 1989; MacKinnon, 1989). If, after an initial adjustment period to the remarriage, the boy is able to develop a positive relationship with his stepfather, the remarriage could have positive effects in the long run, lessening the son's negative attitude toward the mother (Hetherington, 1989, 1993; Vuchinovich, Hetherington, Vuchinovich, & Clingempeel, 1991).

The fifth question asked whether boys exhibit more behavioral problems than girls. The large majority of the judges gave No (28) or neutral responses (24), while only a small minority gave Yes responses (7). The judges' responses are not consistent with the literature which, as noted above, indicates that boys tend to be much more aggressive, non-compliant, and exhibit more behavioral problems than girls (Hetherington, Stanley-Hagan, & Anderson, 1989).

The sixth question asked whether children are more obedient to mothers than fathers. The majority gave No (33) or neutral responses (24), while only two answered Yes. These results are consistent with the literature which indicates that children tend to be more compliant with fathers than with mothers, whether in an intact family or a single parent family (Santrock & Warshak, 1986).

Question 7 asked if joint physical custody is in the best interest of the child. Approximately half of the judges gave negative responses, indicating that they are opposed to joint physical custody, while one fourth of the judges are in favor of this arrangement. The remaining judges chose neutral responses. These findings are consistent with previous reports that judges, for the most part, do not prefer joint physical custody arrangements (Hetherington, 1989; Payne, 1986). These prior reports were based primarily on opinion and speculation, and occasional references to appeals court decisions. The present study is one of the first to document this conclusion with actual data collected from judges. In 1983, the Louisiana legislature adopted a statute which made joint physical custody the preferred plan and created a rebuttable presumption that joint custody is in the best interest of the child. The "best interest of the child" doctrine still allows the judge to consider any factors which he/she may deem relevant to the decision. In spite of the apparent intent of this legislation, the discretion of the court still applies in deciding when and to what extent joint physical custody is in the best interests of the child. The psychological literature indicates that joint custody can be beneficial to the child in many situations. Children tend to show better adjustment following divorce when they have extensive contact with both parents. When parents are able to cooperate with regard to child care arrangements, the children benefit from the parental contact that is available through joint custody arrangements (Meredith, 1985; Phear et al., 1983). Fathers with joint custody tend to have a higher degree of involvement with their children and are more likely to pay child support than noncustodial fathers without joint custody (Grief, 1980; Meredith, 1985). There is also literature indicating that the parents show greater satisfaction with joint custody arrangements than do parents with sole custody plans (Melli, 1986). When continuing hostility is present between the parents, however, joint custody arrangements often exacerbate the child's problems and produce additional emotional distress for the child (Furstenberg & Cherlin, 1991; Johnston, Kline, & Tschann, 1989).

Question 8 asks whether sexual misconduct prior to the divorce should be held against a parent in custody decisions. The non-significant results for this question indicate that the judges exhibited wide disagreement regarding this issue. Approximately half of the judges gave No responses, while one-fourth of the judges gave Yes responses. The psychological literature indicates that parental sexual behavior should only be considered to the extent that it affects the child. If this type of activity is not having a negative impact on the child, it should not be a consideration in custody decisions (Emery, Hetherington, & DiLalla, 1984).

Question 9 asks whether visitation by the non-custodial parent should be tied to the payment of child support. Although this proposal is controversial, it has been suggested by several authors (Hetherington, 1993). As noted earlier, contact with both parents is important to the child's adjustment following a divorce. Anything that would reduce that contact could have a negative impact on the child.

Judges' attitudes and opinions can affect custody arrangements in a number of ways. The most obvious impact occurs in contested cases when judges must make the final decisions, based on the information presented to the court. Judges' attitudes can also have an impact on the process outside of the courtroom. Approximately 90% of custody matters are settled before the parents come to court (Hetherington, 1989). Although these arrangements are considered voluntary, the negotiations are always completed in the context of that which is permitted within the legal system, or as Mnookin and Kornhauser (1979) have described, "bargaining in the shadow of the law." A more accurate description might be "bargaining in the shadow of the law and the judges' presumptions." Thus, if an attorney is aware of the attitudes of a particular judge or a group of judges regarding various custody related issues, this information will have a very definite impact upon the advice that is given to the client with regard to decisions to either reach an agreement out of court or to continue through the legal process in which a judge will make the custody decision. It has even been suggested that a judge's known attitudes may affect the recommendations of court ordered custody investigations by mental health professionals, as the investigator sometimes tries to present recommendations which are consistent with a judge's previous rulings (Levy, 1985). Thus, the attitudes of a judge can reach well beyond the decisions which are actually made by the court in disputed cases (Maccoby & Mnookin, 1992).

REFERENCES

Belsky, J., & Steinberg, L. D. (1978). The effects of day care: A critical review. *Child Development, 49,* 929-949.

Camara, K. A., & Resnik, G. (1988). Interparental conflict and cooperation: Factors moderating children's post-divorce adjustment. In E. M. Hetherington

& J. D. Arasteh (Eds.), *Impact of divorce, single parenting, and step-parenting on children* (pp. 165-195). Hillsdale, NJ: Erlbaum.

Caughy, M. O., DiPietro, J. A., & Strobino, D. M. (1994). Day-care participation as a protective factor in the cognitive development of low income children. *Child Development, 65,* 457-471.

Deleury, E., & Cloutier, A. (1988). The child, the family and the state: Seeking to identify the best interests of the child. In M. E. Hughes & E. D. Pask (Eds.), *National themes in family law* (pp. 211-240). Toronto: Carswell.

Derdeyn, A. P. (1978). Child custody: A reflection of cultural change. *Journal of Clinical Child Psychology, 7,* 169-173.

Emery, R. E., Hetherington, E. M., & DiLalla, L. F. (1984). Divorce, children, and social policy. In H. W. Stevenson & A. E. Siegel (Eds.), *Child development research and social policy* (pp. 189-266). Chicago: University of Chicago Press.

Etaugh, C. (1980). Effects of nonmaternal care on children. *American Psychologist, 35,* 305-319.

Farran, D. C., & Ramey, C. T. (1977). Infant day care and attachment behaviors toward mothers and teachers. *Child Development, 48,* 1112-1116.

Feingold, A. (1994). Gender differences in personality: A meta-analysis. *Psychological Bulletin, 116,* 429-456.

Field, T. M. (1991). Quality infant day care and grade school behavior and performance. *Child Development, 62,* 863-870.

Folberg, J., & Graham, M. (1979). Joint custody of children following divorce. *University of California-Davis Law Review, 12,* 523-542.

Goldstein, J., Freud, A., & Solnit, A. (1979). *Beyond the best interests of the child.* New York: The Free Press.

Hetherington, E. M. (1989). Coping with family transitions: Winners, losers, and survivors. *Child Development, 60,* 1-14.

Irving, H. H., & Benjamin, M. (1991). Shared and sole-custody parents: A comparative analysis. In J. Folberg (Ed.), *Joint custody and shared parenting* (pp. 114-131). New York: The Guilford Press.

Jacob, H. (1988). *The silent revolution.* Chicago: University of Chicago Press.

Kelly, J. B. (1993). Current research on children's post-divorce adjustment. *Family and Conciliation Courts Review, 31,* 29-49.

Levy, R. J. (1985). Custody investigations in divorce cases. *American Bar Foundation Research Journal, 76,* 713-798.

Maccoby, E., & Mnookin, R. (1992). *Dividing the child.* Cambridge: Harvard University Press.

McCahey, J. P., Kaufman, M., Kraut, C., Gaffner, D., Silverman, M., & Zett, J. (1986). *Child custody and visitation law* (Vol. 2). New York: Matthew Bender.

Melli, M. S. (1986). The changing legal status of the single parent. *Family Relations, 35,* 31-35.

Mnookin, R. H., & Kornhauser, L. (1979). Bargaining in the shadow of the law: The case of divorce. *Yale Law Journal, 88,* 950-989.

Nugent, D. C. (1994). Judicial bias. *Cleveland State University Law Review, 1,* 40-63.

Payne, J. D., & Edwards, B. (1991). Cooperative parenting after divorce: A Canadian legal perspective. In J. Folberg (Ed.), *Joint custody and shared parenting* (pp. 275-296). New York: The Guilford Press.

Payne, J. D. (1986). *Payne's commentaries on the Divorce Act, 1985.* Don Mills, Ontario: Richard DeBoo Publishers.

Ryan, J. P. (1986). Joint custody in Canada: Time for a second look. *Reports on Family Law, 49,* 119-148.

Santilli, L. E., & Roberts, M. C. (1990). Custody decisions in Alabama before and after the abolition of the tender years doctrine. *Law and Human Behavior, 14,* 123-137.

Santrock, J. W., & Warshak, R. A. (1986). Development of father custody relationships and legal/clinical considerations in father-custody families. In M. E. Lamb (Ed.), *The father's role: Applied perspectives* (pp. 135-166). New York: Wiley.

Schwarz, E. R. (1996). When neutral doesn't really mean neutral: Louisiana's child custody laws–an attempt to erase gender bias in the name of neutrality. *Loyola Law Review, 42,* 365-390.

Stamps, L. E., & Kunen, S. (1996). Attitudes of Quebec superior court judges regarding child custody and visitation issues. *Journal of Divorce & Remarriage, 25,* 39-53.

Stamps, L. E., Kunen, S., & Lawyer, R. (1996). Judicial attitudes regarding custody and visitation issues. *Journal of Divorce & Remarriage, 25,* 23-37.

U.S. Bureau of Census. (1993). *Statistical abstract of the United States: 1994* (114th ed.). Washington, DC: U.S. Govt. Printing Office.

Weitzman, L. J. (1985). *The divorce revolution: The unexpected social and economic consequences for women and children in America.* New York: The Free Press.

Wexler, J. G. (1985). Rethinking the modification of child custody decrees. *Yale Law Journal, 94,* 757-820.

Evolution of Residential Custody Arrangements in Separated Families: A Longitudinal Study

Richard Cloutier
Christian Jacques

SUMMARY. This study tracks the evolution of three types of residential custody arrangements over a two-year period: sole custody with the father ($n = 59$ children), sole custody with the mother ($n = 69$ children), and joint custody ($n = 69$ children). Three categories of change were defined: (a) no change, (b) minor change (changing the schedule of visits or residence with a parent), and (c) major change (changing the custody arrangement). The results show that a minority of children changed custody arrangement but almost half the children in joint custody changed custody arrangements during the two years of the study. More young children and more girls changed custody arrangements, and girls who changed custody usually went to their mothers. With time, a type of polarization may be observed toward sole custody because there were less parents truly active in child custody at T2 than at T1. *[Article copies available for a fee from The Haworth Document Delivery Service: 1-800-342-9678. E-mail address: getinfo@haworth.com]*

Richard Cloutier, PhD, and Christian Jacques, MPs, are on the faculty, École de psychologie and Centre de recherche sur les services communautaires, Université Laval, Pavillon Charles DeKoninck, Cité Universitaire, Quebec, Canada G1K 7P4.

The present study was conducted while funded by a grant from le Conseil québecois de recherche sociale (CQRS RS-1706 089) and by the Social Sciences and Humanities Research Council of Canada (SSHRC A-498-89-0016).

The authors would like to thank Mark H. Freeston for comments on an earlier version of this article.

[Haworth co-indexing entry note]: "Evolution of Residential Custody Arrangements in Separated Families: A Longitudinal Study." Cloutier, Richard, and Christian Jacques. Co-published simultaneously in *Journal of Divorce & Remarriage* (The Haworth Press, Inc.) Vol. 28, No. 1/2, 1997, pp. 17-33; and: *Child Custody: Legal Decisions and Family Outcomes* (ed: Craig A. Everett) The Haworth Press, Inc., 1997, pp. 17-33. Single or multiple copies of this article are available for a fee from The Haworth Document Delivery Service [1-800-342-9678, 9:00 a.m. - 5:00 p.m. (EST). E-mail address: getinfo@haworth.com].

17

Child custody arrangements determine living conditions offered to the child following parental separation. In the context of parental separation, the adoption of a residential arrangement for the child is often treated as a definitive choice in contrast to the widely acknowledged reality of changing needs of all family members over time. Despite the crucial importance for children, we know little about how the family environment evolves in the years following parental separation. The present study may contribute to correcting the current lack of knowledge in describing the dynamic of the custody over time. Three principal forms of child residential custody may be identified following parental separation: sole custody by the mother, joint custody, and sole custody by the father. In Canada and the United States, more than 85% of children from separated families live in the custody of their biological mother. Although statistics on the prevalence of joint custody vary from one source to another and change over time, it is estimated that 10% of children from separated families reside alternately with their biological mother and their biological father. Finally, less than 5% of children from separated families are in the sole custody of their father (Careau & Cloutier, 1990; Emery, 1988; Greif, 1995; Haurin, 1992; McKie, Prentice, & Reed, 1983; Weitzman, 1985). These results mean that after separation, nine out of ten children live with only one of their biological parents and only see the other for more or less frequent and more or less regular visits. Several studies have observed a significant link between child adjustment after separation and the maintenance of quality relationships with both parents (Arditti, 1991, 1992a; Emery, Hetherington, & Dilalla, 1984; Lemieux & Cloutier, 1992; Peterson & Zill, 1986; Stephen, Freedman, & Hess, 1993; Wallerstein & Kelly, 1980). Some authors have observed that for many children, losing contact with a parent is perceived as the worst aspect of separation (Neugebauer, 1989; Santrok & Warshak, 1979). Children very rarely endorse their parents' separation and generally wish to maintain links with both parents (Barry, Cloutier, Fillion, & Gosselin, 1985; van Wamelen, 1990).

Even if some studies have identified that very strong contacts with the noncustodial parent can interfere with the quality of the relationship between the child and the custodial parent (Johnston, Kline, & Tschann, 1989), it seems that frequent, regular interactions with the noncustodial parent are associated with positive adjustment to parental separation (Amato & Rezac, 1994; Ferreiro, 1990; Hetherington, Cox, & Cox, 1978; Lowenstein & Koopman, 1978; Stewart, Schwebel, & Fine, 1986; Wallerstein & Kelly, 1980).

Despite the importance of maintaining a relationship with both parents, several studies report a decrease in the involvement of the noncustodial parent over time, in this case the father (Arditti, 1992b; Buehler, 1989; Seltzer & Brandreth, 1994). According to Weitzman (1985), the evolution of contacts between the noncustodial father and the child seem to be under the control of a decreasing spiral: the less frequent the child-father contact, the less the father is satisfied with the contact. Reciprocally, the less the father is satisfied with his contact with the child, the less he visits the child. This spiral results in a more or less total withdrawal of noncustodial fathers after several years (Buehler, 1989; Weitzman, 1985). However, the quality of the child-parent relationship appears to be a function of the degree of conflict rather than the custody arrangement: the ex-partners displaying the most bitterness also have the most conflictual relationships with their children, even when the children are in joint custody (Amato & Rezac, 1994; Arditti, 1992a; Arditti & Kelly, 1994; Donnelly & Finkelhor, 1992).

It has also been observed that the gender, both the child's and the parent's, has a significant influence on the quality of the parent-child relationship be it within a custody arrangement or in another (Amato & Rezac, 1994; Crosbie-Burnett, 1989; Healy, Malley, & Stewart, 1991), and it can be hypothesized that gender can also influence the evolution of the custody over time.

Few studies have tracked the changes in custody arrangements over time. Nevertheless, Drolet and Cloutier (1992), in a retrospective study based on the perception of the custodial parent, observed that the custody arrangement changed little in the years following separation. Their data indicated that half (50.1%) the families did not change custody arrangements; 32% made minor changes without changing the basic agreement. Only 17.9% of families changed the basic custody agreement. The authors noted that the changes were motivated more by parental needs and had the effect of decreasing contact between the child and the noncustodial parent.

In a longitudinal study, Kline, Tschann, Johnston, and Wallerstein (1989) reported descriptive data on the evolution of custody arrangements. Their data indicated that only 22% of children initially in joint custody and only 20% of children initially in the custody of their mothers changed custody arrangements. Combining all arrangements together (mother, father, joint, grandparents, etc.), only 25% of the children had changed after two years. Their data also indicate that the number of days/months spent with the least active parent decreased both with custody by the mother (6.8 to 4.2) and with joint custody (16.6 to 10.4). We note that with time, there is a form of polarization of custody toward residence with the principal parent.

Decisions surrounding the choice of a custody arrangement in the context of separation are very important for children because they determine the environment where they will be living and because the decisions have lasting consequences. Many questions remain unanswered. For example, which custody arrangement is most likely to change? Is change associated with the child's age and/or gender? How does the father's involvement change over time? The objective of the present study is to contribute to answering these questions by describing the nature of the changes observed in the family arrangement offered to the child after parental separation and to link these changes to the child's age and gender.

METHOD

The organization of custody arrangements in participating families was assessed twice with the same instruments two years apart in a repeated measures design. Numerically equivalent participation of three types of residential custody was sought to facilitate direct comparison of the residential custody arrangements: (a) families with sole custody by the father, (b) sole custody by the mother, and (c) joint custody. As far as possible, families were also recruited as a function of the target child's age in order to form a group of ten-year-olds and a group of fifteen-year-olds.

The contact time between the child and his parents is used to define the custody arrangement and is calculated only between the child and the father on the basis of the timetable for visits or on the basis of the joint custody residential cycle which could have a maximum duration of two years (1 year with mother–1 year with father). To calculate the contact time we considered the maximum duration covered by the timetable for visits or for the joint custody cycle, for example, seven days in the case where the father sees his child once a week, or 730 days where the custody is shared 1 year–1 year. Next, we considered the number of days when the child was in the father's custody during this period. The formula for calculating the contact time with the father may be assumed as follows: Contact time with the father = number of days with the father/number of days covered by the maximal duration of the timetable or custody cycle. A percentage is then obtained and it is possible to obtain the time with the mother by subtracting from 100 with the exception of children living in apartments at T2. For example, a child who spends two months with the father during the summer holidays has a contact time of 17.3% (63 days/365 days). A further example, a child who spends five days with the mother and two days with the father each week throughout the years has a contact time of 28.6% (2 days/7 days) with the father. The rest of the time is spent with the mother.

Following Drolet and Cloutier (1992), Careau and Cloutier (1990), and Maccoby, Depner, and Mnookin (1990), the parent with residential custody (contact time) more than 72% of the time on an annual basis was considered to have sole custody. On the other hand, families where the custody was between 27% and 73% for both parents were considered as having joint custody arrangements. A fourth custody arrangement was identified at the second evaluation (T2), namely, living in an apartment. This arrangement appeared with the passage of time as a result of some young adults leaving home. Living in an apartment is not a custody arrangement in the sense that the child now takes responsibility for himself or herself. On the other hand, it is also the result of an evolution in the custody arrangement and so it is interesting and useful to define this situation as a custody arrangement.

Subjects

Only families participating in both waves were retained in the present sample. Initially, 225 families participated at T1 but 30 did not complete the second wave, representing a 13.3% drop-out rate. At the initial evaluation (T1) of the 195 children whose families participated in both waves of the study, 29.2% of the children (57/195) lived with custodial fathers. The majority were boys (60%) and were among the fifteen-year-olds (72%). On the other hand, 35.4% (69/195) lived with custodial mothers of which the majority were girls (62%) and were among the fifteen-year-olds (75%). Finally, 35.4% (69/195) lived in joint custody arrangements. Boys (48%) and girls (52%) were equally represented and the majority were from among the ten-year-olds (70%). For the overall sample, there were almost equal numbers of girls (99) and boys (96) and 58.5% were in the fifteen-year-old bracket.

The mean ages of the 118 participating fathers, 153 participating mothers and 195 participating children were 40.7, 39.5 and 12.9 years respectively. On average, 5.8 years had elapsed since the separation (the concept of separation equally includes separations of legally sanctioned and common law or de facto marriages) of the participating families. The mothers had a mean education level equivalent to junior college and a mean income (including ex-partner's or current partner's income if applicable) between $26,000 and $30,000. The fathers had a mean educational level situated between junior college and university and a mean income close to the $36,000-$40,000 bracket. The voluntary participation of French-Canadian families was solicited in the Quebec City region. Data used in this study were collected in the context of a larger study on the child's adjustment to parental separation (Cloutier, 1987).

Questionnaire

The data were collected during a telephone interview. The interview was recorded with the prior approval of the participants (child, mother or father) who had been advised both that all information would be treated anonymously and confidentially and of their right to withdraw from the study at any time. The interviewers, previously trained in the telephone interview procedure, conducted data collection. They were randomly assigned to the families. Recordings of answers to open questions were subjected to content analysis with inter-judge agreements calculated at the beginning, middle, and end of the content analysis process. At each of these stages the percentage agreement varied from 93% to 96% at T1 and from 89% to 91% at T2. For information on visits between the child and the parent, the child's answer was used in the case of disagreement between the child and the parent.

RESULTS

Distribution of Children According to Custody Arrangement at T1 and T2

The distribution of the major custody arrangements (mother, father, and joint) at T2 was analyzed for change using the distribution at T1 as the theoretical distribution in a one-sample Chi squared test (Siegel, 1956). There was significant change over the two-year period, $X^2(2, n = 187) = 15.11, p = .001$. The percentage of children living in sole custody with their mother or in joint custody changed most. At T1, 35.4% (69) of the children lived with a custodial mother and this percentage increased to 44.1% (86) at T2 whereas the percentage of children in joint custody decreased from 35.4% (69) at T1 to 21.5% (42) at T2. Further, the percentage of children in the custody of their father hardly changed from T1 (29.2%: 57) to T2 (30.3%: 59). Finally, 4.1% (8) living in sole or joint custody at T1 were living in apartments at T2.

Types of Changes as a Function of Original Custody Arrangement

The previous data reflect the relative proportions of custody arrangements at T1 and T2 in the study but do not allow the quantification of changes in custody. In order to track the evolution in custody at a child-by-child level, three categories of change were defined: (a) no change,

(b) minor change, and (c) major change. Drolet and Cloutier (1992) ordered these three categories according to the magnitude of change going from the absence of change, via a minor change involving only a modification in the cycle of joint custody between parents or in the scheduling of visits by the visiting parent within the same custody arrangement, and finally to change considered major because the child changes residential arrangements.

We will now relate the types of change in custody arrangement after two years to the original custody arrangement while indicating the impact of the change on the contact time between parent and child. We will use the percentage of time spent with the father as sole indicator of time spent by the child with parents because the percentage of time spent with the mother may be calculated by subtracting time spent with the father from 100%. As the amplitude of change is linked to the contact time (minor versus major) it is foreseeable that the larger differences between T1 and T2 are among subjects who had undergone major change in custody. However, in order to provide a more accurate indication of the continuing degree of parent-child contact, the contact time at T1 was compared to T2 with paired t tests. The alpha level for the t tests was adjusted to $p = .005$ using the Bonferroni technique to control for Type I error.

The upper part of Table 1 presents the distribution of subjects as a function of the custody arrangement at the start of the study together with the category of change after two years (no change, minor change, and major change). These data will be presented for each custody arrangement successively.

Custodial father. As indicated in the first line of Table 1, among the 57 children with custodial fathers at T1, 27 (47.4%) did not change custody arrangement, 16 (28.0%) experienced minor change, and 14 (24.6%) experienced major change. Children who remained with custodial fathers spent close to 88% of their time with the father on both occasions (T1: $M = 87.4\%$ and T2: $M = 88.2\%$). Minor changes in custody did not result in a significant change in contact (T1: $M = 88.1\%$ and T2: $M = 91.3\%$, $t(15) = 1.89, p = .078$). As may be expected, children with custodial fathers at T1 who left this arrangement spent less time with their fathers at T2 (T1: $M = 86.4\%$ and T2: $M = 18.1\%$, $t(15) = -10.80, p = .0001$).

Custodial mother. As indicated in the second line of Table 1, of the 69 children with custodial mothers at T1, 22 (31.9%) did not change custody arrangement, 34 (49.3%) experienced minor changes, and 13 (18.8%) experienced major change. Among children who did not change custody arrangement, the contact time with the father remained stable between T1 ($M = 5.7\%$) and T2 ($M = 4.9\%$). Further, minor changes did not signifi-

TABLE 1. Distribution of Children as a Function of Initial Custody and Category of Change After Two Years

		Change		
Custody Arrangement		None	Minor	Major
(Total Chi square[a])				
	n			
Father	57	27	16	14
Mother	69	22	34	13
Joint	69	24	13	32
Total	195	73	63	59

(Partition of Total Chi square[b])

Subtable

		None	Minor	Major
a	Father	27	16	14
	Mother	22	34	13
	Joint	24	13	32
b	Father	27	16	14
	Mother	22	34	13
	Joint	24	13	32
c	Father	27	16	14
	Mother	22	34	13
	Joint	24	13	32
d	Father	27	16	14
	Mother	22	34	13
	Joint	24	13	32

Note. The borders define the cells used in the comparison.
[a] Total Chi square: $X^2(4, N = 195) = 22.05, p = .0000$.
[b] Chi square for subtable *a*: $X^2(1, n = 99) = 5.38, p = .02$.
Chi square for subtable *b*: $X^2(1, n = 126) = 0.61, p = .436$.
Chi square for subtable *c*: $X^2(1, n = 136) = 2.56, p = .110$.
Chi square for subtable *d*: $X^2(1, N = 195) = 13.15, p = .000$.

cantly modify the contact time between father and child (T1: M = 7.2% and T2: M = 7.7%). Finally, children who had left custodial mothers significantly increased time with their fathers at T2 (T1: M = 11.1% and T2: M = 45.7%, $t(12)$ = 3.59, p = .0037). Note that despite the significant increase, children who left custody with the mother still only spent a mean of 45.7% of their time with their fathers. As we will see in Table 2, the smaller increase in contact time with the father may be explained by the fact that several children (5/13) went to live in an apartment.

Joint custody. The third line of Table 1 shows that among the 69 children in joint custody at T1, 24 (34.8%) did not change custody arrangement, compared to 13 (18.8%) who experienced minor changes before T2, and 32 (46.4%) experienced major changes. For children who did not change custody, the contact time with the father was close to 48% for both waves of the study (T1: M = 47.5% and T2: M = 48.2%). The minor changes did not significantly increase mean contact time between father and child (T1: M = 40.0% and T2: M = 49.1%). Finally, moving from one custody arrangement to another did not significantly change the mean contact between father and child (T1: M = 46.7% and T2: M = 38.1%, $t(31)$ = -1.50, p = .14); the increase among those who went to live with their fathers (11) was cancelled out by those who went to live with their mothers (20).

TABLE 2. Distribution of Children According to Custody Arrangement at T2 Based on Initial Custody Arrangement (T1)

Custody Arrangement	Time 1	Time 2			
		Father	Mother	Joint	Apartment
Father	57	43	10	2	2
Girls	*23*	*14*	*7*	*1*	*1*
Boys	*34*	*29*	*3*	*1*	*1*
Mother	69	5	56	3	5
Girls	*43*	*1*	*36*	*2*	*4*
Boys	*26*	*4*	*20*	*1*	*1*
Joint	69	11	20	37	1
Girls	*33*	*5*	*13*	*15*	*0*
Boys	*36*	*6*	*7*	*22*	*1*

Note. N = 195 children.

Age and change. For the overall sample, more children from the ten-year-old group (38.3%) changed custody arrangements than from the fifteen-year-old group (24.6%), $X^2(1, N = 195) = 4.22, p = .04$. The difference between the age groups is even clearer when the children going to live in apartments at T2 are excluded from the comparison: the number changing custody in the fifteen-year-old group drops to 18.9%, $X^2(1, N = 187) = 8.72, p = .003$. This trend is related to the fact that 54.2% of the changes in custody arrangements were among children who were in joint custody at T1 and that there were more children initially in joint custody in the ten-year-old group (69.6%) than children in other custody arrangements (26.2%), $X^2(1, N = 195) = 34.54, p = .0000$.

Sex and change. Among the children who experienced major change and where the father was involved in custody at T1 ($n = 46$) (i.e., those with custodial fathers or in joint custody), girls (27) changed custody significantly more than boys (19), $X^2(1, n = 46) = 3.78, p = .052$, when the observed frequencies of each gender (in sole custody by the father or joint custody) are compared to frequencies at T1. The frequencies at T1 are then considered as theoretical frequencies (girls: 44.4% and boys: 55.6%) in a single sample Chi-squared test. The link between major change and the inversion of the custodial parent's sex is not found among boys and their mothers because among children whose mother was involved in custody at T1 (i.e., those with custodial mother or in joint custody) there were no more changes among boys (20) than among girls (25) when compared to the expected frequencies from the initial distribution (boys: 49.9% and girls: 55.1%).

Which custody arrangement was most likely to change? The three categories of change (no change, minor, and major) are not distributed proportionally across the three custody arrangements: a X^2 indicated a significant difference between type of custody arrangement at T1 and degree of change at T2 (see Table 1). To interpret this result the frequency distributions were partitioned into four subtables (Reynolds, 1977). Partitioning is a statistical procedure that breaks down the global effect identified by the X^2 into independent subgroups of cells that are then subjected to independent X^2 comparisons. Subtable *a* of Table 1, as indicated by the borders, shows a significant difference between the relative proportions of minor change and no change among custodial fathers and custodial mothers: among custodial fathers there was a higher proportion of no change (62.8% vs. 37.2%) whereas among custodial mothers there was a higher proportion of minor change (60.7% vs. 39.3%). Subtables *b* and *c* of Table 1 did not contribute to the overall effect. Subtable *d* of Table 1 contributed most to the overall effect: there were more major changes (changes of custody arrangement) among the joint custody families (46.4%) than among the combined sole custody families (21.4%). Custody by the father then seemed to be the most stable arrangement, whereas custody by the mother was the arrangement most likely to undergo minor change, and joint custody arrangements were most likely to undergo major changes.

Direction of Changes in Custody Arrangements

The results presented until now concern the types of changes observed according to the initial custody arrangement. We now look only at major changes in the custody arrangement. Two questions will be answered. First, where do children experiencing major changes in custodial arrangement end up at T2? Second, do major changes from T1 to T2 bring parents and children closer together or separate them further? The direction of change will be examined successively for the three types of custody at T1 (Table 2). Data about children living in apartments at T2 will also be presented.

Custodial father. Among the 57 families who initially opted for custody with the father, 14 (24.6%) changed custody arrangements at T2. Only five of the 34 boys (14.7%) left custody with their fathers compared to nine of the 23 girls (39.1%), $X^2(1, N = 57) = 4.417, p = .0361$. Most of the children who left sole custody with the father went to sole custody with the mother (71.4%: 10/14) and most of these were girls (70%: 7/10). One boy and one girl went to joint custody and one boy and one girl went to live in an apartment. These data suggest that for custody with the father, the changes especially involve girls who went to their mothers.

Custodial mother. Among families who opted for sole custody with the mother at T1, only 13 of the 69 children (18.8%) changed custody. Among the 13 children who changed, five (38.5%) went to their fathers, five (38.5%) went to live in an apartment and three (23%) went to joint custody. It was mostly boys who went to their fathers (4/5), mostly girls who went into an apartment (4/5) and two girls and one boy went to joint custody. The low proportion of children who left sole custody with the mother went mostly to their fathers if they were boys or mostly into an apartment if they were girls.

Joint custody. Among the 69 children who were living in joint custody at T1, 32 (46.4%) had changed custody arrangements at T2 (major change). Almost two out of three families (20/32: 62.5%) that changed opted for custody by the mother and in the majority of cases it was the girls who went to their mothers (13/20: 65%). In one out of three families, children went to their fathers (6 boys and 5 girls). Finally, one boy went to live in an apartment. Proportionally more girls went to their mothers than boys.

Apartment living. Among the eight children who were living in an apartment at T2, five were girls and three were boys. Seven were from sole custody: five (1 boy and 4 girls) were with their mothers at T1, two (1 boy and 1 girl) were with fathers, and one boy was in joint custody. All were from the fifteen-year-old group.

The evolution of the custody arrangement shows a polarization toward a single custodial parent. Of the 59 children who changed custody arrangements, 46 (78%) went to sole custody at T2 and 31 (67.4%: 31/46) came from joint custody. On the other hand, only five out of 27 children (17.8%) who left a sole custody arrangement went to joint custody. So, joint custody lost 31 children to sole custody and gained only five. Further, examining the link between gender and custody after major changes shows that 20 girls went to live with their mother and only six went to their fathers whereas the boys who changed custody arrangements went equally to fathers (10) and mothers (10) at T2.

Thus, from T1 to T2 several families left joint custody in favor of sole custody: girls went mostly to live with their mothers whereas among boys, there was no clear pattern of preference for the sex of the custodial parent. Further, it is interesting to note that 13.6% of the children went to live in apartments.

The major changes in custody arrangements had a global effect of distancing the father from the child. In fact, at T1, 126 fathers were involved as a custodian of the child (that is, assuming 28% or more of custodial time annually) and dropped to 101 at T2. This represents a 20% withdrawal of fathers as custodial parents. Among mothers, the proportion of withdrawal was less: at T1, 138 were custodial parents and the number dropped to 128 at T2. The withdrawal was of the order of 7%. Overall, 13% of parents who were active custodians at T1 were noncustodial at T2.

CONCLUSION AND DISCUSSION

The comparison of the custody arrangements of 195 children two years apart revealed that (a) the majority of children (70%) did not change custody arrangement but almost half the children in joint custody did change; (b) younger children changed more often their custody arrangement; (c) girls with a custodial father changed more often custody arrangement; (d) girls who changed custody usually went to their mothers while boys who changed divided equally among mother custody and father custody; and (e) with time, polarization was observed toward sole custody because there were less parents active in child custody at T2 than at T1.

Stability of Custody

The relative stability of custody arrangements observed over a two-year period where 70% did not change has already been reported by Drolet and Cloutier (1992: 82% did not change residence) and by Kline et al. (1989: 75% without changing residence). The differences between these studies may be linked to methodology. In the present study, two arrangements (custody with the father and sole custody) were deliberately overrepresented in the sample in order to obtain numerically equivalent groups for comparison. Now that we know that joint custody is associated with greater change, its overrepresentation provides an artificially high rate of change (and hence lower stability) compared to the general population. In addition, data collection methods may also play a role: Drolet and Cloutier asked subjects for a retrospective consideration of the entire period since separation ($M = 4.3$ years) whereas we used a prospective design and questioned subjects at a two-year interval.

Our results indicate clearly that joint custody is most likely to change. How can the greater mobility in shared custody be explained? It is important to remember that joint custody was judged to be the most satisfying arrangement by the child (Careau & Cloutier, 1990). However, it is certainly plausible that for parents and children alike, alternating residences brings practical difficulties in the long run (Careau & Cloutier, 1990; Donnelly & Finkelhor, 1992; Ferreiro, 1990; Kline et al., 1989; Neugebauer, 1989; Steinman, 1981), notably when there is a large distance between the residences (Arditti, 1992a; Furstenberg, 1988). Further, as children grow older they may prefer a single home with one parent (girls especially prefer to stay with their mothers). It is also possible that greater parental availability in joint custody allows greater openness to change. In other words, there are perhaps less families in sole custody arrangements who have the possibility of change: the noncustodial parent is not available as a custodian. The fact that the arrangement requiring highest level of cooperation among ex-spouses (joint custody) is also showing the highest level of plasticity could be invoked to support the idea that change in custody over time is a desired phenomenon in the separated family.

On the other hand, the mobility of joint custody may also be due to continuing conflict between parents (Goldstein, Freud, & Solnit, 1973; Johnston et al., 1989), dissatisfaction with the arrangement by one parent, notably the mother who often prefers sole custody (Shrier, Simring, Shapiro, Greif, & Lindenthal, 1991), remarriage or relocation of one parent

(Greif, 1990), etc. In the context where maintaining the parental role of both parents has been identified as an adjustment factor among children facing parental separation, more data are needed to explain the greater mobility in joint custody. Two competing hypotheses could then be tested: (a) joint custody is less stable over time because it brings too much strain on the family functioning; or (b) joint custody changes more because it better adapts to the changing needs of the family members.

Minor changes occur especially with sole custody by the mother. These involve changes to visiting schedules within the same custody arrangement. This result is possibly due to the fact that the fathers involved in the minor changes are relatively absent in child custody (less than 8% of contact time on both occasions) and will certainly make it more difficult for the mother and child to change to an arrangement that increases the father's involvement.

Of the three initial arrangements, there was less change with sole custody by the father. Knowing that paternal custody often replaces maternal custody due to the mother's financial, psychological, or parental inability (see Greif, 1990; Greif & Pabst, 1988), it is possible that the greater stability in paternal custody is due, at least in part, to the lack of other choices.

Younger Children and Girls Change More Often

Children who changed custody were younger; most were from the ten-year-old group. The link between age and change is confounded with the initial custody arrangement because there was a higher proportion of younger children in joint custody, the arrangement associated with major change. Thus there is some overlap between age and custody arrangement.

Girls changed custody in greater numbers than boys. The greater mobility among girls was most evident in custody arrangements where contact with the father was frequent, either in paternal or joint custody. Buchanan, Maccoby, and Dornbusch (1992) also observed that girls living with the father have more unstable custody arrangements. A possible explanation of this phenomenon was offered by Warshak and Santrock (1983) who reported that children living with an opposite sex parent wanted to live with the same sex parent when the children, especially the girls, reached a new developmental stage (Greif, 1990). Further, some research supports the idea that custody arrangements with an opposite sex parent are more difficult for the child (Camara & Resnick, 1988; Peterson & Zill, 1986; Santrock & Warshak, 1979; Santrok, Warshak, & Elliott, 1982; Warshak & Santrock, 1983).

Although mainly descriptive, this longitudinal study contributes to better understanding of the dynamics of former spouses' interdependency through the custody of their child and further enhances the relevance of approaching co-parenting in a life-cycle perspective.

REFERENCES

Amato, P. R., & Rezac, S. J. (1994). Contact with nonresidential parents, interparental conflict, and children's behavior. *Journal of Family Issues, 15,* 191-207.

Arditti, J. A. (1991). Child support noncompliance and divorced fathers: Rethinking the role of paternal involvement. *Journal of Divorce & Remarriage, 14*(3/4), 107-119.

Arditti, J. A. (1992a). Differences between fathers with joint custody and noncustodial fathers. *American Journal of Orthopsychiatry, 62,* 186-195.

Arditti, J. A. (1992b). Factors related to custody, visitation, and child support for divorced fathers: An exploratory analysis. *Journal of Divorce & Remarriage, 17*(3/4), 23-42.

Arditti, J. A., & Kelly, M. (1994). Father's perspectives of their co-parental relationships postdivorce. *Family Relations, 43,* 61-67.

Barry, S., Cloutier, R., Fillion, L., & Gosselin, L. (1985). *Child's place in family decisions concerning divorce.* Communication presented at the 8th Biennial Meeting of the International Society for the Study of Behavioral Development, Université François-Rabelais, Tours, France.

Buchanan, C. M., Maccoby, E. E., & Dornbusch, S. M. (1992). Adolescents and their families after divorce: Three residential arrangements. *Journal of Research in Adolescence, 2,* 261-291.

Buehler, C. (1989). Influential factors and equity issues in divorce settlements. *Family Relations, 38,* 76-82.

Camara, K. A., & Resnick, G. (1988). Interparental conflict and cooperation: Factors moderating children's postdivorce adjustment. In E. M. Hetherington & J. D. Arasteh (Eds.), *Impact of divorce, single parenting, and stepparenting on children* (pp. 169-195). Hillsdale, NJ: Lawrence Erlbaum.

Careau, L., & Cloutier, R. (1990). La garde de l'enfant après la séparation: Profil psychosocial et appréciation des familles vivant trois formules différentes [Child custody after separation: Psychosocial profile and family appreciation of three different arrangements]. *Apprentissage et Socialisation, 13,* 55-66.

Cloutier, R. (1987). *Étude longitudinale de la garde et de l'ajustement de l'enfant après la séparation* [Longitudinal study of custody and child adjustment after separation]. Unpublished manuscript, Université Laval, Québec.

Crosbie-Burnett, M. (1989). Impact of custody arrangement and family structure on remarriage. *Journal of Divorce, 13,* 1-16.

Donnelly, D., & Finkelhor, D. (1992). Does equality in custody arrangement improve the parent-child relationship? *Journal of Marriage and the Family, 54,* 837-845.

Drolet, J., & Cloutier, R. (1992). L'évolution de la garde de l'enfant après la séparation des parents [Evolution of child custody after parental separation]. *Santé Mentale au Québec, 17*(1), 31-54.

Emery, R. E. (1988). *Marriage, divorce, and children's adjustment.* Newbury Park, CA: Sage.

Emery, R. E., Hetherington, E. M., & Dilalla, L. F. (1984). Divorce, children, and social policy. In H. W. Stevenson & A. E. Siegal (Eds.), *Child development research and social policy* (pp. 189-266). Chicago: University of Chicago Press.

Ferreiro, B. W. (1990). Presumption of joint custody: A family policy dilemma. *Family Relations, 39,* 420-426.

Furstenberg, F. F. (1988). Child care after divorce and remarriage. In E. M. Hetherington & J. Arastech (Eds.), *Impact of divorce, single-parenting, and stepparenting on children* (pp. 245-261). Hillsdale, NJ: Erlbaum.

Goldstein, J., Freud, A., & Solnit, A. J. (1973). *Beyond the best interests of the child.* New York: Free Press.

Greif, G. L. (1990). Split custody: A beginning understanding. *Journal of Divorce, 13*(3), 15-26.

Greif, G. (1995). Single fathers with custody following separation and divorce. Special Issue: Single parent families: Diversity, myths and realities: I. *Marriage & Family Review, 20,* 213-231.

Greif, G. L., & Pabst, M. S. (1988). *Mothers without custody.* Lexington, MA: Lexington Books.

Haurin, R. J. (1992). Patterns of childhood residence and the relationship to young adult outcomes. *Journal of Marriage and the Family, 54,* 846-860.

Healy, J. M., Malley, J. E., & Stewart, A. J. (1990). Children and their fathers after parental separation. *American Journal of Orthopsychiatry, 60,* 532-543.

Hetherington, E. M., Cox, M., & Cox, R. (1978). The aftermath of divorce. In J. H. Stevens, Jr., & M. Mathews (Eds.), *Mother-child, father-child relations.* Washington, DC: National Association for the Education of Young Children.

Johnston, J. R., Kline, M., & Tschann, J. M. (1989). Ongoing postdivorce conflict: Effects on children of joint custody and frequent access. *American Journal of Orthopsychiatry, 59,* 576-592.

Kline, M., Tschann, J. M., Johnston, J. R., & Wallerstein, J. S. (1989). Children's adjustment in joint and sole physical custody families. *Developmental Psychology, 25,* 430-438.

Lemieux, N., & Cloutier, R. (1992). *L'ajustement à la séparation chez l'enfant: le rôle de la relation coparentale* [Child adjustment to separation: Role of the coparental relationship]. Unpublished manuscript, Université Laval, Québec.

Lowenstein, J. S., & Koopman, E. J. (1978). A comparison of the self-esteem between boys living with single-parent mothers and single-parent fathers. *Journal of Divorce, 2,* 195-208.

Maccoby, E. E., Depner, C. E., & Mnookin, R. H. (1990). Coparenting in the second year after divorce. *Journal of Marriage and the Family, 52,* 141-155.

McKie, D. C., Prentice, B., & Reed, P. (1983). *Divorce: Law and the family in Canada.* Statistics Canada, document no 89502F, Ottawa.

Neugebauer, R. (1989). Divorce, custody, and visitation: The child's point of view. *Journal of Divorce, 12*(2/3), 153-168.

Peterson, J. L., & Zill, N. (1986). Marital disruption, parent-child relationship, and behavior problems in children. *Journal of Marriage and the Family, 48,* 295-307.

Reynolds, H. T. (1977). *The analysis of cross-classifications.* New York: Free Press.

Santrok, J. W., & Warshak, R. A. (1979). Father custody and social development in boys and girls. *Journal of Social Issues, 35,* 112-125.

Santrok, J. W., Warshak, R. A., & Elliott, G. L. (1982). Social development and parent-child interaction in father-custody and stepmother families. In M. E. Lamb (Ed.), *Nontraditional families: Parenting and child development* (pp. 289-314). Hillsdale, NJ: Lawrence Erlbaum.

Seltzer, J. A., & Brandreth, Y. (1994). What fathers say about involvement with children after separation. *Journal of Family Issues, 15,* 49-77.

Shrier, D. K., Simring, S. K., Shapiro, E. T., Greif, J. B., & Lindenthal, J. J. (1991). Level of satisfaction of fathers and mothers with joint or sole custody arrangements: Results of a questionnaire. *Journal of Divorce & Remarriage, 16*(3/4), 163-169.

Siegel, S. (1956). *Nonparametric statistics for the behavioral sciences.* New York: McGraw-Hill.

Steinman, S. (1981). The experience of children in a joint custody arrangement: A report of a study. *American Journal of Orthopsychiatry, 51,* 403-414.

Stephen, E. H., Freedman, V. A., & Hess, J. (1993). Near and far: Contact of children with their non-residential fathers. *Journal of Divorce & Remarriage, 20,* 171-191.

Stewart, J. R., Schwebel, A. I., & Fine, M. A. (1986). The impact of custodial arrangement on the adjustment of recently divorced fathers. *Journal of Divorce, 13,* 55-65.

van Wamelen, C. (1990). Children's ideas about 'divorce and after'. *Journal of Divorce & Remarriage, 14*(2), 125-142.

Wallerstein, J. S., & Kelly, J. B. (1980). *Surviving the breakup: How children and parents cope with divorce.* New York: Basic Books.

Warshak, R. A., & Santrock, J. W. (1983). The impact of divorce in father-custody and mother-custody homes: The child's perspective. In L. A. Kurdek (Ed.), *New directions for child development: No. 19. Children and divorce* (pp. 29-46). San Francisco: Jossey-Bass.

Weitzman, L. J. (1985). *The divorce revolution: The unexpected social and economic consequences for women and children in America.* New York: Free Press.

The Impact of an Educational Seminar for Divorcing Parents: Results from a National Survey of Family Court Judges

Robert L. Fischer

SUMMARY. With a sustained large number of divorces in the U.S. over the last two decades, various educational interventions have been developed for families of divorce. *Children Cope With Divorce* is a parent education seminar that aims to provide divorcing parents with information and resources that will help them decrease the negative effects of the divorce process on their children. Within divorce proceedings, family court judges are important observers of the impact of such parent education seminars. A national survey of judges who have referred divorcing parents to the seminar was conducted. The survey method is discussed and the responding judges' views of the effectiveness of *Children Cope With Divorce* are presented. *[Article copies available for a fee from The Haworth Document Delivery Service: 1-800-342-9678. E-mail address: getinfo@haworth.com]*

Robert L. Fischer, PhD, is Director of Program Evaluation for Families First, a non-profit family and children's service agency in Atlanta, GA.

The author would like to thank Bev Bradburn-Stern, MEd, LPC, and the staff of the CCWD program for valuable assistance and support in the completion of this work.

Address correspondence to the author at Families First, P.O. Box 7948, Station C, Atlanta, GA 30357-0948.

[Haworth co-indexing entry note]: "The Impact of an Educational Seminar for Divorcing Parents: Results from a National Survey of Family Court Judges." Fischer, Robert L. Co-published simultaneously in *Journal of Divorce & Remarriage* (The Haworth Press, Inc.) Vol. 28, No. 1/2, 1997, pp. 35-48; and: *Child Custody: Legal Decisions and Family Outcomes* (ed: Craig A. Everett) The Haworth Press, Inc., 1997, pp. 35-48. Single or multiple copies of this article are available for a fee from The Haworth Document Delivery Service [1-800-342-9678, 9:00 a.m. - 5:00 p.m. (EST). E-mail address: getinfo@haworth.com].

INTRODUCTION

Each year over 1.1 million divorces occur in the United States and in total over one million children experience the divorce of their parents (U.S. Bureau of the Census, 1995). The immediate and longer-term negative effects of the divorce experience on these children have been shown to be considerable and serious for many (Furstenberg & Cherlin, 1991; Wallerstein & Blakeslee, 1989). Generally the experience of divorce leads to lower well-being of children across a variety of domains (e.g., school achievement, conduct, psychological and social adjustment, relationship with parents) (Amato & Keith, 1991). Children in families with higher levels of conflict related to the divorce experience are in even more danger of longer-term negative effects. For example, children of high-conflict divorce are two to four times more likely to be clinically disturbed in emotions and behavior (Johnston, 1994). Children of divorce must cope with an additional set of adjustment tasks on top of the demands of normal child development. In addition, the divorce process can lead to a prolonged disruption of parenting, and it is this disruption that is particularly harmful to children.

With a sustained high rate of divorce over the last two decades, a variety of educational interventions have been developed and delivered (often with court-mandated participation) that focus on the parents, the child, or both. *Children Cope With Divorce* (CCWD) is a parent education seminar that aims to impress upon parents the critical role they play in their child's ability to adjust to the changes surrounding the divorce. The seminar emphasizes their responsibility to form a post-divorce relationship that will provide a nurturing, non-threatening environment for the child. The seminar's aim is to provide divorcing parents with information and resources that will help them decrease the negative effects of the divorce on their children. CCWD now serves approximately 120,000 divorcing (or divorced) parents each year, over 8% of the population of individuals (with children under 18 years of age) seeking divorce in the U.S. annually (U.S. Statistical Abstract, 1995). This article details the results of a national survey of judges who have referred divorcing parents to the seminar (Fischer, 1997).

THE CCWD PROGRAM

The *Children Cope With Divorce* program is a parent education seminar for families experiencing divorce and divorce-related difficulties. CCWD was developed by Families First, a non-profit family and children's service agency (Bradburn-Stern, 1990). In 1988 Cobb County (GA) Superior Court judges implemented a local rule of court requiring attendance at an educational seminar of both parties in divorce, separate maintenance, legitimation, change of custody and visitation actions within 31 days of service upon the defendant. CCWD was selected by the Cobb Judicial Circuit to fulfill this mandatory educational requirement. Since its inception in Cobb County, Georgia, the CCWD program has proliferated in locales around the United States. To date Families First has licensed over 160 non-profit agencies across the country and trained their staff to deliver the program.

The CCWD Model

The four-hour CCWD class provides a means for helping parents better understand the impact of divorce on their children and lessen the negative effects. The seminar is designed to be led by a two-member (male/female) team of masters-level counseling professionals who facilitate the group experience. The class content focuses on the various levels and dimensions of divorce process (emotional, co-parental, legal, economic, community, psychological) and its effects on children (how children react to divorce, child development implications for parental access plans, new family structures, and getting help when needed). See Table A. The program draws on tactics such as group discussion, role play, and video segments to more effectively communicate the content. The seminar offers concrete examples of situations that may occur in a divorcing family and illustrates methods for responding in ways that will better protect the well-being of their child.

In essence, CCWD targets the needs of the children in families experiencing divorce or divorce-related court actions. The seminar seeks to

---

TABLE A. Key Elements of the *Children Cope With Divorce* Program

- Dimensions of the divorce process: emotional, co-parental, legal, economic, community, and psychological
- How children react to divorce
- Child adjustment and parents' role
- New family structures
- Getting help when needed

---

make clear to parents the potential harm that their own behaviors and attitudes may have on their children during the turbulent time of divorce. By discussing the issues surrounding the divorce in a non-judgmental way, the program attempts to benefit parents by providing new perspective on their situation. It offers an educational group experience for parents going through similar difficulties and seeks to help them bolster their own ability to be a good parent to their child. The children and family should benefit directly through the influence the class has on the parent's behavior, attitude, and post-divorce relationship with their former partner. The children should be better able to thrive in their family situations as the concepts are accepted and applied. A secondary set of benefits from the program should accrue to the courts and to taxpayers. Participation in the seminar often leads to fewer interactions with the legal system related to the divorce and the child. This averts additional court action thereby freeing-up space on judges' dockets. In turn, this decreased use of the legal system leads to the lowering of expenses to the court system and the taxpayers.

The CCWD Provider Network

The CCWD provider network of more than 160 licensed non-profit agencies comprises a high degree of variation in regard to location, delivery and local context for the program. A phone survey of all licensed CCWD providers conducted in mid-1996 collected information on the national delivery of the program. The results presented from the phone survey are based on information gathered from 141 of 150 CCWD providers licensed at that time (94% response rate). On a monthly basis, the network of CCWD providers offers 280 seminars nationally, involving 9,886 participants per month on average, or 118,632 per year.

Licensed CCWD providers are located in 38 states but are currently active in only 35 states. See Table B. Several states have numerous CCWD providers. Four states have 10 or more providers and account for 37% of all providers and nearly one-half (48%) of the national monthly CCWD participants: Alabama (14), Georgia (16), Indiana (15), and Texas (15). Five other states have 5 to 9 providers: Florida (9), Louisiana (8), Pennsylvania (7), Virginia (6), and Wisconsin (8). Twelve states have 1 to 4 providers and fourteen states have one provider. Eleven of these single-provider states taken together account for under 3% of the national monthly caseload. The remaining three states, Utah, Vermont, and Washington, have programs of moderate size, amounting to under 5% of the national monthly CCWD participants. Twelve states and the District of Columbia are not represented in the CCWD provider network, including a block of four western states (Idaho, Nebraska, North Dakota, and Wyoming), four

TABLE B. CCWD National Survey of Judges: Distribution of Providers
and Participants

	# Sites	# Sites Active	# Sites Inactive	# CCWD Participants per month	% of CCWD Participants Nationally
Alabama	14	11	3	681	6.9
Arizona	4	1	3	25	0.3
California	1	0	1	0	0
Colorado	2	2	0	390	3.9
Connecticut	3	3	0	60	0.6
Delaware	1	1	0	25	0.3
Florida	9	8	1	1090	11.0
Georgia	16	15	1	1432	14.5
Illinois	1	0	1	0	0
Indiana	15	15	0	1393	14.1
Iowa	4	4	0	394	4.0
Louisiana	8	7	1	109	1.1
Maryland	1	1	0	35	0.4
Massachusetts	3	2	1	41	0.4
Minnesota	1	1	0	40	0.4
Mississippi	1	1	0	25	0.3
Montana	1	1	0	12	0.1
Nebraska	1	0	1	0	0
Nevada	3	3	0	800	8.1
New Jersey	2	2	0	91	0.9
New Mexico	1	1	0	4	>0.0
New York	4	4	0	55	0.6
North Carolina	4	4	0	142	1.4
Ohio	2	1	1	13	0.1
Oklahoma	5	3	2	410	4.1
Oregon	1	1	0	48	0.5
Pennsylvania	7	6	1	277	2.8
Rhode Island	1	1	0	11	0.1
South Carolina	4	3	1	45	0.5
South Dakota	1	1	0	25	0.2
Tennessee	4	4	0	153	1.5
Texas	15	13	2	1288	13.0
Utah	1	1	0	180	1.8
Vermont	1	1	0	184	1.9
Virginia	6	6	0	162	1.6
Washington	3	1	2	125	1.3
West Virginia	3	2	1	15	0.2
Wisconsin	8	6	2	106	1.1
Total	162	137	25	9,886	100.0

southern/midwestern states (Arkansas, Kansas, Kentucky, and Missouri), two eastern states (Maine and New Hampshire), and Alaska and Hawaii. Nationally, providers serve a variety of locales: 62% categorize the area they serve as a mix of rural, urban, and suburban areas; 17% serve primarily rural areas; 14%, mainly urban areas; and 8%, mainly suburban areas.

1996 SURVEY OF REFERRING JUDGES

A key factor in CCWD's ability to help divorcing couples protect their children is the parent's likelihood of attending the seminar. Since many parents are unable to focus on the needs of their children during the time of divorce, the role of the courts in compelling parents to attend the seminar is critical. Individual judges and courts in many jurisdictions have the authority to require parents with minor children to attend a parent education program such as CCWD as a precondition of granting a divorce decree. Due to the critical role of judges in this situation, as advocates for the children involved, the views of individual judges are very valuable in understanding the benefit of CCWD in cases of divorce.

The recognition that the views of key stakeholders are central to the program's viability led to the identification of referring judges as a critical source of feedback about CCWD. As such, judges were seen as having considerable standing in the determination of the program's usefulness. A survey approach was developed to systematically collect information from judges who had referred parents to the CCWD seminar.

Methods

In August 1996 licensed providers of CCWD were asked to provide the names of and appropriate contact information for judges who had referred divorcing parents to their program in the prior six-month period. A database of 641 judges was constructed from the information provided by licensees. A survey was developed to ascertain the judges' views on particular elements of the CCWD program and collect minimal information about the judge. A pilot-test of the survey instrument was conducted with 14 judges in two metro Atlanta counties and refinements of the survey were made thereafter. The survey was mailed to the remaining 627 judges in mid-September 1996. The packet included a cover letter explaining the survey effort, a copy of the survey, and a stamped return envelope. A reminder postcard was sent to all judges who had not responded by early October 1996.

The Judge Sample

Of the original sample of 641 judges, approximately 2.5% (n = 16) should have been excluded from the initial survey mail-out. The original sample erroneously included several judges who were not appropriate recipients of the survey. Several judges reported that they either (1) had not referred parents to the program, (2) did not handle divorce cases, or (3) were unaware of the program. After eliminating these inappropriate recipients from the sample, the revised sample is 625 judges.

A total of 246 judges (39.4%) returned a usable survey. The response rate by state varied from zero to 100%. Eight states had a return of 50% or higher and only five states had a return under 25%. Of these low-return states, three of the five states had a zero return but were represented by only six judges in the sample combined. See Table C for details of the judge sample by state.

Given that the survey population is composed of judges involved in adjudication of family law cases, the level of response (39%) is beyond expectations. Based on the 20% response to a recent large-scale (n = 1200) survey of judges conducted by the National Council of Juvenile and Family Court Judges, the response to the CCWD survey may be viewed as above average (NCJFCJ, 1996). The NCJFCJ survey is useful as a comparison because the population surveyed is most like the judges surveyed about CCWD. Through an inquiry to the American Bar Association, it was determined that little survey work is done with judges in general, and even less with particular subsets of judges (e.g., family law judges). All but three of the responding judges (98.7%) indicated that they had completed the survey personally.

Of responding judges, 80% were male and 20% were female. On average, the respondents had been on the bench for 10.5 years (range: 6 months to 45 years). In addition, the judges report that they have been hearing cases involving divorce for 9 years, on average (range: 6 months to 36 years).

Several states that have active licensed CCWD providers are not represented in Table B because (1) divorcing parents are not referred specifically to CCWD (they were merely given a list of parent education programs), or (2) the provider elected not to participate. These states are Arizona, Delaware, Minnesota, Mississippi, New Mexico, South Dakota, and West Virginia.

Representativeness of Sample

The responding judges represent 24 states, with the heaviest representation in the sample coming from Indiana (20%), Georgia (18%), and Texas

TABLE C. CCWD National Survey of Judges: Distribution of Sample and Respondents and Response Rate by State

	# Judges Full Sample	% of Full Sample	# Judges Responding	% of Total Respondents	% Response by State
Alabama	29	4.6	11	4.5	37.9
Colorado	16	2.6	7	2.8	43.8
Connecticut	5	0.8	2	0.8	40.0
Florida	37	5.9	10	4.1	27.0
Georgia	88	14.1	44	17.9	50.0
Indiana	113	18.1	49	19.9	43.4
Iowa	29	4.6	15	6.1	51.7
Louisiana	30	4.8	10	4.1	33.3
Maryland	2	0.3	1	0.4	50.0
Massachusetts	5	0.8	3	1.2	60.0
Montana	5	0.8	2	0.8	40.0
New Jersey	1	0.2	0	0.0	0.0
Nevada	6	1.0	2	0.8	33.3
New York	7	1.1	3	1.2	42.8
North Carolina	12	1.9	5	2.0	41.7
Ohio	2	0.3	1	0.4	50.0
Oklahoma	44	7.0	17	6.9	38.6
Oregon	6	1.0	1	0.4	16.7
Pennsylvania	21	3.4	8	3.2	38.1
Rhode Island	3	0.5	0	0.0	0.0
South Carolina	8	1.3	1	0.4	12.5
Tennessee	18	2.9	10	4.1	55.5
Texas	98	15.7	28	11.4	28.6
Utah	13	2.1	5	2.0	38.5
Vermont	2	0.3	0	0.0	0.0
Virginia	17	2.7	5	2.0	29.4
Washington	1	0.2	1	0.4	100.0
Wisconsin	7	1.1	5	2.0	71.4
Totals	625	100.0	246	100.0	39.4

(11%). The geographic regions (based on divisions developed by the U.S. Census Bureau) best represented in the sample are the South Atlantic (27%), the East North Central (22%), and the West South Central (22%). See Table D for a comparison of the respondents and the full sample. Given that very little information was available about the judges who did not respond to the survey, a thorough comparison of respondents and nonrespondents is not possible. However, in regard to gender and geo-

TABLE D. Representativeness of Survey Sample

	Full Sample	Respondents
Number of Judges	625	246
Gender		
Female	17.9%	20.3%
Male	82.1%	79.7%
Region		
New England	2.4%	2.0%
Middle Atlantic	4.6%	4.5%
East North Central	19.5%	22.4%
West North Central	4.6%	6.1%
South Atlantic	26.2%	26.8%
East South Central	7.5%	8.5%
West South Central	27.5%	22.4%
Mountain	6.4%	6.5%
Pacific	1.1%	0.8%

graphic region, the responding judges closely mirror the overall sample of 625 judges. However, female judges are slightly overrepresented in the respondent sample (20.3 versus 17.9%). In addition, the West South Central region (Louisiana, Oklahoma, and Texas) is somewhat underrepresented (22.4 versus 27.5%), while the East North Central (Indiana and Wisconsin) and West North Central (Iowa) regions are slightly overrepresented.

In respect to how well the network of CCWD sites is represented in the sample of responding judges, 86% of all participating sites had at least one judge from their area respond to the survey. See Table E for a breakdown by state. Twenty-nine sites elected not to participate in the judge survey and therefore did not submit information about their referring judges. Seven states were not represented in the survey because the single CCWD provider in these states chose not to take part in the survey. In 17 states all licensed sites had at least one referring judge respond to the survey.

The vast majority (94%) of the responding judges refer parents to CCWD under a mandate or requirement of some kind, while the remainder have a situation where participation is voluntary. Most judges who do refer parents under a mandate do encourage parents to attend the seminar, possibly implying the perception of a requirement on the part of parents. On average, the judges have been referring parents to CCWD for approxi-

TABLE E. CCWD National Survey of Judges: Representation of Sites

	# Sites Active	# Sites Participating in Survey	# Sites Represented in Judge Sample	% Sites Represented in Judge Sample
Alabama	11	11	6	54.5
Arizona	1	0	–	–
California	0	–	–	–
Colorado	2	2	2	100.0
Connecticut	3	1	1	100.0
Delaware	1	0	–	–
Florida	8	7	6	85.7
Georgia	15	13	12	92.3
Illinois	0	–	–	–
Indiana	15	14	14	100.0
Iowa	4	4	4	100.0
Louisiana	7	6	6	100.0
Maryland	1	1	1	100.0
Massachusetts	2	1	1	100.0
Minnesota	1	0	–	–
Mississippi	1	0	–	–
Montana	1	1	1	100.0
Nebraska	0	–	–	–
Nevada	3	3	3	100.0
New Jersey	2	1	0	0.0
New Mexico	1	0	–	–
New York	4	2	2	100.0
North Carolina	4	2	1	50.0
Ohio	1	1	1	100.0
Oklahoma	3	3	3	100.0
Oregon	1	1	1	100.0
Pennsylvania	6	5	5	100.0
Rhode Island	1	1	0	0.0
South Carolina	3	2	1	50.0
South Dakota	1	0	–	–
Tennessee	4	4	4	100.0
Texas	13	11	10	90.9
Utah	1	1	1	100.0
Vermont	1	1	0	0.0
Virginia	6	4	3	75.0
Washington	1	1	1	100.0
West Virginia	2	0	–	–
Wisconsin	6	4	3	75.0
Totals	137	108	93	86.1

mately 3 years (range–6 months to 8 years). On average, the judges report referring approximately 85% of the divorce-related cases involving minor children they hear to CCWD. Two-thirds of the judges refer 95% or more of these cases to CCWD.

JUDGES' VIEWS OF CHILDREN COPE WITH DIVORCE

The key emphasis of this survey effort was to assess the views of judges who had referred divorcing parents to the CCWD seminar. The brief survey included (1) five specific questions rated on a six-item scale (including a *No Opinion* category), and (2) four open-ended questions about their impressions of the seminar.

Five Ratings of Effectiveness

In regard to their specific beliefs about the CCWD program, the responding judges had favorable opinions in regard to five dimensions. See Table F. Roughly three-quarters of the respondents believe that the seminar leads to quicker resolution of custody matters (80%), decreased litigation involving the child (79%), and decreased litigation involving the parents for

TABLE F. Ratings of Effectiveness of CCWD by Judges			
The *Children Cope With Divorce* seminar	Strongly Agree or Agree	Mean Response (std dev)	Number of Respondents
1. Increases parents' ability to reach agreement more quickly on custody arrangements	79.7%	3.97 (.69)	222
2. Decreases subsequent litigation between the divorced parents involving the child	79.1%	3.97 (.68)	215
3. Decreases number of times your court sees a case for any reason	73.2%	3.89 (.69)	216
4. Serves to lessen the negative effects of divorce on children of divorcing couples	95.7%	4.43 (.57)	234
5. Benefits the families of parties who participate in the seminar	97.8%	4.43 (.54)	230

any reason (73%). The responding judges overwhelming agreed that the seminar lessens the negative effects of divorce on children (96%) and, more generally, benefits the families of participants (98%). The means and percentages reported are based on the number of responding judges who expressed an opinion on each dimension. The share of judges who reported "no opinion" ranged from 4.9% (item 4) to 12.6% (item 2).

A general trend in the ratings is that male judges rated the seminar higher on all five dimensions, on average. On two questions male judges rated CCWD significantly higher than female judges. On question 3 (subsequent litigation for any reason), 75% of male judges indicated agreement while only 63% of female judges did so ($r = -.129$, $p = .043$, $n = 246$). Likewise, on question 4 (lessens negative effects on children), 97% of male judges agreed versus 89% of female judges ($r = -.160$, $p = .012$, $n = 246$). This finding may be related to years of experience as a judge and in adjudicating divorce cases. The male judges in the sample had significantly more years of experience on the bench than female judges (11.5 versus 6.3 years) ($t = 6.08$, $p = .000$, $n = 242$) and more years handling divorce cases (9.8 versus 5.4 years) ($t = 5.87$, $p = .000$, $n = 235$).

Many judges reported that they prefer to see families in specific types of cases attend the CCWD seminar: divorce (87%), custody (90%), child support (30%), separate maintenance (28%), other (e.g., visitation) (21%). Eighty-one percent of the judges reported that they believed that appropriate parties should be mandated to attend the seminar, 13% thought it should be purely at the discretion of the judge, and the remaining 6% preferred some other arrangement. Only one judge reported the belief that attendance should be purely voluntary.

Open-Ended Comments

The survey included four open-ended questions about the judges' opinions of the CCWD seminar. These questions were posed to allow the judges to offer their own take of the seminar and provide a broader critique of the course. Despite the variety of locales and respondents involved in the survey, several themes were clearly evident across the sample of responses. The themes were identified through a content review of judge comments for each open-ended question conducted by the author. The comments reveal several themes; these are briefly described for each question.

In general, what is your attitude about the program?
CCWD helps the court focus on the needs of the children involved
Seminar benefits many and harms none
Parents believe the seminar is beneficial for them

What do you believe is the greatest benefit of the seminar to your court?
CCWD decreases litigation and facilitates settlement
Seminar lowers hostility and antagonism between parents
Class focuses parents' attention on their children

What do you believe is the greatest need for improvement in the program?
Augment with a children's program and an advanced course for parents
Adjust content to be relevant to never-married parents
Increase communication with court, especially related to research

If you are familiar with other programs, how do you believe the seminar compares to them in terms of effectiveness?
Many judges are unfamiliar with other programs
Information about effectiveness of programs is scarce
CCWD is perceived as better than other programs (by judges who are aware of others)

CONCLUSION

The results of a national survey of judges who have referred divorcing parents to *Children Cope With Divorce* show that responding judges are supportive of the seminar across the country, especially in regard to its lessening subsequent court actions. These judges believe that the seminar is effective in achieving its goals related to protecting the well-being of children in families experiencing divorce and divorce-related change. In addition, they believe that the seminar helps the court focus on the needs of the children involved. Responding judges emphasized three needs for improvement in the seminar: (1) augment with a children's program and an advanced course for parents, (2) adjust content to be relevant to never-married parents, and (3) increase communication with court, especially related to research. Given the proximity of these judges to the individual divorce cases and their role in compelling parents to attend the seminar, their views hold particular value in effectively assessing the benefits of CCWD.

REFERENCES

Amato, Paul R. & Keith, Bruce. (1991). Parental divorce and the well-being of children: A meta-analysis. *Psychological Bulletin, 110(1),* 26-46.
Bradburn-Stern, Bev. (1990). *Children Cope With Divorce* Trainers Manual. Atlanta: Families First.

Fischer, Robert L. (1997). *Children Cope With Divorce–A View from the Bench: Results from a National Survey of Judges.* Atlanta: Families First.

Furstenberg, Frank F. & Cherlin, Andrew J. (1991). *Divided Families: What Happens to Children When Parents Part.* Cambridge, MA: Harvard University Press.

Johnston, Janet R. (1994). High conflict divorce. *Children and Divorce, The Future of Our Children, 4(1).* Los Altos, CA: John and Lucile Packard Foundation, 165-182. Spring.

National Council of Juvenile and Family Court Judges. (1996). Personal communication on December 11, 1996. Reno: NCJFCJ.

U.S. Bureau of the Census. (1995). *Monthly Vital Statistics Report, 43 (13).* Hyattsville, MD: National Center for Health Statistics, October 23.

U.S. Bureau of the Census. (1995). *Statistical Abstract of the United States (115th Ed.).* Washington, DC: U.S. Government Printing Office.

Wallerstein, Judith S. & Blakeslee, Sandra. (1989). *Second Chances: Men, Women, and Children a Decade after Divorce.* New York: Tichnor & Fields.

Children Denied Two Parents:
An Analysis of Access Denial

Lynda Fox Fields
Beverly W. Mussetter
Gerald T. Powers

SUMMARY. Noncustodial parents are often denied access to their children on the grounds that they have failed to comply with court mandated child support payments. This study explores the experiences of a group of noncustodial fathers, many of whom report that access to their children was denied despite the fact that their child support obligations could be confirmed by means of voluntary, automatic Electronic Fund Transfer handled directly through local banking institutions. The article calls for a number of legal reforms designed to protect the rights of noncustodial parents and assure that children have access to both parents. *[Article copies available for a fee from The Haworth Document Delivery Service: 1-800-342-9678. E-mail address: getinfo@haworth.com]*

One of the most disconcerting patterns in contemporary society is that half of all marriages end in divorce (Bureau of Census, 1993). While the divorce process is painful for all family members, children are often the most adversely affected. It is not unusual for them to become pawns in a

Lynda Fox Fields, MSW, is a social work doctoral student and private consultant in Indianapolis, IN. Beverly W. Mussetter, ACSW, is a clinical therapist working with families and children in Indianapolis, IN. Gerald T. Powers, PhD, is Professor and Director of the PhD Program at the Indiana University School of Social Work.

[Haworth co-indexing entry note]: "Children Denied Two Parents: An Analysis of Access Denial." Fields, Lynda Fox, Beverly W. Mussetter, and Gerald T. Powers. Co-published simultaneously in *Journal of Divorce & Remarriage* (The Haworth Press, Inc.) Vol. 28, No. 1/2, 1997, pp. 49-62; and: *Child Custody: Legal Decisions and Family Outcomes* (ed: Craig A. Everett) The Haworth Press, Inc., 1997, pp. 49-62. Single or multiple copies of this article are available for a fee from The Haworth Document Delivery Service [1-800-342-9678, 9:00 a.m. - 5:00 p.m. (EST). E-mail address: getinfo@haworth.com].

power struggle in which custody is viewed as the ultimate measure of victory.

Most observers agree that any divorce is likely to have profound consequences on children, the nature and quality of which is largely dependent upon how the parents handle their differences (Bradburn-Stern & Morley, 1991). This is especially true in relation to matters involving the disposition of custody. Sometimes parents manage to negotiate a mutually acceptable agreement within the parameters established by the bench. Unfortunately, the breakdown of "shared meaning" that inevitably leads to separation and divorce, as well as the subsequent litigation, often tends to mitigate against the establishment of functional relationships (Depner, Leino, & Chun, 1992).

The correlation between parental conflict and various behavioral, psychological and social indicators of child adjustment is well established (Hanscom, 1992). This is particularly true in situations that culminate in divorce (Klatner, 1987; Klatner, Kloner, Schreier, & Okla, 1989; Kurdek & Siesky, 1980). Among the many factors that have been found to negatively affect a child's adjustment to their parents' divorce is the separation from the noncustodial parent (Bloom & Hodges, 1984). In the vast majority of cases, the noncustodial parent is the father and the court typically awards all legal rights regarding children to the mother who subsequently retains sole custody for the duration of the court order (Hillery, 1993). This power differential involving visitation rights is often a continuing source of conflict between the contending parties with the court traditionally aligning itself on the side of the custodial parent (Ramos, 1979). Although noncustodial parents (NCPs) are routinely required to provide child support, there are rarely comparable provisions to assure that the custodial parent will either provide reasonable access to the children or be held accountable for the expenditures related to financial transfers (Ramos, 1979). In many states, NCPs are legally obligated to financially support their children but are denied equal rights with respect to shared or co-parenting.

In the state of Indiana, the site of the present study, it became a misdemeanor to deny access of a child to a noncustodial parent in 1991. Despite this criminal statute, however, there is no evidence to indicate that any successful prosecution of access denial has occurred. It is not surprising, therefore, that existing statutes dealing with custody and child support issues are perceived by many NCPs as patently unfair and unresponsive to both their needs and those of their children.

THE SOCIAL/PSYCHOLOGICAL EFFECTS OF DENIAL

It has been suggested that divorce "parentectomizes" the noncustodial parent from his/her children (Williams, 1990). When this occurs, it represents a significant stressor with respect to the child's continued emotional and cognitive development (Bloom & Hodges, 1984). One study concluded that the "worst effects," with respect to a child's symptoms and developmental retardation, correlate positively with the "continued conflict and blame between the divorcing parents, and with lack of access to the absent parent" (Committee on the Family of the Group for the Advancement of Psychiatry, 1980). Conversely, the positive adjustment of children following divorce has been found to be associated with the noncustodial parent's continuing, frequent coparenting relationship with the former spouse and the NCP's inclusion in the child's life after divorce (Koch & Lowery, 1984). These findings underscore the importance of learning more about the factors that affect familial relationships in such highly volatile situations.

Little has been written concerning the feelings of noncustodial parents following divorce, especially with respect to issues involving their parental identity, separation from family, and access denial. In a survey of male NCPs, it was found that some fathers perceived a marked decrease in their ability to sustain their child's feeling of being a member of a family after the divorce (Greif, 1979). "Parental Influence" was found to be functionally related to the amount of contact between the child and father following the divorce—the less contact, the less perceived influence by the father. The study concluded that "children of divorce, as do children of intact families, need loving relationships with two parents, and that joint custody arrangements should be encouraged."

Issues related to post-divorce adjustment were also explored in a series of interviews in which it was discovered that divorced men seeking psychiatric help reported that they experienced profound feelings of sadness, depression, and emptiness accompanied by a sense of personal loss and a decrease in self-esteem (Jacobs, 1982). Some of the fathers reported that they could not bear the agony of separation from their children and that the imposition of periodic visitations was considered intolerable.

THE RELATIONSHIP BETWEEN CHILD SUPPORT
AND ACCESS

It is commonly assumed that the primary reason noncustodial parents are denied access to their children is because they fail to comply with court mandated child support payments. This assumption has been confirmed in a study of attitudes involving custodial parents and domestic court officials (Thiessen, 1985). Both these groups generally believed that the amount of access granted NCPs regarding visitation correlates positively with the level of child support compliance. If this is accurate, it would follow that NCPs who comply with court mandated child support payments would likely encounter relatively few access problems. The present study tests that assumption with a group of noncustodial fathers for whom there exists an electronic record of their child support payments. Specifically, it addresses the question, *"Do noncustodial parents who comply with court ordered child support payments perceive that they are denied access to their children by custodial parents?"*

THE METHODOLOGY

This study is the product of a secondary analysis of extant data collected by the Coalition for Children's Access to Parents (C-CAP). This Indiana-based organization advocates on behalf of "the rights of children to have meaningful relationships with both parents." Toward that end, this coalition of human service professions works "to develop and make available educational resources for divorced parents through a variety of providers such as legislators, courts, social services, schools and others who deal with the disruption of the family unit" (C-CAP, 1992).

The original questionnaire was developed and pretested by C-CAP in an effort to explore a variety of issues ranging from access denial to attempts at remediation. It was also designed to address some of the perceived needs of noncustodial parents including topics such as judicial reform, revised visitation schedules, improved legal counsel and the availability of emotional support groups. The revised questionnaire consisted of a mixture of sixty-seven closed and open ended items.

Because accurate information is not available on all noncustodial parents living in the State of Indiana, a decision was made to focus the study on subjects who were participating in a voluntary Electronic Fund Transfer (EFT) program. This limitation raises a number of questions with respect to representativeness and ultimately the generalizability of the results. Nevertheless, the use of what might be thought of as a "convenience sample" had an important advantage with respect to the present study. It made it possible to control the critical variable of "child support" as it relates to the broader issue of access denial. Since electronic fund transfers are handled through a local banking institution, permanent records are maintained on all transactions involving child support payments.

This made it possible to isolate a subset of NCPs who were known to be meeting their court ordered obligations regarding child support.

At the time of the survey, there were approximately 2,000 noncustodial parents participating in an EFT program. A twenty-five percent random sample of this number was selected for inclusion in the study. Ninety-eight of the questionnaires were returned unanswered because the subjects no longer lived at the designated address. Of the remaining 402 questionnaires, a total of 96 were completed and returned. Because 23 of these questionnaires were answered by someone other than the noncustodial father, they were eliminated from the study in an effort to keep the sample as "clean" as possible. The remaining 73 questionnaires, or approximately 20% of the usable pool, were included in the final data analysis.

While the intent of the original survey was primarily descriptive in nature, this secondary analysis focuses specifically on the perceptions of NCPs regarding their visitation experiences when questions regarding the payment of child support are removed as possible justifications for access denial. It explores three factors that appear to be related to the NCPs' level of satisfaction with the enforcement of court ordered visitation arrangements: power differentials in the relationship between the custodial and noncustodial parents; the role of the court in enforcing visitation arrangements; and perceptions of fairness in the resolution of access disputes.

CHARACTERISTICS OF THE SAMPLE

Who are the subjects that participated in this study? The majority of the sample is comprised of divorced or remarried white males. The typical marriage had lasted almost eight years followed by a separation or divorce of five years duration. Most of these unions produced two children whose average age was nine years, four months at the time of the study. The average annual personal income of the NCP was $30,913 (median: $30,000) with a reported average annual total family income of $43,379 (median: $38,000). The positively skewed distribution of the family income variable is due to a clustering of higher incomes for married couples with dual incomes. Weekly child support payments averaged $117 (median $109), varying positively in relation to the number of children ($r = 0.67$, $p < .01$).

While it is impossible to determine whether the present sample is representative of the broader population of noncustodial parents, some demographic comparisons with similar cohorts can be informative. For example, it is possible to compare the above mentioned variables with similar data collected in a recent study of five visitation enforcement programs located in different parts of the country (Pearson & Anhalt, 1992). In 1990, The Center for Policy Research in Denver conducted a national survey of visitation enforcement in American courts. Five such programs in the states of Arizona, Michigan, Florida, Kansas and California were selected for intensive study. The averaged demographics for these programs provide a useful profile of the NCP for comparative purposes. (See Table 1.)

Generally, the demographics for the Indiana sample are similar to the aggregate figures for the five visitation enforcement programs. However, there are two notable exceptions. The subjects in the Indiana sample had been divorced or separated twice as long as their national counterparts. This explains the 2.1 year difference in the average age of the dependent children between the two groups. As the divorce/separation interval for couples increases, so, too, does the age of their children ($r = 0.52$, $p <$ .01). The Indiana sample also enjoyed an average annual family income more than $5,000 higher than the average for the five programs included in the national study. This may account for why the average amount of child support was substantially higher for the Indiana sample. This may also be accounted for by the finding that Indiana has the country's highest financial child support guidelines (Pirog-Good, 1993). It was found

TABLE 1. A Comparison of Selected Marriage and Divorce Characteristics Between the Indiana Sample and Clients Served by Five Visitation Enforcement Programs

	5 STATE AVG.	:	IN
Percent ever married	91%	:	89%
Average years married	7.4	:	7.8
Average years divorced	2.6	:	5.3
Average number of children	1.6	:	1.7
Average age of children	7.3	:	9.4
Percent remarried (fathers)	47%	:	33%
Family income (median)	$32,643	:	$38,000
Average amount of support	$3,084	:	$5,616
Number of subjects	66-107	:	66-73

that support levels correlate positively with personal income ($r = 0.57$, $p < .001$).

The available data are not particularly helpful in explaining these exceptions. Since the most obvious differences are of a financial nature, however, they may be partially explained by the fact that the Indiana sample was comprised solely of males while all the other samples included females. It is also possible that the observed differences may be program specific (for instance, the Indiana sample only included those in an EFT program, which may be more likely to be utilized by higher income individuals), or they may simply reflect regional variations with respect to the populations from which the samples were drawn. Whatever the explanation, the magnitude of these differences are sufficiently large to suggest caution with respect to any generalizations that might be drawn relative to other programs or areas of the country.

FINDINGS

There is little question but that many children do not receive child support following divorce (Weitzman, 1985). The Stanford Child Custody Project confirmed the findings of earlier studies that visitation and child support are functionally related (Peters, Argys, Maccoby, & Mnookin, 1990). Fathers who see their children regularly tend to be more responsible in meeting their child support obligations. Seltzer (1991) found that fathers who maintained contact with their children were more than three times as likely to make child support payments than were those who had no contact.

Functional relationships, however, do not necessarily imply causation. It is exceedingly difficult to unravel the complex causal sequence among potentially related variables. On the face of it, one might be tempted to conclude that contact with children somehow motivates fathers to be more responsible with respect to child support. But it is also plausible that fathers who meet their child support obligations may feel a stronger sense of entitlement with respect to visitation rights. It has also been argued that both contact and child support levels may be caused by some third variable such as parental attachment. According to Ferguson (1990), "It makes sense that a man does not visit because he pays, or pays because he visits, but instead does both because he cares about the children and has a reasonable relationship with them." The logic of Ferguson's argument notwithstanding, it has also been found that following the divorce, both the number of parent/child contacts and the level of child support tend to decrease with the passage of time (Pearson, Anhalt, & Thoennes, 1991).

With so many confounding variables, it is apparent that research regarding the relationship between visitation behavior and child support is confusing at best. The phenomenon may be so complex that it may prove impossible to clearly differentiate between independent and dependent variables or totally rule out the possibility of spurious relationships. In the present study, however, we have attempted to control one of the variables in the functional relationship—*support payments*—in an effort to more carefully explore the experiences that fathers have with respect to the other—*access*.

The data from this study suggests that, despite a process that guarantees the regular payment of child support, noncustodial parents harbor a number of very strong negative feelings regarding the nature of their visitation arrangements. For most NCPs, the conditions governing visitation are established by the court. In the majority of cases this means biweekly visits and access to children for portions of at least some of the major holidays. The court also establishes the level of support payments which, for the subjects of this study, is handled voluntarily through automatic electronic fund transfers (EFT) funneled through local banking institutions. While 23.3% of the respondents admit to having missed one or more support payments in the past, all of them were participating in an EFT program at the time of the study.

It was found that only a third of the NCPs in the sample were satisfied with the visitation arrangements as established by the court. Fifty-four percent attempted to have the arrangements legally modified—generally without success. Despite the fact that 75% of the respondents considered the visitation arrangements to be "unfair," more than half (54.3%) of the respondents claim that they religiously follow the schedule established by the court. The remaining 46% admit that they routinely or sometimes disregard the court ordered guidelines. Of those who do not follow the guidelines, 25% (or a total of seven respondents) state that they actually see their children "more often" than provided for by the established visitation schedule. Typically this occurs only with the consent of the custodial parent. Unfortunately, the remaining 75% of the NCPs who do not follow the guidelines indicate that they see their children "less" than prescribed by the court ordered schedule, or "not at all." There are a number of possible reasons for this disconcerting finding. While part of the problem may be due to a lack of interest on the part of the NCP, a large majority of the respondents (80%) attribute their failure to follow the prescribed visitation schedule to systemic factors over which they feel they have little or no control.

Sixty-nine percent of the NCPs are dissatisfied with the visitation arrangements as they currently operate. They feel that the arrangements are essentially dictated by the custodial parent, even in situations in which the court may have issued orders to the contrary. They see an imbalance in power and an unwillingness on the part of the court to intervene on their behalf even when it is clear that their rights are being violated. They consider the courts to be biased in favor of the custodial parent, a circumstance that undermines any efforts they may make to be a responsible parent.

Many NCPs feel very vulnerable regarding their relationship with their children. They attribute much of this vulnerability to the unfair advantage enjoyed by their custodial counterparts when it comes to the resolution of visitation disputes. More than two-thirds (68.1%) of the NCPs indicate that they regularly have "serious disagreements" with their ex-spouses regarding visitation. Fifty-five percent claim to have been denied visitation sometime during the past year. Forty-three percent allege that such denials occurred at least seven times during that period. A third of the respondents believe that their ex-spouses have made up untrue stories about them in order to justify the withdrawal of visitation rights. An even larger percentage (69.7) claim that their ex-spouses have attempted to alienate their children by telling lies about the NCP. Forty-one percent allege that their ex-spouses have threatened to move out of state, and another 37% claim that their ex-spouses have even gone so far as to hide the children as a means of denying visitation.

Because of what they consider to be the unfair advantage enjoyed by their custodial counterparts, many NCPs do not feel that they are able to play a viable role in the lives of their children. They say that they would like to spend more time and have greater involvement with their children, but are powerless to do so. In fact, the depth of their frustration appears to be so great that as many as 80% of the respondents would support a statute that would empower the police to enforce court mandated visitation orders.

These reports are consistent with an earlier study which found that angry feelings on the part of former spouses can serve to hinder effective involvement on the part of fathers. In an effort to avoid painful encounters with their former wives, embittered fathers often discontinue or decrease the number of visits they have with their children (Kelly, 1981). This observation is consistent with our failure to identify any relationship between the number of hours a NCP spends with his child(ren) and the amount of child support provided ($r = -0.04$, NS).

The overriding concern of the participants in this study has to do with what they perceived to be a fundamental issue of fairness. It should be noted that, while less than 25% of the respondents feel that the visitation arrangements as dictated by the court are inherently fair, there is no relationship between perceived fairness and the amount of child support paid (Point-biserial r = .03, NS). Fairness seems to have more to do with the critical events surrounding visitation than with any presumed entitlement associated with the payment of child support. Most of the respondents would like to have more involvement in the care and decisions that affect their children. One NCP argues that such involvement "requires more visitation with the child to better understand the child's needs."

The data seem to suggest that perceptions of fairness and satisfaction with visitation are functionally related to a series of critical issues that set the tone for the visitation experience: (1) Are there serious disagreements about visitation; (2) Does conflict occur at the time of transfer; (3) Does the custodial parent ever attempt to hide the child(ren) from the NCP; (4) Does the custodial parent tell lies about the NCP? Whenever any one or combination of these issues are perceived by the NCP to exist, questions of fairness and satisfaction with the visitation process are more prevalent. While none of these issues are related to the NCP's level of child support, all four of them correlate significantly with the NCP's level of satisfaction with the visitation arrangements as illustrated in Table 2.

Overall, NCPs expressed satisfaction with visitation arrangements when they felt that they were being treated fairly by their custodial ex-spouses. Conversely, they expressed dissatisfaction when matters of basic fairness

TABLE 2. The Relationship of Four Critical Issues with the NCP's Level of Child Support and Satisfaction with Visitation Arrangements

	Child Support		Visitation Sat.	
	Pt. Bi-Serial r :	X^2	Phi.	Prob.
Disagreements about visitation	0.07 (NS) :	6.18	.31	.013
Conflict at time of transfer	−0.13 (NS) :	7.94	.36	.005
Custodial parent hides children	0.04 (NS) :	7.84	.35	.005
Custodial parent tells lies about NCP	0.09 (NS) :	6.83	.34	.009

were perceived to be disregarded (Phi Coefficient = 0.74, p < .001). It is difficult to determine how the issue of fairness impacts the overall quality of the relationship between ex-spouses. It may be that prior negative relationships are more likely to generate power struggles that tend to be perceived as issues of fairness. A level playing field may simply reflect a more positive relationship or the ability of the contending parties to rise above their differences on behalf of the children. In either case, when the NCP feels that he is being treated fairly, the visitation arrangements tend to go more smoothly, conflict is kept to a minimum, and the NCP identifies himself more fully with the parenting role. It is reasonable to assume that, when this occurs, the best interests of the child are more likely to be served.

CONCLUSIONS

It has been suggested that one of the primary reasons custodial mothers deny access is because their ex-spouses frequently fail to meet mandated child support responsibilities. Such behavior is believed to exacerbate any negative feelings that may already exist between the divorced couple. This study explores the perceptions of a group of noncustodial fathers for whom the possible contaminating effects of the child support variable has been removed from the visitation scenario. Despite voluntary participation in an automatic electronic fund transfer program, the majority of the fathers who participated in this study report that they experience serious problems with respect to issues related to visitation. The data do *not* support the prevailing assumption that the primary reason for access denial is non-payment of child support.

Most noncustodial fathers feel that their ex-spouses possess a disproportionate share of the power when it comes to the management of their children's welfare. They feel that their former wives often tend to abuse that power and that such violations are routinely ignored by the courts. They feel powerless to do anything about the situation, and for them, matters related to visitation often involve fundamental issues of fairness. As a result, they often feel disenfranchised and ineffectual in their efforts to carry out what they consider to be the responsibilities associated with their role as fathers.

Any research that contributes to a better understanding of the factors involved in the access denial controversy is likely to be of interest to professionals who engage in the process of counselling or mediating custody disputes. Comparative analyses designed to explore various dimensions of the access issue would contribute to this aim, including the exploration of topics such as: regional variations in legal regulations and their relative effectiveness in combatting visitation abuses; the effectiveness of alternative intervention strategies such as parenting classes as a means of preventing and/or resolving access disputes; and finally, the use of mandatory mediation as an alternative to the more traditional adversarial models. Also, since this study was conducted exclusively with noncustodial *fathers,* it would be useful to study a comparable group of noncustodial *mothers* to determine if that population perceives access issues in the same manner as their male counterparts. Power may be used in different ways when the gender of the custodial parent is varied.

It should also be emphasized that this study focused solely on the perceptions of only one of the parties involved in the access controversy. There are always at least two sides to every story and perceptions of any given individual do not necessarily represent reality. It is possible that as the level of conflict between divorcing parents increases, the tendency for them to distort reality may increase as well. One of the very few comparative studies on the subject found that when the same questions are asked of both parents, significantly different responses tend to emerge (Baver, Wolchik, Sandler, Fogas, & Zvetina, 1991). While their responses were found to correlate, each party tended to respond in ways that favored his or her particular perspective. For example, in a related study custodial parents maintained that they received 27% less child support than the noncustodial parents reported having provided (Baver, Fitzpatrick, & Bay, 1991). Truth probably falls somewhere between the extremes. Despite whatever perceptual distortions may prevail, however, for the fathers in this study, reality is defined by what they believe rather than by what actually exists. For them, there is little cause for optimism without some significant changes in the policies and attitudes that surround the enforcement of visitation statutes.

The most pressing needs fall into the realm of legal reforms, including rigorous enforcement of current visitation guidelines as well as the continuing scrutiny and modification of those guidelines to assure increased and consistent access for children to both parents. An important corollary of any policy revision would include the implementation of a state-wide system designed to track all components of the divorce process (including the judicial enforcement of visitation orders and accountability with respect to child support payments). Other possible reforms might include the establishment of presumptive joint *legal* custody and mandatory mediation as additional means of ensuring that children of divorce have access to both parents. While legal reforms cannot be relied upon to resolve all the problems associated with the access dilemma, they would seem to be a necessary first step if we ever hope to resolve the dilemma in a way that serves the best interests of the child.

REFERENCES

Baver, S.H., Wolchik, S.A., Sandler, I.N., Fogas, B.S., & Zvetina, D. (1991). Frequency of visitation by divorcing fathers: Differences in reports by fathers and mothers. *American Journal of Orthopsychiatry,* 61, 448-454.

Baver, S.L., Fitzpatrick, P.J., & Bay, R.C. (1991). Non-custodial parent's report of child support payments. *Family Relations,* 40, 180-185.

Bloom, B.L., & Hodges, W.F. (1984). Parents' report of children's adjustment to marital separation: A longitudinal study. *Journal of Divorce,* 8, 33-50.

Bradburn-Stern, B., & Morley, R.C. (1991). *Children cope with divorce: Parent handbook.* Indianapolis, IN: Visiting Nurse Service, Inc.

Coalition for Children's Access to Parents. (1992). Organizational Brochure. Indianapolis, IN.

Committee on the Family of the Group for the Advancement of Psychiatry. (1980). *New trends in child custody determinations.* Washington, DC: Mental Health Materials Center.

Depner, C.E., Leino, E.V., & Chun, A. (1992). Interparental conflict and child adjustment: A decade review and meta-analysis. *Family and Conciliation Courts Review,* 30, 323-340.

Ferguson, R. (1990). *Non-custodial fathers: Factors that influence payment of child support.* Unpublished manuscript.

Greif, J.B. (1979). Fathers, children, and joint custody. *American Journal of Orthopsychiatry,* 49, 311-319.

Hanscom, J. (1992). "She loves Amy more than her cat!" An essay on the need to change language of divorce. *Family and Conciliation Courts Review,* 30, 342-351.

Hillery II, A. (1993). The case for joint custody. In D. Levy (Ed.), *The best parent is both parents: A guide to shared parenting in the 21st century.* Norfolk, VA: Hampton Roads Publishing Company, Inc.

Jacobs, J.W. (1982). The effect of divorce on fathers: An overview of the literature. *American Journal of Psychiatry,* 159, 1235-1241.

Kelly, J. (1981). Current research on children's post-divorce adjustment: Research findings and clinical implications. *Family and Conciliation Courts Review,* 31, 29-47.

Klatner, N. (1987). Long term effects of divorce on children: A developmental vulnerability model. *American Journal of Orthopsychiatry,* 57, 587-600.

Klatner, N., Kloner, A., Schreier, S., & Okla, S.G. (1989). Predictors of children's postdivorce adjustment. *American Journal of Orthopsychiatry,* 59, 605-618.

Koch, M.A.P., & Lowery, C.R. (1984). Visitation and the noncustodial father. *Journal of Divorce,* 8, 47-63.

Kurdek, L.A., & Siesky, A.E. (1980). Effects of divorce on children: The relationship between parent and child perspectives. *Journal of Divorce,* 4, 85-99.

Pearson, J., & Anhalt, J. (1992). *The visitation enforcement program: Impact on child access and child support.* Denver, CO: The Center for Policy Research.

Pearson, J., Anhalt, J., & Thoennes, N. (1991). *Child support in Colorado: The results of a 1991 household survey.* Denver, CO: The Center for Policy Research.

Peters, E., Argys, L., Maccoby, E., & Mnookin (1990). *Changes in child support payments after divorce: Compliance and modifications.* Washington, DC: U.S. Department of Health and Human Services.

Pirog-Good, M.A. (1993). Child support guidelines and the economic well being of children in the United States. *Family Relations,* 42, 453-462.

Ramos, S. (1979). *The complete book of child custody.* New York: G.P. Putnam's Sons.

Seltzer, J. (1991). Relationships between fathers and children who live apart: The father's role after separation. *Journal of Marriage and the Family,* 53, 79-101.

Thiessen, R.L.V. (1985). *Noncustodial parents: An investigation of some personality, demographic, and interactional correlates of child support compliance and father's perceptions of the post divorce situation.* Austin, TX: University of Texas, Unpublished Dissertation.

U.S. Department of Commerce, Economics and Statistics Administration, Bureau of Census, Statistical Abstract of the United States. (1993). *The National DataBook,* 113th Edition.

Weitzman, L. (1985). *The divorce revolution: The unexpected social and economic consequences for women and children in America.* New York: Free Press.

Williams, F.S. (1990). *Child custody and parental cooperation: The importance of preventing parentectomy (the removal of a parent from the child's life) following divorce.* Washington, DC: Keynote Address, Fifth Annual Conference, National Council for Children's Rights.

An Evaluation of the New Hampshire Child Support Guidelines: Using Social Science Research to Shape Child Support Policy

Walter L. Ellis

SUMMARY. An initiative was introduced in the 1996 New Hampshire Legislature that would grant a reduction in child support payments based on the number of overnight stays with children. This paper presents a case study discussing the process in which data on the court's usage of child support guidelines were obtained from divorce records and attorneys in two New Hampshire counties and used by a legislative committee to assess the merits of incorporating this bill into the guidelines. Findings in this child support policy research revealed nothing compelling for amending the guidelines. Final action taken by this legislative committee, therefore, was the recommendation that there be no further legislation on this initiative. *[Article copies available for a fee from The Haworth Document Delivery Service: 1-800-342-9678. E-mail address: getinfo@haworth.com]*

Policy makers have increasingly used social science research to support the view they themselves hold, or to criticize the view that others recom-

Walter L. Ellis, PhD, is Assistant Professor, Department of Social Work, Murkland Hall, 15 Library Way, University of New Hampshire, Durham, NH 03824.

The author gratefully acknowledges Paul Wilson, Visiting Associate Professor of the Department of Social Work, for his invaluable comments on earlier drafts of this manuscript.

[Haworth co-indexing entry note]: "An Evaluation of the New Hampshire Child Support Guidelines: Using Social Science Research to Shape Child Support Policy." Ellis, Walter L. Co-published simultaneously in *Journal of Divorce & Remarriage* (The Haworth Press, Inc.) Vol. 28, No. 1/2, 1997, pp. 63-75; and: *Child Custody: Legal Decisions and Family Outcomes* (ed: Craig A. Everett) The Haworth Press, Inc., 1997, pp. 63-75. Single or multiple copies of this article are available for a fee from The Haworth Document Delivery Service [1-800-342-9678, 9:00 a.m. - 5:00 p.m. (EST). E-mail address: getinfo@haworth.com].

mend to them (Rein, 1978). Rein reported that social science research plays a definite part in the complex process by which society constructs its perceptions of reality, defines what its problems are and determines what principles of intervention should guide its action and inaction. This complex process makes it possible for empirical data to help towards making better policy decisions. The purpose of this child support policy research is to obtain empirical data to be used by a legislative committee in deliberations concerning a child support initiative.

CHILD SUPPORT INITIATIVE

A child support bill, Senate Bill (SB) 648, was introduced in the 1996 New Hampshire Legislature that would grant noncustodial parents a reduction in their child support payments should they exceed spending 62 overnights with their children. The assumption behind this decrease is that such a visitation schedule entails extraordinary expenses. The 62 overnights were arrived at by a New Hampshire Child Support Study Committee (1995) that examined the relationships among child support, custody and visitation. This committee also developed a specific formula for reducing child support payments.

Voting History of SB 648

On March 6, 1996, the Senate Judiciary Committee voted 4 to 2 that SB 648 ought to pass with an amendment. The full Senate, by voice vote on March 7, 1996, recommended that the bill ought to pass. On April 11, 1996, the House Judiciary and Family Law Committee voted 10 to 6 recommending that SB 648 be sent to interim study. This action was over a minority report recommending passage of SB 648. In a vote of 201 to 105, the full House on April 18, 1996 went along with the majority of the House Judiciary and Family Law Committee recommending that SB 648 be sent to interim study.

OBJECTIVE OF THIS CHILD SUPPORT POLICY RESEARCH

Many members of the House Judiciary and Family Law Committee argued that courts in New Hampshire already have power to make adjustments to support awards for special circumstances, including extraordinary expenses involving exercise of custodial or visitation rights. As such, these policy makers took the stance that SB 648 was not warranted. While the Interim Study Committee had information about other states that had adopted mathematical formulas that take into account the percentage of the year that children reside with each parent when setting child support award amounts, there was no assembled information documenting the court's usage of child support guidelines in New Hampshire. The author, therefore, was recruited by the Interim Study Committee to provide such documentation so that this information would be available during deliberations in the interim study process.

The objective of this child support policy research is to address two questions relative to SB 648; to what extent do judges and marital masters deviate from the 1989 New Hampshire Child Support Guidelines? And, in cases of deviations from guidelines, what are the special circumstances under which deviations are made? By answering these questions and in light of the history of child support legislation and empirical studies of child support reform, a more informed decision can be made with respect to SB 648.

RELEVANT CHILD SUPPORT LEGISLATION

In an attempt to make the child support system equitable, the U.S. Congress in 1984 required states to: (1) deduct child support from wages and other income of absent parents; (2) reduce state income tax refunds to absent parents by the amount of the past due child support; (3) impose liens against real and personal property for amounts of past due child support; (4) include medical support as part of child support orders whenever health care coverage is available to the absent parent at reasonable cost; (5) establish State Commissions on child support; and (6) establish non-binding guidelines for setting child support award amounts within the state (Public Law 98-378, 1984).

Still recognizing that in some situations the child support system is inequitable, the U.S. Congress with the passage of the Family Support Act of 1988, mandated even stricter child support regulations (Public Law 100-485, 1988). Rather than having advisory (non-binding) guidelines as in the 1984 reform, guidelines are now to be presumptive; meaning that judges can only depart from them on written evidence that they are unfair to either the children or to one or both of the parents. While the 1984 reform required states to withhold child support payments from income when payments were one month overdue, withholding is now required at the time support was ordered. In addition, states are now required to review award levels periodically to assure that the custodial parent continues to receive an equitable share of the noncustodial parent's income for the children. Provisions covering paternity are also included in this recent child support legislation.

New Hampshire Child Support Guidelines

The Family Support Act of 1988 sets guidelines and minimum requirements for states. Each state is to develop its own program for implementation of this new child support reform policy. In conformity with federal mandates, lawmakers in New Hampshire developed guidelines to be used in determining the amount of child support awarded (New Hampshire Revised Statutes Annotated [RSA], 1992). The guidelines currently in use are the 1989 New Hampshire Child Support Guidelines.

These guidelines are based on the "income shares" model. As reported in section 458-C:3 of the RSA, the determination of amount is based upon the parents' combined adjusted income. Subtracted from this sum are state income taxes paid and the amount of standard deductions for federal income tax and F.I.C.A. withholding as published and adjusted on an annual basis by the Office of Child Support Enforcement Services. This sum is then multiplied by the percentage of each parent's income.

The total child support obligation is divided between the parents in proportion to their respective incomes. Work-related child care expenses are deducted from the adjusted gross income of the parent incurring the expense.

As indicated in section 458-C:4 of the RSA, there is a rebuttable presumption; the presumption being that the amount of the award which would result from the application of guidelines is the correct amount of child support. To rebut the presumption, court officials have to indicate in the record that a circumstance exists which would make the application of guidelines either unjust or inappropriate in a particular case. Such judgements are made on the basis of the following criteria, though they are not limited to these criteria. Satisfaction of these conditions is deemed sufficient for deviating from guidelines.

Section 458-C:5 of the RSA spells out the following criteria under which there can be adjustments in the application of guidelines:

a. ongoing extraordinary medical, dental or education expenses, including expenses related to the special needs of a child, incurred on behalf of the involved children;

b. significantly high or low income of the obligor or obligee;

c. the economic consequences of the presence of stepparents or stepchildren;

d. extraordinary costs associated with the obligor's exercise of his/her physical custodial rights;

e. the economic consequences to either party of the disposition of a marital home made for the benefit of the child;

f. the opportunity to optimize both parties' after-tax income by taking account of federal tax consequences of an order of support;

g. state tax obligations;

h. split or shared custody arrangements; and

i. other special circumstances found by the court to avoid an unreasonably low or confiscatory support order taking all relevant circumstances into consideration.

Empirical Studies Related to Deviations from Presumptive Guidelines

The research evidence indicates that the setting of child support award amounts is *not* presumptive. Using a sample of 1,153 marital dissolutions representing 10 Minnesota counties, Rettig, Christensen and Dahl (1991) found considerable deviations from the Minnesota Child Support Guidelines. An overwhelming 87.4 percent of these awards deviated from the guidelines amount. Only 12.6 percent of court-ordered child support awards were exactly at the guidelines amount. It is important to note that 39.4 percent deviated above what the guidelines indicated, and 48 percent deviated below what the guidelines called for.

Meyer, Bartfeld, Garfinkel and Brown (1996) gathered data from court records in 21 counties in Wisconsin, and examined over 14,000 cases of paternity and divorce from 1980 to 1991. When examining 1,986 divorce cases involving sole physical custody, these researchers found that between 1988 and 1991 (during which time the Percentage-of-Income Standard was presumptive) 58.5 percent of the child support orders were in guidelines range. Ten percent of the orders were above what the guidelines called for, and 16.4 percent were below guidelines requirements.

Ray (1993) examined 1,627 child support cases in 9 New York counties. Ray found that in 21.7 percent of the cases the judgement was within the New York Child Support Guidelines range, which means that 78.3 percent deviated. Of the cases that deviated, 40.1 percent were above the guidelines and 38.2 percent were below the guidelines range.

METHODOLOGY

To provide the Interim Study Committee information about the court's usage of child support guidelines in New Hampshire, divorce case data were obtained from Strafford County and Carroll County Superior Courts. To complement data in these divorce cases, information was obtained via mail questionnaire from attorneys representing parties in these cases. Strafford County and Carroll County Superior Courts were primarily chosen to ensure a representation of both urban and rural court data on divorce. Strafford County is located in the New England County Metropolitan Area (Slater & Hall, 1996). Carroll County consists mainly of small towns.

Administrators of the New Hampshire Superior Court mandated that commencing September 1, 1995, judges and marital masters begin using a Uniform Support Order to record rulings on application of guidelines as set forth in section 458-C:5 of the RSA. Data were collected from all final divorce cases involving minor children between September 1, 1995 and May 21, 1996. The total population was 159. Included in this population were old divorce cases that had been reopened for either review or modification of awards. Data were obtained from those cases that were filed between 1988 and 1996.

Divorce case records contain the Uniform Support Order which provides detailed information on child support including: (1) whether or not child support was ordered, (2) whether or not orders were in compliance with guidelines, (3) and reasons for making any adjustments to guidelines.

A questionnaire was mailed to 109 attorneys involved in these divorce cases. Six of the questionnaires were returned as undeliverable. Of the 103 questionnaires that were presumed to have been received, 55 were returned representing a 53 percent response rate. The questionnaire provided information on: (1) attorneys' opinions about amending child support guidelines, and (2) divorcing parties' request to attorneys to deviate from guidelines due to extraordinary expenses associated with the exercise of custodial or visitation rights.

RESULTS

Adherence to Guidelines

Of the 85.5 percent of cases in which child support was ordered, a little over half (52.7 percent) were found to comply with guidelines (Table 1). This percentage is in range with research reported by Meyer et al. (1995). These researchers found 58.5 percent of their child support orders to be within guidelines range.

Close to half (47.3 percent) of the child support orders were found to deviate from guidelines (Table 1). This large percentage of cases that deviated from guidelines is similar to results found by other researchers (Rettig et al., 1991; Meyer et al., 1996; Ray, 1993) that have examined the use of presumptive guidelines.

Reasons for Deviating from Guidelines

As discussed above, section 458-C:5 of the RSA spells out criteria under which there can be adjustments to the application of guidelines. Of the cases that deviated from guidelines, almost half (49 percent) deviated on the basis of the "other" criterion, not the specified criteria spelled out in the RSA. This finding concurs with Ray (1993). Ray reported that when a reason was given to an acknowledged variation case the most common justification used was "other," which accounted for 47 percent of the reasons given.

The fact that the "other" criterion was so prevalent suggests that the criteria spelled out in the RSA are not the ones that divorcing parties pursue when they want adjustments to the guidelines. Instead, this finding implies that divorcing parties bring unique family circumstances to the court's attention and seek adjustments to the guidelines based on these circumstances.

Only 3 of the 9 designated criteria listed in the RSA (i.e., significantly high/low income of obligor or obligee, the economic consequences to either party of the disposition of a marital home made for the benefit of the child, and split or shared custody) accounted for more than 10 percent of the deviations. The special circumstance, extraordinary costs associated with the obligor's exercise of his/her physical custodial rights, that was of

TABLE 1. Child Support Orders

Ordered by Court		
	#	%
No	23	14.5
Yes	136	85.5
Orders Adhered to Guidelines		
	#	%
No	70	47.3
Yes	78	52.7

special interest to the Interim Study Committee was cited as a reason for making an adjustment to the guidelines in only 4.3 percent of the cases that deviated.

Divorcing Parties' Request to Attorneys to Deviate from Guidelines

Attorneys were asked to indicate the percentage of time in their cases that divorcing parties had requested them to deviate from the guidelines due to extraordinary expenses associated with the exercise of custodial or visitation rights. As reported in Table 2, divorcing parties made this request less than a quarter of the time. Apparently, this is not a major issue in these attorneys' case loads.

Attorneys' Opinions About Amending Guidelines

Attorneys were also asked whether or not they agree that the 1989 New Hampshire Child Support Guidelines should be amended to take into consideration noncustodial parents who spend a significant amount of time (if defined as exceeding 62 nights per year) with their children. While half (50.9 percent) of the attorneys were opposed to such change, a large number (47.2 percent) were in favor of amending the guidelines (Table 3); the conclusion being that among these attorneys there was no consensus on this issue.

However, attorneys responded differently when asked whether or not they agree that the 1989 New Hampshire Child Support Guidelines should be amended to take into consideration noncustodial parents who spend a

TABLE 2. Percentage of Time Divorcing Parties Request Attorneys to Deviate from Guidelines Due to Extraordinary Expenses Associated with the Exercise of Custodial or Visitation Rights

% of time	#	%
0	8	15.1
1-25	35	66.0
26-49	4	7.5
50	1	1.9
51-75	2	3.8
76-99	1	1.9
100	2	3.8

significant amount of time with their children, thus reducing the regular expenses of the custodial parents. Well over half (60.8 percent) of the attorneys agreed to such change and 37.2 percent disagreed that the guidelines should be amended (Table 4).

DISCUSSION

This child support policy research addressed two questions relative to SB 648; to what extent do judges and marital masters deviate from the 1989 New Hampshire Child Support Guidelines? And, in cases of deviations from guidelines, what are the special circumstances under which deviations are made? The guidelines were deviated from in close to half (47.3 percent) of the cases. Of these cases, the most common (49 percent) reason given for making an adjustment to the guidelines was "other."

TABLE 3. Attorneys' Opinions About Amending Guidelines to Take into Consideration Noncustodial Parents Who Spend a Significant Amount of Time (if Defined as Exceeding 62 Nights per Year) with Their Children

	#	%
Strongly Agree	14	26.4
Agree	11	20.8
No Opinion	1	1.9
Disagree	14	26.4
Strongly Disagree	13	24.5

TABLE 4. Attorneys' Opinions About Amending Guidelines to Take into Consideration Noncustodial Parents Who Spend a Significant Amount of Time with Their Children, thus Reducing the Regular Expenses of the Custodial Parents

	#	%
Strongly Agree	14	27.5
Agree	17	33.3
No Opinion	1	2.0
Disagree	11	21.5
Strongly Disagree	8	15.7

As discussed above, this criterion is not listed in the RSA. Thus, rather than simply abiding by criteria spelled out by lawmakers, judges and marital masters are exercising their judicial discretion in these rulings. Moreover, in cases where adjustments were made to guidelines, not only were deviations downward, but they were also upward. For example, in one case it was ruled that, "the amount of child support is in excess of the guidelines to take into account fluctuations in the obligor's income as a self-employed realtor."

This example and the rest of the data examined in this child support policy research indicate that judges and marital masters are adjusting child support payments, both upward and downward, to take account of the best interests of the child and the special circumstances of the parents. There is nothing in this data which indicates that deviations from the guidelines are arbitrary. Given the wide variations in individual family circumstances, it seems reasonable that judges and marital masters have latitude to exercise independent judgement. Only in this way can the best interests of the child and equity between parents be adequately served, since no list of guidelines or rules could be comprehensive enough to meet all circumstances. In conclusion, this child support policy research reveals nothing compelling for a change in the 1989 New Hampshire Child Support Guidelines.

This child support policy research was undertaken to help inform a decision concerning SB 648. Obviously, this child support policy research does not take into consideration all of the factors that could enter into such a decision. However, on the basis of the findings in this child support policy research, the following child support policy alternatives are proposed.

CHILD SUPPORT POLICY ALTERNATIVES

Policy Alternative #1

Do nothing. Leave the guidelines as they are and depend on judges and marital masters to continue to exercise their judicial discretion to accommodate various unique family circumstances.

Policy Alternative #2

Extend the current criterion in section 458-C:5 of the RSA which provides for deviations from guidelines in response to "extraordinary costs associated with the obligor's exercise of his/her physical custodial rights."

This criterion might be met with 62 overnights per year. However, in the interest of equity and to avoid risk of financial hardship to the custodial parent, it would seem advisable that in lowering the amount of child support paid by the noncustodial parent, two conditions should be met: (1) the extraordinary costs of 62 overnights borne by the noncustodial parent should be documented, and (2) that the reduction in child support payments should be offset by a demonstrable reduction in costs of child support borne by the custodial parent. An example:

> Mother and father pay $50 per month for child support. Let us suppose that in this, as in all such support judgements, there is a presumption that the child needs $100 per month for adequate support. It takes the $100 to provide for food, clothing, school expenses, entertainment, transportation, and so forth. If either parent's child support payment is reduced, the $100 per month is still needed to provide these essential outlays.
>
> If, under this policy alternative, the noncustodial parent has the child overnight for 62 nights per year, he or she can claim a reduction in his or her child support payment. If the reduction is $15 per month and if this $15 reduction is not offset by a reduction in the financial outlay of the custodial parent, then the presumption that the $100 per month is required for adequate support is not met. The custodial parent is therefore required to make up the shortfall or the child's living requirements must be reduced, resulting in either inadequate support of the child or an inequitable burden on the custodial parent.

CHILD SUPPORT POLICY OUTCOME

On October 24, 1996, the Interim Study Committee in executive session voted 8 to 4 recommending no further legislation on SB 648. This recommendation corresponds to policy alternative #1 above. The child support policy outcome, therefore, is to leave the guidelines as they are and depend on judges and marital masters to continue to exercise their judicial discretion to accommodate various unique family circumstances.

IMPLICATIONS FOR FUTURE CHILD SUPPORT INITIATIVES

This child support policy research began with a discussion of a child support initiative (SB 648), evolved through a research process (formulating research questions, developing a methodology for collecting data, and analyzing data) whereby two alternative child support policy options for addressing this child support bill were proposed, and communicated via oral presentation and written research report to an Interim Study Committee (Majchrzak, 1984). Majchrzak noted that policy research is specifically directed at providing policy makers with the options and information they need to solve social problems.

There were three lessons learned in this child support policy research. First, the time span for completing the research process was rather short. The research process commenced in May 1996, and the deadline for communicating with the Interim Study Committee was set in October 1996.

Second, there was the need to get the Interim Study Committee to "buy" into this child support policy research and not have it tainted with any connection to special interest groups. Around the state there were many of these groups with a vested interest in the outcome of SB 648. A decision was made to decline invitations from these groups to speak about SB 648 until communications with the Interim Study Committee had taken place.

Third, personal values came into play during the research process. This was particularly evident when it came to analyzing the data and stating a conclusion. The thought of presenting raw data to the Interim Study Committee and letting the committee arrive at its own conclusion about the merits of SB 648 was seriously entertained.

Social science research can be very valuable to policy makers. One member of the Interim Study Committee expressed to the author that, "it appeared that the previous thrust of assembled materials had been an effort to validate a stated problem on the basis of anecdotal testimony rather than by objective assessment and analysis." Perhaps, this child support policy research prevented the committee from attempting to "fix" something (child support guidelines) that was not broken to begin with.

REFERENCES

Majchrzak, A. (1984). *Methods for policy research*. Newbury Park, California: Sage Publications.

Meyer, D., Bartfeld, J., Garfinkel, I., & Brown, P. (1996). Child support reform: Lessons for Wisconsin. *Family Relations, 45*, 11-18.

New Hampshire Child Support Study Committee. (1995). *Report of the New Hampshire child support study committee*. Concord, New Hampshire: New Hampshire Senate.

New Hampshire Revised Statutes Annotated. (1992). *New Hampshire revised statutes annotated*. Salem, New Hampshire: Butterworth Legal Publishers.

Public Law 100-485. (1988). Family support act of 1988. *United States statutes at large 102*. Washington, DC: United States Government Printing Office, 2343-2361.

Public Law 98-378. (1984). Child support enforcement amendments of 1984. *United States statutes at large 98*. Washington, DC: United States Government Printing Office.

Ray, M. (1993). *New York state child support standards act: Evaluation project report*. Albany, New York: New York State Department of Social Services.

Rein, M. (1978). *Social science & public policy*. Kingsport, Tennessee: Kingsport Press, Inc.

Rettig, K., Christensen, H., & Dahl, C. (1991). Impact of child support guidelines on the economic well-being of children. *Family Relations,* 40, 167-175.

Slater, C. & Hall, G. (1996). *1996 county and city extra: Annual metro city and county data book*. Lanham, Maryland: Bernan Press.

CUSTODIAL ISSUES FOR FATHERS, MOTHERS AND GRANDPARENTS

Noncustodial Fatherhood: Research Trends and Issues

Kris Kissman

SUMMARY. Research on non-custodial fathers is progressing from the negative effects of father absence to the development of successful models of co-parenting where absentee fathers share responsibilities for childrearing. Theoretically-based analyses of the obstacles and factors that promote father involvement need to be placed within the context of diverse families and interactions between biological parents living apart. Assessment of the impact of father presence on child well-being is especially important in light of the high proportion of children living in one-parent families without father support and the high rate of poverty among children raised by mothers. *[Article copies available for a fee from The Haworth Document Delivery Service: 1-800-342-9678. E-mail address: getinfo@haworth.com]*

Kris Kissman, PhD, is Associate Professor, Department of Social Work, Room 1231, Peck Building, Southern Illinois University at Edwardsville, Edwardsville, IL 62026-1455.

[Haworth co-indexing entry note]: "Noncustodial Fatherhood: Research Trends and Issues." Kissman, Kris. Co-published simultaneously in *Journal of Divorce & Remarriage* (The Haworth Press, Inc.) Vol. 28, No. 1/2, 1997, pp. 77-88; and: *Child Custody: Legal Decisions and Family Outcomes* (ed: Craig A. Everett) The Haworth Press, Inc., 1997, pp. 77-88. Single or multiple copies of this article are available for a fee from The Haworth Document Delivery Service [1-800-342-9678, 9:00 a.m. - 5:00 p.m. (EST). E-mail address: getinfo@haworth.com].

The social science literature on noncustodial fatherhood has proliferated in the past few years, with terms used to describe these fathers as nonresident, absentee and undercover fathers. Growing interest in noncustodial parenthood is partly in response to changing family structure and the rapid increase in children raised in one-parent families, most often by mothers. Currently 27% of all children in the U.S. are raised in one-parent families and over one half of these children are poor (U.S. Bureau of the Census, 1995b).

Changing family structure and the contemporary political climate encouraging family self-sufficiency have prompted investigations of what constitutes successful models of co-parenting where absentee fathers share responsibilities for child-rearing. Child support obligation of fathers, based on share of income devoted to children in two-parent families, has been estimated to equal 17% of fathers' income for one child and 25% for two children (Garfinkel et al., 1992). Yet, while $11.9 billion in child support was paid during 1991, $17.7 billion remains uncollected; and if court orders matched noncustodial fathers' ability to pay, the amount overdue in child support would be close to $50 billion in one year (U.S. Bureau of the Census, 1995a; Sorensen, 1995). Financial support of children is important in its own right and especially so in light of findings that fathers who provide financial and material support also tend to emotionally nurture and take active roles in caring for their children (Kissman & Shapiro, 1992).

Whether separated, divorced, never-married, adolescent or older, noncustodial fathers of minor children experience various impediments to their involvement in the lives of their children. Failure to obtain employment to meet their children's financial needs constitutes one of the major obstacles to father involvement, especially for the high proportion of African American fathers who experience high rates of unemployment and underemployment (Hendricks, 1988). The greater the persistence of poverty, the less the involvement of fathers, so that children who need support the most are least likely to receive it (Harris & Marmer, 1996). Young fathers often do provide in-kind or material support such as food and clothing for their children when they cannot provide much financial support (Danziger & Radin, 1990). But lack of resources to carry out a provider role and other factors such as fathers' new family responsibilities decrease fathers' ability and/or willingness to carry out co-parental responsibilities (Furstenburg & Cherlin, 1991).

Research on how fathers' financial and emotional support affects child well-being should be contextualized within a family systems framework that takes into account realities of diverse family forms, such as role taking and the external ecology in which families interact. Society's changing attitudes toward fatherhood, for example, will continue to impact fathers' perceptions of their roles and responsibilities. Exploration of how fathers perceive and carry out the role of parent, how available they are to their children and what responsibility they take for their care can be guided by theoretical frameworks that help assess multiple factors involved in role taking within families. In families where biological parents live apart, roles and responsibilities are bound to "deviate" from the traditional family model which has often been idealized as the preferred model from which diverse family forms are compared. The impact of parental relationships on father involvement is likely to differ in families, for example, where mothers facilitate or impede father visitation with children. Father/child relationships in these families are contingent on the level of conflict in the parental dyad and whether fathers developed relationships with their children prior to a divorce. Post-divorce fathers visit their children more frequently than do fathers of children born outside marriage and father involvement is also likely to be affected by fathers forming new families and the length of time fathers have resided away from their children (Ahrons & Miller, 1993).

THEORETICAL FRAMEWORKS

The process of developing successful models of co-parenthood where nonresident parents share responsibilities for childrearing requires identification of factors that influence paternal involvement and analyses of how these factors interact. Unemployment, for example, is likely to impact father's perception of his role as father, especially because fatherhood has traditionally been closely linked to the provider role. Similarly, how fathers perceive the impact of their involvement on their child's educational and psychological development and what they think is necessary to make contribution to their children's well-being are important areas of analysis (Child Trends, 1996). Fathers' perceptions of their roles and responsibilities are therefore likely to be influenced by economic resources (provider role) and how they perceive their impact on child well-being (caretaker role). Assessment of how these variables interact and how they impact frequency and quality of father visits and financial assistance to nonresident children can be guided by theoretical frameworks that explain how the meaning of roles impacts action (involvement).

Symbolic interactionism formulated by Blumer (1969) provides a helpful framework for the conceptualization of the provider/caretaker roles in absentia. Blumer states that people act on the basis of the meaning various roles have for them and that meanings emerge through social interaction with others. Fathers' perceptions of their paternal roles can be conceptualized as contingent on their interaction with biological mothers of their children in that father/child interaction is positively impacted when biological parents maintain a functional level of cohesion (Esposito, 1995; Hoffman, 1995). Role taking in binuclear and two-parent families may not differ in this respect because parental cooperation is a requisite to all families carrying out their goals of support and socialization of children.

Fathers' role perceptions have been found to change when they form new families and either live with biological children or stepchildren. The presence of these coresident children results in fathers reporting that fatherhood is increasingly more important to them and that they find parenting more manageable (Seltzer & Brandreth, 1994). It is not clear whether these changes in fathers' perception of parenthood, based on interactions with children in newly formed families, create stronger relationships between father and children from previous relationships. Increased responsibilities associated with new family formation may well offset potential benefits to the father/nonresident child relationship as resulting from fathers being exposed to parenting. Ahrons and Miller's (1993) finding that the longer fathers live away from their children, the less time they tend to spend with them may be partly a function of children's age; the older the child, the less time noncustodial fathers tend to spend with them. Conversely, older children have been found to be more affected by father presence than are younger children (Pruett, 1993; The National Center on Fathers and Fathering, 1996).

Family systems theory helps frame the constellation of factors that impact how biological parents living apart carry out the goals of the family; nurturance and socialization of children. Diverse families interact within the context of changing societal norms about fatherhood. Both parents' perceptions of fathers' roles and responsibilities toward co-parenthood are changing as fathers are increasingly gaining and sharing custody of their children. As expectations of fathers' co-parental responsibilities increase, lack of involvement appears to be more a violation of social norms, even where the social context in which the family resides provides limited opportunities for fathers to carry out provider roles, and the provider role is inextricably linked to caretaking.

As fathers increasingly gain custody of biological children society's changing perception of the role of fatherhood, including noncustodial fatherhood, is likely to impact the caregiver/provider role positively. Although fathers have been found to perceive parenthood as increasingly important as they are more exposed to parenting, and more manageable as they gain more experience with childrearing, simply engaging fathers in parental skills training and imparting to them knowledge about child development is not likely to be as effective in socializing males to the parenting role as is direct exposure to the parenting role.

Less is known about to what extent guilt and self-blame hinder fathers' abilities to co-parent. Studies have found that non-custodial mothers often suffer debilitating guilt feelings after relinquishing custody of their children (West & Kissman, 1991). Along the same lines, research findings are unclear about how the presence of a stepfather in the child's home affects fathers' role perception and to what extent fathers tend to feel less obligated for their children's care where stepfathers are viewed as preempting the paternal role.

Roles and responsibilities within the boundaries of diverse families are inextricably linked to the external context in which families interact, not only to stepfathers in the home but also the role of extended families and the world of work. The support of extended families, including grandfathers and other significant males, in support and socialization of children and fathers' abilities to provide for their children are among the multiple factors that are part of the external boundary of the one-parent family.

The desirability of father involvement, notwithstanding, where family dynamics of abuse, indifference and numerous other pathological interactions abound, father involvement is often not possible or desirable. Nor should nonresident fathers be encouraged to be involved in the lives of children in order to rescue families headed by mothers from the "non-intact" or broken state into which they are often categorized (Walters et al., 1989). Although one-parent families are much more vulnerable to economic impoverishment than are two-parent families, the strength of these families in carrying out support and socialization of children is often minimized by negative comparison with idealized two-parent families and failure to control for economic status which accounts for some of the negative outcomes in child well-being and achievement.

Cross-national comparisons, for example, indicate that child poverty is reduced to less than 3%, compared to over 20% in the U.S. in countries where income transfer, family policies and gender equality in wages are geared toward strengthening families (Males, 1996).

NONCUSTODIAL FATHERS AND THE ONE-PARENT FAMILY

Family systems theory provides a framework for conceptualization of families headed by mothers as interacting within the context of support, albeit often minimal support, from nonresident fathers and extended family. The role of extended family extends beyond the ability to nurture and to provide for children. Burton's (1996) findings that family norms about fatherhood are handed down multi-generationally have implications for research about extended family influences in socializing males to the fathering roles, particularly the identification of factors that facilitate inter-generational transmission of norms that promote co-parenthood and factors that inhibit paternal involvement.

Minton and Pasley's (1996) qualitative data from matched pairs of mothers and fathers, for example, sheds light on how fathers' roles differ from that of mothers in that fathers generally come to see their roles as more associated with playful interaction with children rather than discipline or caregiving. Gender-based division of labor within families extends to other significant males in the child's life, including grandfathers who are more likely to engage in play with their children than are grandmothers who tend to assume caregiving roles, as reported by Radin et al. (1991). Male parental roles within families are often ambiguous but noncustodial fatherhood is even more complex, leaving many fathers unsure about what roles they are able to play in co-parenting their children (Minton & Pasley, 1996).

Because information about noncustodial fathers is all too often obtained from mothers, further areas of research into noncustodial fatherhood should include matched samples of mothers and fathers to explore factors such as what fathers think is necessary to make contributions to their children's educational and psychological development (National Center on Fathers and Families, 1996). Securing information from both parents who live apart is particularly important because of incongruence in reports by mothers and fathers living apart where fathers have tended to rate higher their involvement in their children's lives after divorce than do mothers (Seltzer & Brandreth, 1994).

Research on co-parental relationship as it affects child well-being is scarce and data is all too often obtained from mothers' perspective because fathers are difficult to locate and it is difficult to elicit information about family life from fathers (Furstenburg & Cherlin, 1991). Parental conflicts have been found to influence children's behavior in families where biological parents live apart. Contact with the nonresident parent, most often father, has been found to be associated with increased behavioral problems in boys when parental conflict was high (Ahrons & Miller, 1993). Along similar lines, Arditti and Kelly (1994) found that more positive relationships with ex-wives was the strongest predictor of fathers assuming co-parental responsibilities in terms of increased frequencies of visits and quality of the interaction between parent and child. The impact of father involvement on child well-being is also mitigated by parental conflict which has been found to have an adverse effect on child well-being, indicating the need for investigation of the quality of father involvement in children's lives (Cohen, 1995).

Research on noncustodial father involvement has tended to be confined to post-divorced parental relationships. There is a dearth of research on the increasing number of never-married fathers who have been found to have an even lower level of involvement than do post-divorce fathers.

FATHER INVOLVEMENT AND THE IMPACT ON MINOR CHILDREN

The most compelling reason for gathering additional data on fathers and fathering is the impact of father involvement on child educational and psychological well-being (Child Trends, Inc., 1996). Studies of the impact of father presence on child well-being are scant, but frequency of father visits has been associated with higher academic achievement, self-esteem, social competence and overall well-being of children (Ahrons & Miller, 1993). The presence of fathers seems to be important for adolescent boys' development of initiative and industry, specifically in planning problem solving, building and exploring (Pruett, 1993; Belsky & Eggebeen, 1991). Father presence has been found to impact adolescent girls' delay of sexual activity (National Center on Fathers and Fathering, 1996). Although most recent studies agree that the socioeconomic status of the family impacts the development and behavior of young children more than does father absence, the importance of having two parents provide for material needs of the child reduces the probability that poverty will impact child well-being (Crockett et al., 1993; Wade, 1994).

The findings that children who receive material and emotional support from fathers also tend to receive support from extended family and friends of the family (Kissman & Allen, 1993) point to the need for study of family interactions and norms that promote paternal support and support from extended family members, including other significant males. The benefits of male involvement on child well-being extend to grandfathers. Children whose grandfathers spend time with them have been found to score higher on child development scales, for example (Radin et al., 1991).

Early childhood development and educational programs conceptualize male involvement as including fathers, grandfathers, uncles, friends and other men in the child's immediate environment (Comprehensive Child Development Project, 1996). Comprehensive services are provided by these programs to fathers, male extended family members and friends who are encouraged to develop skills to use in their own life as well as in childrearing. Program components are geared toward implementing changes deemed important to the development of nurturing males and include job training and placement, parental skills, understanding child development and parental responsibilities. The program's emphasis on providing essential services to create maximum involvement of males in the nurturing of children breaks down traditional polarization of work and family life. Males who need to develop skills in nurturing also need resources to provide nurturing.

Father involvement must be perceived within the larger context of social inequality, and lack of resources that disproportionately affect diverse family forms and especially ethnic families. The special obstacles of male unemployment and underemployment, particularly in inner city communities, serve as powerful obstacles to male involvement as reported by Hendricks (1988), especially since provision of material resources has been linked to nurturing of children. According to Newman and Chauncy's (1995) work on job finding in inner city areas, an average of 14 people had applied for every job opening in the local McDonald's restaurant during a five-month period and 73% of those rejected for the jobs had not found work a year later. The National Jobs for All Coalition (1996) suggests that the true state of the national unemployment be determined by the Department of Labor by collection of data on the number, location and quality of job vacancies across the United States.

Because the availability of economic resources is a powerful predictor of male involvement, income variations should receive as much attention as does age in social science research. However, current studies tend to emphasize age differences, adolescent and older fathers, more than differences based on income and marital status, never-married and post-divorced. Noncustodial fathers share similar obstacles and challenges across age, race and socioeconomic lines, although there are some unique aspects of race and ethnicity that should be emphasized. McAdoo (1988) and Peters (1988) have stressed the importance of African American fathers providing appropriate ethnic socialization of their children and sensitization to the negative consequences of ethnocentrism of others (Peters, 1988).

CONCLUSION

Successful models of co-parenthood where fathers share responsibilities for raising their children should be conceptualized within the context of one-parent families, most often headed by mothers. These families share many of the characteristics of the "traditional" two-parent families, such as varying gender role assignments where fathers tend to take less responsibility for childrearing than do mothers. The fact that male roles often differ from that of mothers in level and type of parenting is likely a function of different expectations and socialization processes because fathers are usually able to provide caregiving when they assume custody of their children.

Findings that fathers spend less time in discipline and care, more time on playful interactions and rate higher the time spent with their nonresident children than do mothers may be related to traditional gender role assignment where nonresident father caregiving is rated as rather anomalous with subsequent inflation in value. Matched samples of fathers and mothers to assess the incongruence between perceptions of co-parental responsibilities have been difficult to obtain due to lack of access to nonresident fathers who tend to eschew opportunities to share information about family lives. Qualitative as well as quantitative data obtained through in-depth interviews would help determine both parents' views of the impact father involvement has on children's well-being and psychological development. Anecdotal data that augment information obtained through structured interview surveys can enable parents who live apart to fully share their stories about obstacles and facilitators to co-parenting.

As fathers increasingly gain custody of their children, expectations of fathers' involvement in childrearing are likely to increase. Similarly, the presence of coresident children in reconstituted families represents increased opportunities for fathers to engage in parental roles which are nevertheless marked by a great deal of ambiguity, particularly for never married fathers who have not established close relationships with their children. While mothers often suffer from guilt and self-blame subsequent to relinquishing custody of their children, it is not clear to what extent such feelings play a part in fathers' inability to interact with their children.

The quality of interactions between parents living apart has been found to be one of the best predictors of father involvement. Conflicting relationships between parents can have adverse results on child well-being in families where parents live apart as well as in two-parent families. Research studies that increasingly focus on how women "orchestrate" men's relationships with the children by scheduling/facilitating or preventing visitation by fathers have implications for how interventions such as conflict resolution skills can facilitate parental cooperation. Parental relationships are a key factor in successful co-parenting but fathers should not be perceived as rescuers of inadequate one-parent families. Nonresident fathers comprise important parts of support systems that strengthen the family's ability to support and socialize children. But in many mother-headed families, nonresident fathers are unable or unwilling to provide support and in cases where abuse and severe conflict have been part of the family history, support may not be desirable.

The distinguishing feature of the one-parent family is that its support system has many forms, at times comprising extended family members and friends, surrogate fathers, grandfathers and other significant males rather than nonresident fathers. Extended families also play an important role in shaping intergenerational patterns of fatherhood in absentia, including expectations of what constitutes "good enough" fatherhood and handing down information such as child management skills and knowledge of child development. Nonresident father involvement should be assessed within the context of support and expectations of extended families' kinship and societal expectations as well as obstacles such as geographic distance between parents, fathers' new family responsibilities and presence of stepfather in the child's home that represent distinguishing characteristics of reconstituted and one-parent families.

Members of diverse families interact within a societal context where changing expectations and norms about fatherhood impact family members' beliefs about what roles and responsibilities fathers have toward their children's care. These beliefs are then mitigated by fathers' means to carry out responsibilities of fatherhood and their views of what impact they have on their children's well-being, psychological and educational development. Research on noncustodial fathers is evolving toward identification of within-in-group variations based on income, age, and race. While fathers are increasingly being held responsible for providing for their children regardless of their relationships with mothers of their children or their new family responsibilities for new families, unemployed or underemployed fathers face special obstacles to carrying out the provider/caretaker role. Adolescent fathers and African American fathers are overrepresented in poverty statistics with scarce resources creating strong reliance on extended kinship networks, grandfathers, uncles and family friends as part of the male caregiver/provider system that provides bi-cultural socialization of children. Similarly, as investigations progress beyond the boundaries of post-divorced families toward how never-married biological parents interact to promote child well-being, marital status becomes an increasingly prominent factor in the development of successful models of co-parenthood.

Theoretical frameworks such as family systems and symbolic interactions can help guide analyses of father role perceptions and societal changing expectations of father responsibilities as provider and caregiver of his children. Some of the changing expectations are reflected by increasing numbers of court orders for child support awards commensurate with fathers' abilities to pay and greater efforts to collect these awards from fathers by various means ranging from tracking down fathers who are in arrears and garnisheeing their wages to withholding licensures. Fathers who provide for their children also tend to spend time with and nurture them, but the relationship between provider and caregiver roles may not hold true for fathers who are mandated to provide for the material needs of their children.

REFERENCES

Ahrons, C.R. & Miller, R.B. (July, 1993) The effect of post-divorce relationship on paternal involvement. *American Journal of Orthopsychiatry*, 63,3: 441-4540.

Arditti, J.A. & Kelly, M. (January, 1994) Contract with non-resident parents. Interparental conflict and children's behavior. *Journal of Family Issues*, 15:191-207.

Belsky, J. & Eggebeen, D. (1991) Early and extensive maternal employment and young children's social and emotional development. Children of the National Longitudinal Survey of Youth. *Journal of Marriage and the Family*, 53:1083-1110.

Blumer, H. (1969) *Symbolic Interactionism: Perspectives and Methods*. Englewood Cliffs, NJ.

Burton, L.M. (June 1996) *"Under Cover" Parenting: Reframing Paradigms for Studying African American Fathers*. Paper presented at the Ethnographic Conference on Fathers and Fathering, NICHD, Washington, DC.

Child Trends, Inc. (May, 1996) *Improving Federal Data on Fathers: A Summary of the Town Meeting on Fathering and Male Fertility*, Washington, DC.

Cohen, O. (1995) Divorced fathers raising children. *Journal of Divorce & Remarriage*, 23, 1/2:55-73.

Comprehensive Child Development Program, Leslie Bates Davis Neighborhood House. Description of Services. East St. Louis, IL.

Crockett, L.J., Eggebeen, D.J. & Hawkins, A.J. (September, 1993) Father's presence and young children's behavioral and cognitive adjustment. *Journal of Family Issues*, 14, 3:355-377.

Danziger, S.K. & Radin, N. (1990) Absent does not equal uninvolved: Predictors of fathers in teen mother families. *Journal of Marriage and the Family*, 52:626-42.

Esposito, S.A. (1995) Cohesion and adaptability in the noncustodial father-child relationship: The effects of interaction quality. *Journal of Divorce & Remarriage*, 23 (1/2): 21-37.

Furstenburg, F.T. & Cherlin, A.J. (1991) *Divided Families: What Happens to Children when Parents Part*. Cambridge, MA: Harvard University Press.

Garfinkel, I., Meyer, D.R. & Sandefur, G.D. (December, 1992) The effect of alternative child support systems on Blacks, Hispanics and non-Hispanic Whites. *Social Service Review*, 66, 4:524-546.

Harris, K.M. & Marmer, J.K. (September, 1996) Poverty, paternal involvement and adolescent well-being. *Journal of Family Issues*, 17, 5:614-40.

Hendricks, L.E. (1988) Outreach with teenage fathers: A preliminary report on three ethnic groups. *Adolescence*, 23, 91:711-720.

Hoffman, C.D. (1995) Pre- and post-divorce father-child relationships and child adjustment: Noncustodial fathers' perspectives. *Journal of Divorce & Remarriage*, 23 (1/2) 3-20.

Kissman, K. & Allen, J.A. (1993) *Single Parent Families*. Newbury Park, CA: Sage Publications.

Kissman, K. & Shapiro, J. (1990) The composites of social support and well-being among adolescent mothers. *International Journal of Adolescent and Youth*, 2, 3:165-73.

Males, M.A. (1996) *The Scapegoat Generation: America's War on Adolescents*. Monroe, ME: Common Courage Press.

McAdoo (1988) The roles of black fathers in the socialization of black children. In H.P. McAdoo (Ed.), *Black Families* (2nd Ed., pp. 257-269). Newbury Park, CA: Sage Publications.

Milton, C. & Pasley, K. (January, 1996) Fathers parenting role identity and father involvement: A comparison of nondivorced fathers. *Journal of Family Issues*, 17, 1:26-45.

National Center on Fathers and Families: Core Learnings (1996) Graduate School of Education, University of Pennsylvania, Philadelphia, PA.

National Jobs for All Coalition (1996) *Welfare "Reform": Where Are the Jobs?* New York, NY.

Newman, K.S. & Chauncy, J. (1995) *Finding Work in the Inner City: How Hard Is It Now?* New York: Columbia University Press.

Peters, M. (1988) Parenting in black families with young children. In H. P. McAdoo (Ed.), *Black Families* (2nd Ed., pp. 228-241) Newbury Park, CA: Sage Publications.

Pruett, K.D. (1993) The paternal presence. *Families in Society*, 74:46-50.

Radin, N., Oyserman, D. & Benn, R. (1991) Grandfathers, teen mothers and children under two. In P.K. Smith (Ed.), *Psychology of Grandparenthood*. London: Routledge Press.

Seltzer, J.A. & Brandreth, Y. (March, 1994) What fathers say about involvement with children after separation. *Journal of Family Issues*, 154:49-77.

Sorensen, E. (July, 1995) *A National Profile of Noncustodial Fathers and Their Ability to Pay Support*. Washington, DC: The Urban Institute.

U.S. Bureau of the Census (1995b) Child support for custodial fathers and mothers (Current Population Reports P60-187). Washington, DC: U.S. Government Printing Office.

U.S. Bureau of the Census (1995a) Income, poverty and valuation of non-cash benefits, 1993 (Current Population Reports Series P20 #478). Washington, DC: U.S. Government Printing Office.

Wade, J.C. (November, 1994) African American fathers and sons: Social, historical, and psychological considerations. *Families in Society*: 561-570.

Walters, M. (1988) Single parent, female-headed households. In M. Walters, B. Carter, P. Rapp. & O. Silverstein (Eds.), *The Invisible Web: Gender Patterns in Family Relationships*. New York: Free Press.

Why Do Fathers Become Disengaged from Their Children's Lives? Maternal and Paternal Accounts of Divorce in Greece

Charlie Lewis
Zoe Maka
Amalia Papacosta

SUMMARY. After divorce almost 50% of fathers lose touch with their children. Two explanations have been offered. The continuity hypothesis states that post-divorce relationships match pre-divorce contact. The discontinuity hypothesis, following Kruk (1991), states that fathers who have been highly involved are more likely to become disengaged because of the pain of separation from their children. In two Greek studies, mothers (Study 1) and mothers and fathers (Study 2) were interviewed about the precursors of the father's current relationship with the child. The results from both studies provide strong support for the continuity hypothesis. Discrepancies be-

Charlie Lewis, PhD, is on the faculty, Department of Psychology, Lancaster University, UK. Zoe Maka, MSc, and Amalia Papacosta, MSc, are graduate students in the Department of Psychology, Lancaster University.

The authors are grateful to Edward Kruk for allowing them to use his interview schedule for this research. The first author also appreciates the generous hospitality offered to him by Liam Kruk-Pulkingham when he visited Canada in order to write part of this paper.

Address correspondence to: Charlie Lewis, Department of Psychology, Lancaster University, LA1 1YF, U.K. Email (c.lewis@lancaster.ac.uk).

[Haworth co-indexing entry note]: "Why Do Fathers Become Disengaged from Their Children's Lives? Maternal and Paternal Accounts of Divorce in Greece." Lewis, Charlie, Zoe Maka, and Amalia Papacosta. Co-published simultaneously in *Journal of Divorce & Remarriage* (The Haworth Press, Inc.) Vol. 28, No. 1/2, 1997, pp. 89-117; and: *Child Custody: Legal Decisions and Family Outcomes* (ed: Craig A. Everett) The Haworth Press, Inc., 1997, pp. 89-117. Single or multiple copies of this article are available for a fee from The Haworth Document Delivery Service [1-800-342-9678, 9:00 a.m. - 5:00 p.m. (EST). E-mail address: getinfo@haworth.com].

tween these and Kruk's data may be explained by the impact of expectations and practices concerning fathers in different cultures upon their involvement after divorce. In Greece disengagement appears to be the consequence of low paternal investment in parenting. *[Article copies available for a fee from The Haworth Document Delivery Service: 1-800-342-9678. E-mail address: getinfo@haworth.com]*

The amount and nature of contact between fathers and their children after divorce has received increasing attention in the literature (see, e.g., Arendell, 1995; Hetherington and Stanley-Hagan, 1997). Following marital disruption, children typically spend at least five years of their lives in a single-parent household (Bumpass and Sweet, 1989; Furstenberg et al., 1983; Hofferth, 1985). In 90% of divorced families mothers are granted sole custody of the children and fathers are granted visitation (Loewen, 1988). In this paper we explore just why large numbers of men still lose contact with their children after a separation has occurred.

Survey research has demonstrated a decrease in the quantity and quality of contact between children and their non-custodial fathers. Demographic evidence from the National Survey of Children (Furstenberg, Peterson, Nord and Zill, 1983; Furstenberg and Nord, 1985; Furstenberg, Morgan and Allison, 1987) and the National Survey of Families and Households (Seltzer, Schaefer and Charng, 1989; Seltzer and Bianchi, 1988; Seltzer, 1991) shows us the extent of paternal "disengagement." Furstenberg et al. (1983) found that in 52% of divorced families with children aged 11-16 the last contact between fathers and their children had been one or more years before. One quarter had no contact over the previous five years, with the proportion rising to 64% among those separated for 10 years or more. Only one out of six children averaged a weekly contact with their father.

A more recent estimate of fathers' absence indicates an increase in fathers' post-divorce contact with children over the 1980s (Seltzer, 1991). It is reported that approximately 30% of children whose parents divorced had no contact with them at all, during the previous year. However, Seltzer noted that less than one-third of children who had contact with their fathers had spent extensive periods of time with them. Under one-third visited at least once a week or spent over three weeks a year with their fathers. Even among those fathers in weekly contact with their children, only 17% of them had a substantial influence on decisions about children's rearing, such as health care matters and education (Seltzer, 1991). Such data provide confirmation for the conclusion made by Furstenberg and Cherlin (1991, p. 35-36) that ". . . over time, the vast majority of children will have little or no contact with their fathers."

A similar story of non-custodial fathers becoming less nurturant and more detached from their children is found in studies using observational and interview data (e.g., Arditti and Allen, 1993; Arendell, 1986, 1995; Dudley, 1991; Hess and Camara, 1979; Hetherington, Cox and Cox, 1976, 1985; Kruk, 1991; Stephens, 1996; Umberson and Williams, 1991; Wallerstein and Kelly, 1980). All these confirm the pattern of modest contact immediately after the separation, followed by a sharp decline in their involvement in childrearing over time. Many suggest negative consequences of fathers' absence on all family members, especially for children (Amato, 1993; Hetherington, Stanley-Hagan and Anderson, 1989).

The quality of the relationship between the ex-spouses has been reported as a strong predictor (Ahrons, 1983; Ahrons and Miller, 1993; Arditti and Allen, 1993; Arendell, 1995; Dudley, 1991; Furstenberg et al., 1983, 1985, 1987; Kruk, 1991; Minton and Pasley, 1996; Seltzer, 1991; Seltzer and Brandreth, 1994; Stephens, 1996). A positive relationship with the ex-spouse has been associated with higher levels of contact as well as contributing to the child's post-divorce adjustment (Koch and Lowery, 1984). When there is a high level of conflict between the ex-couple, the non-custodial father may avoid contact with the child in order to avoid further conflicts with the ex-spouse (Furstenberg et al., 1985). Furthermore, Ahrons (1983) has stressed the mediating role of mothers in the relationship between fathers and children and the payment of maintenance (e.g., Stephen, Freedman and Hess, 1993) on the issue of paternal disengagement is important.

Just why do fathers drift away from their children's lives? Should researchers just look at the inter-parent relationship or are other factors important? Much of what is known about fathers comes from survey research and from interviews with divorced mothers. As Arendell (1995) indicates, both are inadequate to express fathers' own views and experiences of the divorce aftermath. Knowledge is limited as to how many non-custodial fathers are likely to become disengaged from their children's lives. Too little attention has been given to the link between the fathers' involvement in their children's care during marriage and their roles in their children's lives after marital dissolution. A few studies have addressed the continuity of men's parenting before and after divorce, but the findings appear to be controversial. Two views are apparent.

Firstly, there is what we term the *continuity hypothesis*, which would perhaps be better described as the continuity assumption. This states that the pre- and post-divorce father-child relationship patterns are quite similar. A number of studies (Friedman, 1980; Hodges et al., 1991; Lowery, 1986; Rosenthal et al., 1981) appear to confirm this "common sense" assumption. Furstenberg et al. (1988) proposed that the fathers' level of knowledge of their children and early paternal involvement in child care are highly related to paternal post-divorce contact. It is widely assumed that fathers who are much involved in their children's lives during marriage form strong emotional bonds with them, which they may actively seek to maintain after separation. The degree to which men invest in their children can be measured by the levels of their involvement in childrearing, the strength of their psychological attachments, their ability to understand their children's needs and paternal influence on children's development. This sense of investment in parenting during marriage may have a strong positive effect on the fathers' ongoing relationships with their children after marital dissolution.

However, a second explanation for paternal disengagement has been receiving increased attention over the past few years. We term this the *discontinuity hypothesis*. Hetherington (1979) found that some non-custodial fathers who had been relatively uninvolved with their children during marriage become concerned fathers following divorce, while others who had been intensely attached withdrew from their children. Similarly, Wallerstein and Kelly (1980), examining a clinical sample of parents and their children, found no correlation between the level of paternal attachment during marriage and the paternal relationship both 18 months following divorce and in a five-year follow-up study. Drawing upon these findings, Kruk (1991, 1992, 1993) performed a cross-national study of 80 non-custodial fathers. He proposed that a striking discontinuity exists between the level of paternal investment during marriage and fathers' parenting following divorce. According to Kruk's model, fathers who invest highly in their relationship with children are *more* likely to become disengaged from their children's lives after a divorce, whereas fathers only peripherally involved may remain in contact. The process of disengagement is " . . . the result of a combination of structural constraints and fathers' own psychological response to the loss of the pre-divorce father-child relationship" (Kruk, 1991, p. 225). Men who are highly attached to their children may experience great emotional distress stemming from the perceived "loss" of their children and from their inability to construct a new role as non-custodial fathers. Furthermore, the constraints imposed on them by the divorce courts and the absence of a social support network often result in a complete loss of the relationship with their children. In contrast, fathers who are much less attached to, and involved with, their children are more likely to remain in touch since the "visiting" relationship may actually enhance contact with their children.

This paper reexamines Kruk's (1991) interesting claim that, paradoxically, fathers who become disengaged from their children had been more involved as parents before the separation took place. Two studies are presented which examine this issue. Using Kruk's interview schedule they explore whether (1) mothers give the same opinion as the fathers in Kruk's study about the process of, and reasons for, paternal disengagement; (2) mothers and fathers agree about the causes of disengagement; (3) the patterns of change witnessed in Kruk's paper are evident in a culture outside the English-speaking world. Both studies reported here were conducted in Greece. There were two reasons why this location was chosen. Firstly, we wished to extend Kruk's findings in another context. Too much research is conducted within limited cultural domains and geographical areas, particularly North America, albeit with a few exceptions (e.g., Hatzichristou, 1993). Secondly, our choice of Greece was made in part because the population is restricted to a confined geographical area. Some 50% of Greeks live in Athens, thus reducing the likelihood that paternal disengagement will occur because of increased physical distance between family members (see, e.g., Umberson and Williams, 1991).

STUDY 1

While we acknowledge that research on fathers after divorce has relied too much on mothers' accounts (Arendell, 1995), this study was planned to see if mothers gave the same reasons for their ex-husbands' disengagement from their children as had the fathers in Kruk's (1991) study. Kruk relied purely upon paternal accounts and a maternal perspective seemed to be warranted. He studied a mixture of separated and divorced families. In order to match his sample as closely as possible this study chose two selection procedures. From lawyers' records successive divorce cases were selected— all divorces in Greece involve lawyers and this seemed to be an easy way to get a population sample. In order to obtain a further mixture of divorced and separated families individual teachers from state secondary schools were approached to locate the children in their classes who were known to come from such families. The sample was completed using the familiar snowballing technique (e.g., Biernacki and Waldorf, 1981). The aim was to compare the parenting histories of the fathers in the sample who were identified as "disengaged" (i.e., had no contact with their child over the last month) with the involvement of men still in regular contact with their child.

METHOD

Sample

Forty-four mothers were recruited in two locations in Greece. Twenty lived in Athens, while 24 came from Larisa, a small city in the north of

Greece. Forty-three had exclusive or major custody, while in one family the children resided with the father. They were located initially through two lawyers and three teachers in Larisa and four lawyers in Athens. Further respondents were located via the snowball procedure. Seventy-three percent of those contacted by telephone agreed to participate. In two of the initial families, the fathers were deceased. Their ex-wives were interviewed, but excluded from this analysis (none of the results change if they are included). In the final sample of 42, 18 were recruited via lawyers, nine through teachers and 15 through snowballing.

Following Kruk (1991) the main focus of the study was the amount of contact the father had with his children at the time of the interview. He asked fathers the question "How many times in the past month have you been in contact with them; that is, actually physically being with them?" Responses were coded from (1) "not at all" to (6) "more than five." This analysis uses resident mothers' reports to distinguish between "contact" and "disengaged" fathers. The 21 "disengaged" fathers were those who had had no contact with their children in the month prior to the time of the interview; "contact" fathers were those who had at least one physical contact with their children. Nineteen (of 21) contact fathers were reported to see their children regularly (seven of them daily), while only six disengaged men were reported to see their child usually, on a monthly basis, and 13 had contact less than yearly or never.

Seventeen fathers had one child, 22 families had two children, four families had three children and one family in Athens had four children. Most of the demographic characteristics of the respondents resembled those of Kruk's (1991) sample, which are reported here in parentheses. The mothers' mean age was 39.5 years ranging from 26 to 61. The mean age of fathers was 44.14 years (39 years and 3 months in Kruk, 1991) ranging from 31 to 69 (24 to 56 in Kruk). Of the 42 mothers, one (2%) had remarried (8% in Kruk). The rest remained divorced or separated. Twenty-five couples (59%) were legally divorced (49% in Kruk). The mean length of their marriage was 8 years and 5 months (8 years and 3 months in Kruk) ranging from 5 months to 20 years (4 months to 24 years in Kruk). The mean length of the separation at the time of the interview was 8 years and 4 months, ranging from 2 months to 24.75 years. This is longer than the period in Kruk's sample (3 years and 4 months, ranging from 3 months to 6 years, 11 months) and covariance techniques were employed in part to control for this difference.

In 31 (74%) cases (68% in Kruk) the wife initiated the separation, the husband did so in six (15%) cases (23% in Kruk) and there was a mutual decision in six (12%) instances (10% in Kruk). As in Kruk's study, the sample spanned a range of occupational groups. Two mothers were unemployed, 22 were in white collar occupations and 18 were in blue collar jobs. Of the 42 fathers, seven were unemployed, 20 were white collar and 15 were blue collar.

Data Collection and Measures

The semi-structured face-to-face interview designed by Kruk (1991) was modified for use with this sample. Firstly the questions, originally addressed to the father, were rephrased so that mothers were asked about their ex-spouse as a father. Secondly, some questions in the questionnaire which were not addressed in the original paper were omitted. Data were obtained on:

- Demographic information about all family members as well as information regarding the family history.
- Assessments of the pre-divorce father-child relationship with an emphasis on the father's physical involvement with, and emotional attachment to, his children.
- Information regarding the transition period during the divorce process including how custody and access were arrived at and fathers' satisfaction with these arrangements.
- Data about the post-divorce father-child relationship including information regarding changes in various areas of influence in children's development and the current relationship between the ex-spouses.
- Evaluations of the positive and negative aspects of the divorce process for the children and for the fathers themselves.

RESULTS

Demographic Characteristics and Statistical Design

The three main parts of this section examine father-child relationships in the two types of family (contact vs. disengaged) before, during and after marital dissolution. Preliminary analyses comparing the responses of mothers in the two locations (Athens and Larisa) revealed no major differences, so the data were pooled. Next, demographic comparisons of the two types of father were made. There were no significant differences between contact and disengaged men in relation to length of marriage (99.47

months vs. 108.95 months, respectively), maternal age (37.61 years vs. 41.38 years), the reported initiator of separation, fathers' current marital and economic status, and the ages, sex constellations and numbers of children. However, paternal post-divorce contact was significantly associated with the length of separation and the age of the father. Disengaged fathers had been separated on average 124 months, as opposed to 77 months for contact fathers, F (1,40) = 4.45, p < .05. Disengaged fathers (age: 48) were also older than contact (age: 40) ones, F (1,40) = 9.69, p < .005. Given these differences and the same contrast between this and Kruk's study, length of separation and paternal age were controlled for by loading each factor as covariates in the following analyses of variance. Most measures were on continuous scales and, after checks for normality, were examined by a one-way analysis of covariance (contact vs. disengaged). Categorical variables (concerning the demographic and personal characteristics of the parents and their marital history) were analyzed using chi-square tests.

Pre-Divorce Factors

The following issues were explored: paternal involvement in infant care, fathers' attachment to children, their influence on children's development and growth and attitudes towards gender role divisions in the home. Table 1 provides a summary of the general scales which were constructed to assess these areas of paternal involvement, comparing maternal assessments of contact vs. disengaged fathers. Appendix 1 presents the same comparisons (contact vs. disengaged) for every question which comprised those scales.

Paternal involvement in infant care was assessed on eight activities. Responses for each were coded on a six-point scale, with a range of 1 "No Involvement" to 6 "Exclusive Involvement." The scale of total "Involvement in Infant Care" was a combination of each question, with a range of 8-48. As with the other scales, reported as follows, the overall scores were low, suggesting a limited or "traditional" role for fathers. A significant overall difference was obtained, indicating that fathers who had maintained contact with their children after divorce were described by their ex-wives as having been relatively more involved in their children's early care (see Table 1, section a). On individual child-care tasks contact fathers were significantly more involved than disengaged fathers in the following areas: changing diapers, feeding, bathing, playing and lulling the baby to sleep (see Appendix 1, section a: all p < .05).

Table 1, section b, presents the total reported amount of contact between fathers and their children in the year before the separation, as

TABLE 1. Mothers' Mean Assessment of Paternal Relationship with Children Pre- and Post-Divorce by Current Contact (Disengaged vs. Contact)

		Paternal Post-Divorce Contact				
		Disengaged (N = 21)		Contact (N = 21)		
Variables	Range	M	SD	M	SD	
a. Paternal Involvement in Infant Care	8-24	11.58	3.96	16.43	8.44	$F(1.38) = 7.4, p < .01$
b. Pre-Divorce Contact	0-35	5.09	7.41	11.57	11.56	$F(1.38) = 4.66, p < .05$
c. Attachment	4-16	6.29	2.07	9.67	4.78	$F(1.38) = 5.71, p < .05$
d. Paternal Influence on Children's Development Before Separation	9-31	15.29	6.84	22.77	10.88	$F(1.38) = 7.36, p < .01$
e. Paternal Influence on Children's Development After Separation	9-35	13.29	5.97	23	11.89	$F(1.38) = 9.83, p < .01$

measured by the number of hours per week alone with the child and the time with others also present. It shows that contact fathers were reported to have spent twice as many hours per week with the child than disengaged men (12 hours vs. 5 hours per week). This significant difference was accounted for in time spent alone with the child (see Appendix 1.b).

Following Kruk (1991), fathers' emotional attachment to their children was measured by combining four questions about their relationships in the year before the divorce (questions about thinking about and wanting to be with the children when not with them and both comforting and talking with the children when in distress). A specific question about the father's emotional attachment to his children was also estimated on the same five-point scale (1 = not attached − 5 = very strongly attached), but was not included in the scale. Table 1.c shows that mothers significantly distinguished the two groups of men, with contact fathers being more attached to their children. In addition to the direct question "How strongly was the father emotionally attached to children," disengaged fathers were reported to be less attached but this difference was not quite significant, $F(1,38) = 3.58, p = .06$.

The influences that fathers had in various areas of children's development and growth were measured on six-point scales with a range of 1 "no influence" to 6 "very high influence." These were daily care and safety, teaching, giving the child a feeling of being part of the family and the development of the child's intellectual abilities, physical skills, personality, emotional adjustment, religious beliefs and morals. A measure of total Paternal Influence on the Children's Development was constructed by adding the nine items. Table 1.d shows that both groups were reported to be relatively uninvolved (the maximum possible score on the scale was 54). However, contact fathers were reported to be more influential. Significant differences between contact and disengaged fathers emerged in the following areas: daily care and safety, personality development and moral development (Appendix 1.d).

Kruk (1991, p. 205) reported significant differences in fathers' ideologies before divorce, with a higher proportion of disengaged men recalling no difference between maternal and paternal roles. However, the same questions in this study failed to distinguish between the two groups of fathers. Mothers were asked about their ex-husbands' attitudes towards gender role division within the family, with the questions "Was the father feeling uncomfortable doing things about children which he feels are unmanly?" and "Would your ex-husband say that there is a fundamental difference in roles between the father and the mother in the family?" With respect to the latter question, 81% of contact fathers and 71% of disengaged men were reported to be in favor of sex-role division in the home.

Factors During Divorce

In keeping with Kruk's study, there was no relation between the amount of paternal post-divorce contact and spousal disagreement over the issues of custody, access, property settlements and child support. However, three sets of results differed from Kruk's original study. Firstly, no significant difference between contact and disengaged fathers was found in their satisfaction with the legal custody arrangement, at least as reported by their ex-wives–Kruk had found disengaged fathers to be more dissatisfied. Second, in this study but not its predecessor, significant differences between the two sub-groups of fathers emerged in relation to the way in which child custody and access were arranged. Most disengaged fathers (20 of 21) were reported to have wanted the custody to be assigned to the mother, while nine of 21 contact fathers wanted to be assigned either complete or joint custody, χ^2 [1, N = 42] = 8.4, p < .01. Furthermore, 18 (of 21) contact fathers and six (of 21) disengaged fathers were reported to have wished to visit their children at the time of separation, χ^2 [1, N = 42] = 15.01, p < .001. Thirdly, there was a strong significant difference between contact and disengaged fathers related to the implementation of access arrangements. Mothers reported that most (71%) disengaged fathers had not implemented any joint or court decisions, while most (95%) contact fathers had at least implemented part of them, χ^2 [1, N = 42] = 19.48, $p <$ .001.

Factors After Divorce

A number of significant differences emerged in relation to the couples' post-divorce negotiations over the children. The respondents were asked to rate their relationship with their ex-partners, on a six-point scale, ranging from "nonexistent" to "very friendly." There was a clear difference between contact and disengaged fathers, $F(1,38) = 7.22$, $p < .01$. Fifteen ex-wives of disengaged fathers rated their relationship with their ex-partners as "very unfriendly." On the other hand, for 11 of 21 contact fathers, their ex-wives asserted that they maintained friendly relationships with them. However, no significant difference was found in relation to the fathers' feelings for their ex-wives, F (1,38) = 0.27, ns. Paternal contact was also not associated with former wives' encouragement or discouragement of fathers' contact with their children after divorce (71% of wives of disengaged men and 90% of contact fathers said that they were highly encouraging, F (1,38) = 3.6, *nqs.*

Table 1.e shows the mothers' responses to questions about paternal influence after separation. The same nine issues as discussed with reference to the fathers' pre-divorce influence (Table 1.d) were addressed on six-point scales. A significant difference between contact and disengaged fathers emerged, F (1,38) = 9.03, $p < .01$. Disengaged men were reported to be almost completely uninvolved in their children's development, while contact fathers were reported to have some influence.

Paternal contact was not significantly associated with the adequacy of their residential accommodation. Half of each group was reported to have insufficient number of bedrooms to house the child or children. However, proximity was found to be a factor affecting paternal post-divorce contact. At the time of the interview 95% of contact fathers were living in the same town as their children, while 43% of disengaged fathers were living in a different town, χ^2 [1, N = 40] = 8.4, $p < .01$. Eighty-eight percent of mothers did not consider fathers' work schedule or finances to be significant obstacles to their post-divorce contact with children and most of them stated that for both groups of fathers the effects of divorce on their work were insignificant.

Like the fathers in Kruk's study, these mothers reported negative effects of the divorce on the psychosocial adjustment of the majority of fathers (55%) and children (62%). However, unlike Kruk, there were no differences in reported symptoms between contact and disengaged men.

DISCUSSION

The results of this study give clear support for the idea of continuity between pre-divorce family relationships and the involvement of fathers after they become separated from their wives. On almost every individual and combined measure contact fathers were rated by their ex-wives as more involved in family life. As Table 1 and Appendix 1 show, fathers who became disengaged were recorded as having been less participant in infant/child care, to have developed weaker attachments to their children, spending less time with them and being less influential on significant aspects of their development. Such patterns continued after the separation and until the father became disengaged.

Why do these results differ so markedly from those of Kruk (1991), whose questionnaire was used in this study? We delay an analysis of the location of this study until the General Discussion. One obvious reason for the discrepancy may be that the respondents in this study were mothers while fathers were the focus of attention in Kruk's research. There might be two interpretations of the continuity and change in the paternal relationship over divorce—"his" vs. "hers" (Seltzer & Brandreth, 1994). A further study is needed to examine this issue before general issues in Study 1 can be discussed.

STUDY 2

This study compares the views of both mothers and fathers about their shared experiences of divorce. It utilizes the same measures that were employed in Study 1 and Kruk (1991) to examine whether mothers and fathers give similar or different accounts of the causes of paternal disengagement. If mothers and fathers disagree, then this study will show the importance of examining both perspectives in an attempt to understand paternal contact with children after separation. If, however, they agree, then this will enable us to explore further the differences between Study 1 and that of Kruk (1991).

Care was taken in Study 1 to match the sample with that of Kruk (1991). In this study no such attempts were made. Indeed it was hoped that differences between this and the other samples could be capitalised upon.

METHOD

Sample

Forty divorced families in Athens were selected through the records of two lawyers. Both ex-spouses were contacted by telephone, the study was described (including the fact that we would need to interview both parents) and they were asked if they wished to participate. Both parents had to agree to do so. Fifty percent consented to be interviewed–a figure lower than that in Study 1 but not uncharacteristic of divorce research. The final sample was composed of 20 divorced couples. In all cases apart from one the mother retained physical and legal custody of the children.

In keeping with the first study it was decided to use maternal evaluations of paternal disengagement in response to the question about the last contact between the father and child. In any case a high level of agreement between parents' responses to this question was found (r = .72). Eleven fathers (55%) had had contact in the last month and eight of these usually saw their children at least weekly. In nine cases (45%) fathers had not seen their children in the past month and were classified as disengaged. In this group five saw the child "yearly" and four never.

Seven (35%) fathers had one child and 13 (65%) had two children. The ages of the fathers and mothers were older than those in Study 1 (49.25 years for fathers and 44.25 years for the mothers). As a result of our use of lawyers for recruitment, all the couples were legally divorced. Seven (35%) had remarried since the divorce, six of whom were classified as disengaged. Seven (35%) mothers had also remarried.

The mean length of the marriage was 12 years, ranging from 4 years, 6 months to 20 years. The mean length of separation at the time of the interview was 8 years, 3 months, ranging from 1 year, 9 months to 17 years, 1 month. The mean length of divorce at the time of the interview was 6 years, 3 months, ranging from 10 months to 15 years, 6 months. In eight (40%) cases, the wife initiated the separation, the husband did so in nine (45%) and there was a mutual decision in three (15%) instances. As in Study 1 and Kruk's research, the sample spanned a range of occupational groups. Three (15%) fathers were classified as blue collar and 17 (85%) were white collar.

Data Collection and Measures

The same interview that was used in Study 1 (with a few modifications described in the Results section) was employed with the mothers in this sample. The fathers' interview was a direct translation of the relevant sections of Kruk's original interview.

RESULTS

Demographic Characteristics and Statistical Design

As with Study 1 preliminary analyses were conducted to examine whether the contact and disengaged fathers were distinguishable in demographic terms. There were no apparent differences between the two groups in relation to the lengths of their marriage, separation and divorce. The number, age and gender of children were not significantly associated with paternal post-divorce contact. No observable differences between contact and disengaged fathers were found in respect to both the parents' ages, their economic statuses[1] and their working hours. There was no apparent difference in relation to the mother's marital status. However, a significant difference between contact and disengaged fathers emerged for the father's marital status. Six (of 9) disengaged fathers had remarried but only one (of 11) contact father had remarried: Fisher's Exact Test: $p < .05$. Given that the two statuses of divorced vs. remarried were binary this variable was not used as a covariate in the following analyses.

The major aim was to determine whether conclusions about the factors that predict paternal post-divorce contact with children depend on who the respondent is; 2 (sex of respondent) by 2 (contact vs. disengaged) analyses of variance were conducted, with sex of parent treated as a within subjects factor. The measures of paternal involvement were comparable to those used in Study 1 with a few exceptions, listed below. Categorical variables were analyzed using Fisher's Exact Test because of the small numbers in each group. Pearson correlations were also employed to test the size of the relationship between parents' assessments. Table 2 provides a summary of the mean scores of fathers on all the variables assessing their relationship with children. Given that there were significant main effects for groups (disengaged vs. contact) and sex of parent but no interactions, in the following sections we will discuss each group difference first, followed by the comparison of mothers' and fathers' accounts. The scale scores of the mothers and fathers are presented in Table 3.

Pre-Divorce Factors

Paternal Involvement in Infant Care

Section a of Table 2 shows the parents' (mothers and fathers combined) assessments of the fathers' involvement in infant care. As with Study 1 this measure consisted of a combination of eight activities assessed on six-point Likert scales. As Table 2.a shows, contact fathers scored twice as highly on this scale. Table 3.a shows that fathers' assessments of their

---

1. There were more white collar workers in the contact group and blue collar workers in the disengaged group but, as there were no differences in income, these differences were not examined further.

TABLE 2. Overall Comparison Between Contact and Disengaged Fathers

		Paternal Post-Divorce Contact				
		Disengaged (N = 9)		Contact (N = 11)		
Variables	Range	*M*	*SD*	*M*	*SD*	
a. Paternal Involvement in Infant Care	8-31	11.06	2.31	20.95	6.01	*F(1.18) = 29.9, p < .001*
b. Paternal Contribution in Running the Household	6-21	11.17	2.31	15.59	6.01	*F(1.18) = 18.18, p < .001*
c. Pre-Divorce Contact	0-30	3.39	2.47	11.73	6.5	*F(1.18) = 22.19, p < .001*
d. Attachment	4-20	9.22	2.5	15.18	3.41	*F(1.18) = 11.48, p < .001*
e. Paternal Influence on Children's Development Before Separation	9-54	22.28	7.18	37.41	8.99	*F(1.18) = 22.46, p < .001*
f. Paternal Influence on Children's Development After Separation	9-51	13.83	4.47	30.45	10.36	*F(1.18) = 28.30, p < .001*

TABLE 3. Overall Differences Between Parents' Perspectives

		Sex of respondent				
	Fathers (N = 20)		Mothers (N = 20)			
Variables	*M*	*SD*	*M*	*SD*		
a. Paternal Involvement in Infant Care	18.2	7.55	14.8	6.24	*F(1.18) = 7.95, p < .01*	
b. Paternal Contribution in Running the House-hold	14.53	3.8	12.22	3.8	*F(1.18) = 6.01, p < .05*	
c. Pre-Divorce Contact	10.55	8	5.4	5.11	*F(1.18) = 10.18, p < .01*	
d. Attachment	13.95	4.6	11.05	4.1	*F(1.18) = 11.48, p < .01*	
e. Paternal Influence on Children's Development Before Separation	36.1	10.81	25.1	11.63	*F(1.18) = 30.57, p < .001*	
f. Paternal Influence on Children's Development After Separation	25.3	12.63	20.65	11.33	*F(1.18) = 3.79, NQS*	

involvement were consistently higher than those of their ex-wives. This was a significant main effect, but the difference in overall scoring was 3.4 on a scale with a possible range of 48 points. The lack of an interaction (here and in subsequent analyses) suggests that men consistently report higher involvement. However, a high agreement between each ex-spouse was also found (r (19) = .72, $p < .01$, 2-tailed), which explains the absence of an interaction. We next examined each of the eight individual measures of infant care. On almost every one a difference between contact and disengaged fathers was reported by both parents. Appendix 2.a presents comparisons of each of the activities as reported by the fathers. It shows that contact fathers reported significantly higher levels of involvement on each measure (all $p < .05$). In the mothers' assessments, significant differences between the two sub-groups of fathers emerged in six areas of infant care concerning feeding, bathing, preparing meals, lulling, playing and taking the baby to the doctor (all $p < .05$).

Paternal Involvement in Domestic Activities

Reports on the paternal contribution to running the household were also taken, using the same "Paternal Involvement" scale. Table 2.b compares the contact and disengaged fathers and indicates a significant main effect for group. Table 3.b shows that fathers report greater paternal involvement than do mothers. However, there was a modest and significant agreement between ex-spouses on the part played by the father (r (19) = .42, $p < .05$, 2-tailed). Appendices 2.b and 3.b present the data on the individual tasks that comprised the scale of domestic activities. They show that according to the men the contact fathers had been involved more in shopping, cooking meals, and cleaning the house (all $p < .05$). While the maternal responses each showed higher scores for contact fathers, none was significant.

Weekly Hours of Contact Between Father and Child Before the Divorce

With regard to the amount of pre-divorce contact between fathers and children, the analysis of variance revealed significant main effects for both group (see Table 2.c) and sex of parent (see Table 3.c). According to both parents the contact fathers were reported to have spent over three times longer with their children than the men who would become disengaged. Fathers' estimates were almost twice as long as those of mothers. Again there was a significant agreement between parents (r(19) = .5, $p < .05$, 2-tailed). Appendices 2.c and 3.c present the data from specific questions about time. They show that contact fathers reported more time alone and with others present, while this was only the case for time alone when their ex-wives were used as respondents–replicating the pattern found in Study 1.

Fathers' Emotional Attachment to the Children Before the Separation

As with Study 1 the measures used formed a 20-point scale of paternal attachment, which was the combination of four questions, and also a direct question about the father-child attachment. Tables 2.d and 3.d summarize the scale scores and main effects. Parents rated disengaged fathers as less attached to their children and mothers rated fathers less highly. Mother-father scores were significantly correlated ($r(19) = .65, p < .65$). Appendices 2.d and 3.d show that, on all four scale questions and the direct attachment probe, contact fathers reported themselves to have been more involved than disengaged men (all $p < .01$), while their ex-wives reported contact men to have been more closely attached, to have thought about their children more often and comforted them when in distress (see Appendix 3.d).

Fathers' Influence on Their Children's Development Before the Separation

The influence that fathers were reported to have was assessed in the same overall scale as used in Study 1, with the exception that concern with religious activity was replaced by help with financial matters. As before, the nine six-point scales (ranging from 1 "no influence" to 6 "very high influence") formed a composite measure with a maximum possible score of 54. Table 2.e shows that contact fathers scored almost twice as high on these assessments than disengaged men. The significant sex of parent effect was caused by fathers' scores being consistently higher (see Table 3.e). Mothers' and fathers' scores were highly correlated ($r(19) = .71, p < .01$, 2-tailed). On all nine issues contact fathers remembered themselves as having been more influential (see Appendix 2.e) and their ex-wives concurred with them on all but two measures–contact fathers were not deemed to have had a greater effect on their children's intellectual development or on their children's health and safety.

Paternal Role Ideologies

Parents' perceptions of gender role differences within the family were obtained by asking them directly (Would you [/ your ex-husband] say that there is a fundamental difference in roles between the father and the mother in the family?). Responses were recoded on a binary measure

(1: no, and 2: yes). However, logistic regression analyses performed on fathers' and mothers' scores revealed no significant differences between the two groups–eleven (55%) men and 14 (70%) of their ex-wives stated that the father believed in role differentiation.

Factors During Divorce

Following Kruk's paper and Study 1, the interview examined how the divorce unfolded. It covered legal aspects of the divorce experience and each partner's involvement in, and reaction to, the decision to separate, access arrangements, custody, property and child support. No significant differences were found between the two groups of non-custodial fathers or parents, nor were there any interactions.

Factors After Divorce

Paternal involvement was assessed in the same way as before, first by examining the nine areas of "influence" on children's development, in a composite measure of total "Paternal Influence on Children's Development." There was a significant main effect for groups, with contact fathers scoring over twice as high as disengaged men (see Table 2.f). The mothers rated paternal involvement lower but on this measure the difference was not quite significant (see Table 3.f). The mothers' and fathers' scores were significantly correlated ($r(19) = .64$, $p < .01$). Appendix 2.f shows that disengaged men reported less influence than contact fathers in eight of the nine areas discussed, the exception being financial matters. Appendix 3.f shows that the ex-wives of contact fathers rated them more influential on five of the nine measures–the exceptions were influences on the child's physical, personality and emotional development and in financial matters. As would be expected, comparison of sections e and f of Tables 2 and 3 shows that paternal influence was reported to decline after the separation.

Fathers' desire to visit their children post-divorce was coded on a binary scale with 1 = yes and 2 = no. There was a significant difference between the two subgroups. All the contact fathers reported that they wanted to see their children regularly, while most disengaged fathers (6 of 9) said that they were now not willing to visit their children, Fisher's Exact Test: $p = .005$. Their ex-wives gave very similar responses on this issue. Almost half (4 of 9) the disengaged men reported being unwilling to visit their children because they did not want to have any contact with their ex-wives. With regard to the fathers' satisfaction with their post-divorce contact with children, a significant difference between contact and disengaged fathers was found on a five-point scale from wanting to see the children "much less" to "much more," $F(1,18) = 19.9, p < .01$. Five (of 9) disengaged fathers reported that the amount of time they currently spend with their children is "about right," while the vast majority of contact fathers (10 of 11) said that they wanted to see their children a lot more than they usually do.

A single scale assessed the post-divorce relationship between the ex-couple from 1 (indifferent) to 6 (very friendly). A significant difference between contact and disengaged fathers emerged in relation to their feelings about their ex-wives, with $F(1,18) = 5.97, p < .05$. Four (of 9) disengaged fathers felt "indifferent." On the other hand, the majority of contact fathers (7 of 11) described their feelings in positive terms. Consistent with these findings, 5 of 9 disengaged fathers answered that they have no relationship with their ex-spouses concerning children, while 7 of 11 contact fathers indicated that on many occasions they take mutual decisions with their ex-wives concerning issues affecting their children's lives. Scores on a scale of quality of contact about the children (again from 1 = non-existent, to 6 = very friendly) again showed group differences, $F(1,18) = 27.89, p < .01$. However, in keeping with Study 1, both parents stated that the mothers were encouraging of the fathers' post-divorce contact with children.

According to both parents' perspectives, paternal post-divorce contact was not significantly associated with the adequacy of fathers' accommodation, their work schedules, financial matters or with the distance between fathers' residence and that of their children. In 90% of the cases (7 out of 9 disengaged fathers and 11 out of 11 contact fathers) children were living in the same town as father.

DISCUSSION

The findings of this study suggest two conclusions. In the first place the reported father-child interaction replicates the pattern of continuity which is suggested in Study 1, but not that of Kruk (1991). The fathers in this sample who had lost touch with their children were reported both by their wives (as in Study 1) and by themselves as consistently less involved in the practical aspects of child care, in building a strong and reciprocal attachment with their children and influencing their development. The high level of agreement between spouses, as shown in the significant correlations between the maternal and paternal reports on every measure, provides us with sufficient inter-rater reliability to suggest that the parental assessments were correct, at least in terms of how they construct reasons for the father's current involvement with the children.

Secondly, the consistent main effects for sex of parent (see Table 3) provide support for the claim that differences of opinion between divorcees should be respected. In this study there were consistent sex of parent effects, but no interactions. The main effects show that in divorce mothers consistently state that fathers were less involved than fathers do, irrespective of whether the man keeps in contact with the child or the mother-father relationship after divorce. However, the agreement between parents shows that differences between them are quantitative rather than qualitative. These patterns replicate Seltzer and Brandreth's (1994) finding of general agreement between ex-spouses, but a difference of opinion over the amount of involvement, particularly in some aspects of their interaction like the financial provision for the children.

GENERAL DISCUSSION

Why did these studies produce data which consistently showed the opposite pattern of results to that of Kruk (1991)? There are two areas of possible explanation which we must consider in order to address this question. The first concerns methodological issues upon which the studies might have differed. The second concerns possible cultural differences between the two samples. We will address each of these areas in turn.

The first area concerns methodological issues. To begin with, discrepant results must raise the issues of replicability, bias in measures and basic differences between samples. Perhaps these studies, Kruk's or both projects, fail to provide replicable results? This seems unlikely given the structure of both papers. In Kruk's a comparison is made between two sub-samples in Scotland and Canada. In this paper there is the congruence not only between studies 1 and 2 but also between the mothers and fathers in the latter.

Given that the research in both papers uses the same questionnaire, the suggestion that this measure contains a consistent bias can probably be ruled out, because of the opposite results produced in the two papers. Although both used the same measure, the questionnaire might have been dramatically altered in its translation. This is highly unlikely, however, as both interviewers (A.P. and Z.M.) are bilingual and the response patterns were similar over the scores of questions examined twice in this paper. In addition, we collected some qualitative data which show that the respondents interpret the questions in ways which indicate that the intended implication of each was communicated.

On the issue of basic sampling issues, there is little to choose between the two papers in terms of their sampling techniques and the number of respondents (80 in Kruk's paper and 82 in this). Kruk has the advantage of a cross-national comparison, but this paper examined fathering in two regions of the same country and capitalized on both fathers' and mothers' responses (Study 2).

Perhaps there are deeper sampling issues involved here? In Study 1 of this paper care was taken to match the sample with that of Kruk. Although most demographic aspects were similar, the sample discussed here was older and the couples have been separated for longer. We feel that these differences are unlikely to account for the contrast in the results from both papers for three reasons. Firstly, both investigations used retrospective techniques. While the respondents in this study had to remember events and relationships over a longer time period, the high inter-parent reliabilities are encouraging. Secondly, in Study 1 covariance procedures were used to reduce any effects of the age of father and length of separation. Thirdly, the sample in Study 2 was very different to those in Kruk and in Study 1. The fathers were older, had been married for longer and were mostly in white collar jobs. Yet the results obtained closely matched those of Study 1. Taken together, these factors suggest that we can not simply explain away the conflicting findings by pointing out methodological incompatibilities.

The second area of explanation for the differences between this study and Kruk's concerns the cultures in which they were located. It may be that the experience of divorce is different for men in Greece than it is for their equivalents in English-speaking countries. There are two areas of support for this suggestion. In the first place, the respondents in Greece gave very different responses to questions about men's and women's domestic roles to those obtained in British or North American samples. For example, 69% of men in the Greek samples were reported to be in favor of a clear difference between mothers and fathers. This contrasts with 26% in Kruk's study. Secondly, the reported levels of involvement of the fathers in these Greek studies were very low not only in terms of practical care but also in terms of their psychological relationships with their children. Such patterns match the low involvement of men found in Greek families in general (Thorpe, Dragonas and Golding, 1992). It could well be, therefore, that the discrepancies between this and Kruk's study are caused by different types of relationship between fathers and children in the two types of culture. Given the low levels of paternal investment by the Greek fathers, perhaps they do not become attached enough in order to face the problems experienced in the respondents interviewed by Kruk?

It seems highly possible that the discrepancies between the two papers reveal interesting features of father-child relationships after divorce which would benefit from further exploration. Firstly, the issue of cultural differences should be examined further. If these contrasts can be replicated then they need to be explained. It may be the case that the reasons why some men become disengaged from their children vary according to differences in cultural practices. Perhaps these practices give rise to different levels of paternal engagement and disengagement? Secondly, any cultural differences could be utilized to examine the relative influences of paternal involvement during marriage vs. the ex-spousal relationship after divorce upon the man's relationship with his children. The differences between these and Kruk's data show how such factors might be teased apart.

In conclusion, the contrast between these studies and Kruk's suggest that paternal disengagement is more complex than has previously been argued. Perhaps there is a U-shaped function of men's involvement in marriage as a predictor of their post-divorce contact? Some married fathers develop moderate involvement in their children's lives, in which their duties are restricted to those of provider and benign playmate. In such families the father may retain such a role after divorce. However, paternal disengagement may be the result either of fathers continuing to be only marginally involved in family relationships (and therefore drifting away easily after separation) or as a result of the psychological and structural issues which arise from their increased involvement, as suggested by Kruk (1991). Further research should explore this possibility.

REFERENCES

Ahrons, C.R. (1983). Predictors of paternal involvement post-divorce: Mothers' and fathers' perceptions. *Journal of Divorce*, 6, 55-69.

Ahrons, C.R., & Miller, R.B. (1993). The effect of the post-divorce relationship on paternal involvement: A longitudinal analysis. *American Journal of Orthopsychiatry*, 63 (3), 441-450.

Amato, P.R. (1993). Children adjustment to divorce–Theories, hypotheses, and empirical support. *Journal of Marriage and the Family*, 55: 1, 23-38.

Arditti, J.A., & Allen, K.R. (1993). Understanding distressed fathers' perceptions of legal and relational inequities post-divorce, *Family and Conciliation Courts Review*, 31: 4, 461-476.

Arendell, T. (1986). *Mothers and divorce: Legal, economic and social dilemmas*. Berkeley: University of California Press.

Arendell, T. (1995). *Fathers and divorce*. Beverly Hills: Sage Publications.

Biernacki, P., & Waldorf, D. (1981). Snowball sampling. *Sociological Methods and Research*, 10, 141-163.

Bumpass, L.I., & Sweet, J.A. (1989). Children's experience in single-parent families: Implications of cohabitation and marital transitions. *Family Planning Perspectives*, 21, 256-260.

Dudley, J.R. (1991). The consequences of divorce proceedings for divorced fathers. *Journal of Divorce & Remarriage*, 16, 171-193.

Friedman, H.J. (1980). The father's parenting experience in divorce. *Psychiatry*, 137, 1177-1182.

Furstenberg, F.F., Jr. (1988). Good dads–bad dads: Two faces of fatherhood. In A.J. Cherlin (Ed.), *The changing American family and public policy* (pp. 193-218). Washington, DC: Urban Institute.

Furstenberg, F.F., Jr., & Cherlin, A. (1991). *Divided families: What happens to children when parents part*. Cambridge, MA: Harvard University Press.

Furstenberg, F.F., Jr., Morgan, S.P., & Allison, P.D. (1987). Paternal participation and children's well-being after marital dissolution. *American Sociological Review*, 52, 695-701.

Furstenberg, F.F., Jr., & Nord, C.W. (1985). Parenting apart: Patterns of childrearing after marital disruption. *Journal of Marriage and the Family*, 47, 893-204.

Furstenberg, F.F., Jr., Peterson, J.L., Nord, C.W., & Zill, N. (1983). The life course of children of divorce: Marital disruption and parental contact. *American Sociological Review*, 48, 656-668.

Hess, R.D., & Camara, K.A. (1979). Post-divorce family relationships as mediating factors in the consequences of divorce for children. *Journal of Social Issues*, 35, 79-96.

Hetherington, E.M. (1979). Divorce: A child's perspective. *American Psychologist*, 34, 851-858.

Hetherington, E.M. (1986). Family relations, six years after divorce. In K. Pasley & Ihinger Tallman (Eds.), *Research and theory*. New York: Guilford Press.

Hetherington, E.M., Cox, M., & Cox, R. (1976). Divorced fathers. *Family Coordinator*, 25 (October): 417-428.

Hetherington, E.M., Cox, M., & Cox, R. (1978). The aftermath of divorce. In J.H. Stevens, Jr., & M. Mathews (Eds.), *Mother/child, father/child relationships* (pp. 149-176). Washington, DC: National Association for the Education of Young Children.

Hetherington E.M., Cox, M., & Cox, R. (1985). Long term effects of divorce and remarriage on the adjustment of children. *Journal of the American Academy of Child Psychiatry*, 24: 5, 518-530.

Hetherington, E.M., Hagan, M.S., & Anderson, E.R. (1989). Marital transitions: A child's perspective. *American Psychologist*, 44, 303-312.

Hetherington, E.M., & Stanley-Hagan, M.M. (1997). The effects of divorce on fathers and their children. In M.E. Lamb (Ed.), *The role of the father in child development*. New York: Walley.

Hodges, W.F., Landis, T., Day, E., & Oderberg, N. (1991). Infant and toddlers and post-divorce parental access: An initial exploration. *Journal of Divorce & Remarriage*, 16 (3-4), 239-252.

Hofferth, S.L. (1985). Updating children's life course. *Journal of Marriage and the Family*, 47, 93-115.

Koch, M.A., & Lowery, C. (1984). Visitation and the non-custodial father. *Journal of Divorce*, 8, 47-65.

Kruk, E. (1991). Discontinuity between pre- and post-divorce father-child relationships: New evidence regarding paternal disengagement. Custodial patterns and influences. *Journal of Divorce & Remarriage*, 16, 195-227.

Kruk, E. (1991). *Divorce and disengagement. Patterns of fatherhood within and beyond marriage.* London: Sage Publications.

Kruk, E. (1992). Psychological and structural factors contributing to the disengagement of non-custodial fathers after divorce. *Family and Conciliation Courts Review, 30:* 1, 81-101.

Kruk, E. (1993). *Divorce and disengagement. Patterns of fatherhood within and beyond marriage.* Fernwood Halifax: Canada.

Kruk, E. (1994). The disengaged non-custodial father: Implications for social work practice with the divorced family. *Social Work*, 39: 1, 15-25.

Loewen, J.W. (1988). Visitation fatherhood. In P. Bronstein & C.P. Cowan (Eds.), *Fatherhood Today: Men's changing role in the family* (pp. 195-213). New York: John Wiley.

Lowery, C.R. (1986). Maternal and joint custody: Differences in the decision process. *Law and Human Behaviour*, 10, 303-315.

Minton, C., & Pasley, K. (1996). Fathers' parenting role identity and father involvement. A comparison of non-divorced and divorced non-resident fathers. *Journal of Family Issues*, 17, 26-45.

Rosenthal, K., & Keshet, H. (1981). *Fathers without partners: A study of fathers and the family after marital separation.* Totowa, NJ: Rowman and Littlefield.

Seltzer, J.A. (1991). Relationships between fathers and children who live apart: The father's role after separation. *Journal of Marriage and the Family*, 53, 79-101.

Seltzer, J.A., & Bianchi, S.M. (1988). Children's contact with absent parents. *Journal of Marriage and the Family*, 50, 663-677.

Seltzer, J.A., & Brandreth, Y. (1994). What fathers say about involvement with children after separation. *Journal of Family Issues*, 15: 1, 49-77.

Seltzer, J.A., Schaeffer, N.C., & Charng, H.W. (1989). Family ties after divorce: The relationship between visiting and paying child support. *Journal of Marriage and the Family*, 51, 1013-1031.

Stephen, E.H., Freedman, V.A., & Hess, J. (1993). Near and far: Contact of children with their non-custodial fathers. *Journal of Divorce & Remarriage*, 20: 3/4, 171-191.

Stephens, L.S. (1996). Will Johnny see daddy this week? An empirical test of three theoretical perspectives of post-divorce contact. *Journal of Family Issues*, 17:4, 466-494.

Thorpe, K.J., Dragonas, T., & Golding, J. (1992). The effects of psychosocial well-being during early parenthood: A cross national study of Britain and Greece. *Journal of Reproductive and Infant Psychology*, 10: 4, 205-217.

Umberson, D., & Williams, C.L. (1991). Non-custodial parenting and fathers' mental health. Report submitted to the Hogg Foundation for Mental Health.

Wallerstein, J.S., & Kelly, J.B. (1980). *Surviving the break up: How children and parents cope with divorce.* New York: Basic Books.

APPENDIX 1

Mothers' Assessment of Paternal Relationship with Children Pre- and Post-Divorce by Current Contact (Disengaged vs. Contact) in Study 1.

Paternal Post-Divorce Contact

Variables:	Disengaged (N = 21)		Contact (N = 21)		
	M	SD	M	SD	
a. Early Involvement in Infant Care					
Change Diapers	1.19	0.40	2	1.58	$F(1.38) = 5.09, p < .05$
Feed the Baby	1.28	0.56	1.76	1.13	$F(1.38) = 4.6, p < .05$
Bathe the Baby	1.23	0.53	2.04	1.65	$F(1.38) = 5.09, p < .05$
Take the Baby out for Walk	1.76	1.04	2.04	1.53	$F(1.38) = 1.88, NQS$
Prepare Baby's Meals	1.19	0.67	1.33	0.79	$F(1.38) = 1.88, NQS$
Lull the Baby to Sleep	1.14	0.47	2.23	1.54	$F(1.38) = 8.48, p < .01$
Play with the Baby	1.8	0.87	2.66	1.23	$F(1.38) = 4.29, p < .05$
Take the Baby to the Doctor	1.95	1.35	2.33	1.46	$F(1.38) = 2.34, NQS$
b. Pre-Divorce Contact (in amount of hours per week)					
Alone with Children	0.38	1.35	2.19	3.47	$F(1.38) = 4.17, p < .05$
With Others Present	4.71	7.47	9.38	9.29	$F(1.38) = 2.46, NQS$
c. Attachment Indices					
Thinking about Children	2.04	1.02	2.85	1.52	$F(1.38) = 1.52, NQS$
Wanting to be with Children	1.71	0.78	2.57	1.39	$F(1.38) = 3.01, NQS$
Comforting Children	1.52	0.74	2.38	1.35	$F(1.38) = 4.43, p < .05$
Talking with Children	1.23	0.62	2.09	1.37	$F(1.38) = 5.78, p < .05$
Attachment	1.95	0.97	2.76	1.26	$F(1.38) = 3.58, NQS$
d. Paternal Influence on Children's Development Before Separation					
Daily Care and Safety	1.38	0.97	2.76	1.94	$F(1.38) = 7.83, p < .01$
Intellectual Development	1.57	1.32	1.95	1.71	$F(1.38) = 0.47, NQS$
Physical Development	1.38	1.20	2.09	1.64	$F(1.38) = 1.93, NQS$
Personality Development	1.47	1.03	2.66	1.87	$F(1.38) = 6.41, p < .05$
Teaching Behaviour	2.28	1.61	3.14	1.82	$F(1.38) = 1.74, NQS$
Emotional Development	1.57	1.24	2.38	1.71	$F(1.38) = 3.22, NQS$
Religious Development	1.61	1.16	1.57	1.24	$F(1.38) = 0.01, NQS$
Moral Development	2.09	1.64	3.38	1.8	$F(1.38) = 8.73, p < .01$
Giving Child a Feeling of Being Part of the Family	1.9	1.57	2.8	1.99	$F(1.38) = 3.69, NQS$
e. Paternal Influence on Children's Development After Separation					
Daily Care and Safety	1.52	1.2	2.9	1.86	$F(1.38) = 11.38, p < .01$
Intellectual Development	1.66	1.19	1.9	1.67	$F(1.38) = 0.52, NQS$
Physical Development	1.61	1.16	2.04	1.71	$F(1.38) = 0.17, NQS$
Personality Development	1.42	0.87	2.66	2	$F(1.38) = 5.81, p < .05$
Teaching Behaviour	1.52	1.12	3.04	1.96	$F(1.38) = 6.54, p < .05$
Emotional Development	1.33	0.85	2.61	1.85	$F(1.38) = 5.98, p < .01$
Religious Development	1.23	0.76	1.52	1.12	$F(1.38) = 0.37, NQS$
Moral Development	1.57	1.24	3.42	1.83	$F(1.38) = 16.97, p < .001$
Giving Child a Feeling of Being Part of the Family	1.38	0.97	2.85	1.9	$F(1.38) = 8.85, p < .01$

APPENDIX 2

Fathers' Mean Assessment of Their Relationship with Children Pre- and Post-Divorce by Current Contact (Disengaged vs. Contact) in Study 2.

Paternal Post-Divorce Contact

Variables:	Disengaged (N = 9)		Contact (N = 11)		
	M	SD	M	SD	
a. Early Involvement in Infant Care					
Change Diapers	1	0.001	2.18	1.07	*F(1.18) = 10.69, p <.01*
Feed the Baby	1.22	0.44	2.45	0.82	*F(1.18) = 16.33, p <.01*
Bathe the Baby	1	0.001	2.36	0.67	*F(1.18) = 36.45, p<.001*
Take the Baby out for Walk	1.66	0.7	3.27	0.9	*F(1.18) = 18.86, p<.01*
Prepare Baby's Meals	1.11	0.3	2.36	0.67	*F(1.18) = 25.72, p<.001*
Lull the Baby to Sleep	1.33	0.5	3.18	1.16	*F(1.18) = 19.47, p<.01*
Play with the Baby	2.11	0.78	3.9	1.3	*F(1.18) = 13.21, p<.001*
Take the Baby to the Doctor	2.22	1.56	3.81	1.16	*F(1.18) = 6.83, p <.05*
b. Paternal Contribution in Running the Household					
Shopping	2.88	1.69	4.54	1.03	*F(1.18) = 7.27, p<.05*
Earning Money	5.55	0.88	4.9	0.94	*F(1.18) = 2.46, NQS*
Cooking Meals for the Family	1	0.1	2.09	1.04	*F(1.18) = 9.72, p<.01*
Cleaning the House	1	0.1	1.72	0.64	*F(1.18) = 11.26, p<.01*
Taking out the Rubbish	1.88	1.61	3.45	1.91	*F(1.18) = 3.79, NQS*
c. Pre-Divorce Contact (in amount of hours per week)					
Alone with Children	2.11	1.45	6.63	3.98	*F(1.18) = 10.4, p <.01*
With Others Present	2.88	1.53	8.54	5.95	*F(1.18) = 7.63, p <.05*
d. Attachment Indices					
Thinking about Children	2.88	1.05	4.45	0.93	*F(1.18) = 12.39, p<.01*
Wanting to be with Children	2.11	0.6	4.09	1.22	*F(1.18) = 19.62, p<.001*
Comforting Children	3	0.86	4.63	0.92	*F(1.18) = 16.4, p<.001*
Talking with Children	2.22	0.6	3.81	1.25	*F(1.18) = 11.82, p<.01*
Attachment	2.66	0.7	4.9	0.3	*F(1.18) = 91.26, p<.0001*
e. Paternal Influence on Children's Development Before Separation					
Daily Care and Safety	2.44	0.52	4.81	1.16	*F(1.18) = 31.6, p <.001*
Intellectual Development	2.55	0.88	4.72	1.55	*F(1.18) = 13.8, p <.01*
Physical Development	2.11	1.26	3.81	1.72	*F(1.18) = 6.1, p <.05*
Personality Development	2.88	1.26	4.9	1.37	*F(1.18) = 11.4, p <.01*
Teaching Behaviour	3.22	1.2	4.81	1.4	*F(1.18) = 7.2, p <.01*
Emotional Development	2.88	1.26	4.63	0.8	*F(1.18) = 14, p <.01*
Moral Development	3.33	0.86	5.09	1.44	*F(1.18) = 10.2, p <.01*
Giving Child a Feeling of Being Part of the Family	3.44	1.23	5.36	0.67	*F(1.18) = 19.5, p <.001*
Financial Matters	4.11	0.6	5.36	0.67	*F(1.18) = 18.8, p <.001*
f. Paternal Influence on Children's Development After Separation					
Daily Care and Safety	1	0.001	2.36	1.68	*F(1.18) = 5.8, p <.05*
Intellectual Development	1	0.001	3.72	1.4	*F(1.18) = 29.8, p <.001*
Physical Development	1	0.001	2.72	1.6	*F(1.18) = 10.1, p <.01*
Personality Development	1.22	0.44	4.36	1.2	*F(1.18) = 54.6, p <.001*

APPENDIX 2 (continued)
Paternal Post-Divorce Contact

Variables:	Disengaged (N = 9)		Contact (N = 11)		
	M	SD	M	SD	
f. Paternal Influence on Children's Development After Separation					
Teaching Behaviour	1.55	1.01	4.36	1.2	*F(1.18) = 30.8, p < .0001*
Emotional Development	1.22	0.44	4.18	1.16	*F(1.18) = 51.3, p < .0001*
Moral Development	1.22	0.44	4.45	1.29	*F(1.18) = 10.9, p < .0001*
Giving Child a Feeling of Being Part of the Family	1.22	0.44	3.81	1.6	*F(1.18) = 22, p < .001*
Financial Matters	4.66	1.5	4.45	1.43	*F(1.18) = 0.1, NQS*

APPENDIX 3

Mothers' Mean Assessment of Paternal Relationship with Children Pre- and Post-Divorce by Current Contact (Disengaged vs. Contact) in Study 2.

Paternal Post-Divorce Contact

Variables:	Disengaged (N = 9)		Contact (N = 11)		
	M	SD	M	SD	
a. Early Involvement in Infant Care					
Change Diapers	1	0.001	1.63	1.02	*F(1.18) = 3.42, NQS*
Feed the Baby	1.11	0.3	1.9	0.94	*F(1.18) = 5.79, p < .05*
Bathe the Baby	1	0.001	1.72	1	*F(1.18) = 4.62, p < .05*
Take the Baby out for Walk	1.66	0.7	2.54	1.21	*F(1.18) = 3.67, NQS*
Prepare Baby's Meals	1	0.001	2	1	*F(1.18) = 8.91, p < .01*
Lull the Baby to Sleep	1.33	0.5	2.27	1.19	*F(1.18) = 4.85, p < .05*
Play with the Baby	1.66	0.5	3.09	1.13	*F(1.18) = 12.12, p < .01*
Take the Baby to the Doctor	1.66	1	3.18	1.07	*F(1.18) = 10.41, p < .01*
b. Paternal Contribution in Running the Household					
Shopping	2.33	1	3.27	1.79	*F(1.18) = 1.95, NQS*
Earning Money	3.88	1.76	4.72	1.1	*F(1.18) = 1.68, NQS*
Cooking Meals for the Family	1.1	0.3	1.72	0.9	*F(1.18) = 3.72, NQS*
Cleaning the House	1	0.001	1.54	0.93	*F(1.18) = 3.03, NQS*
Taking out the Rubbish	1.77	1.64	2.45	1.75	*F(1.18) = 0.78, NQS*
c. Pre-Divorce Contact (in amount of hours per week)					
Alone with Children	0.44	0.88	4.9	4.36	*F(1.18) = 9.1, p < .01*
With Others Present	1.44	2.06	3.72	3.71	*F(1.18) = 2.69, NQS*
d. Attachment Indices					
Thinking about Children	1.88	0.78	3.9	1.04	*F(1.18) = 23.01, p<.001*
Wanting to be with Children	2.22	0.83	3.27	1.48	*F(1.18) = 3.54, NQS*
Comforting Children	2.33	1	3.63	0.92	*F(1.18) = 9.14, p < .01*
Talking with Children	1.77	0.6	2.54	1.03	*F(1.18) = 3.67, NQS*
Attachment	2.22	0.66	3.81	0.98	*F(1.18) = 17.2, p < .001*

APPENDIX 3 (continued)

Paternal Post-Divorce Contact

Variables:	Disengaged (N = 9)		Contact (N = 11)		
	M	*SD*	*M*	*SD*	
e. Paternal Influence on Children's Development Before Separation					
Daily Care and Safety	2.11	1.16	2.9	1.51	*F(1.18) = 1.6, NQS*
Intellectual Development	1.88	1.26	3.27	1.79	*F(1.18) = 3.7, NQS*
Physical Development	1.44	0.52	2.81	1.66	*F(1.18) = 5.6, p < .05*
Personality Development	1.66	1	3.81	1.47	*F(1.18) = 13.9, p < .01*
Teaching Behaviour	1.88	1.05	3.36	1.56	*F(1.18) = 5.7, p < .05*
Emotional Development	1.88	1.53	3.36	1.43	*F(1.18) = 4.9, p < .05*
Moral Development	2.11	1.45	3.81	1.53	*F(1.18) = 6.4, p < .05*
Giving Child a Feeling of Being Part of the Family	2.11	1.69	4.45	1.63	*F(1.18) = 9.8, p < .01*
Financial Matters	2.44	2	3.45	1.86	*F(1.18) = 1.3, NQS*
f. Paternal Influence on Children's Development After Separation					
Daily Care and Safety	1.11	0.33	2.54	1.63	*F(1.18) = 6.6, p < .01*
Intellectual Development	1.44	1.33	3	1.84	*F(1.18) = 4.4, p < .05*
Physical Development	1.33	1	2.09	1.37	*F(1.18) = 1.9, NQS*
Personality Development	1.88	1.53	3.09	1.3	*F(1.18) = 3.5, NQS*
Teaching Behaviour	1.44	1.01	2.9	1.7	*F(1.18) = 5.1, p < .05*
Emotional Development	1.88	1.83	3.27	1.73	*F(1.18) = 2.9, NQS*
Moral Development	1.22	0.44	3.72	1.61	*F(1.18) = 20, p < .001*
Giving Child a Feeling of Being Part of the Family	1.55	1.13	3.18	1.83	*F(1.18) = 5.3, p < .05*
Financial Matters	1.66	1.32	2.63	1.68	*F(1.18) = 1.9, NQS*

Post-Divorce Father Custody:
Are Mothers the True Predictors
of Adult Relationship Satisfaction?

Steven T. Olivas
Cal D. Stoltenberg

SUMMARY. This study examined the effects of different custodial arrangements following divorce and the impact they have on the adult romantic functioning of the children. It used 72 undergraduate participants coming from mother custody, father custody, or non-divorced backgrounds. Results indicated that custodial arrangement had largely no significant effect on the satisfaction felt in relationships, or in general attachment style. The gender of the participant was found to be a factor, with females exhibiting more security in romantic relationships and males showing a tendency to place relationships as secondary in their lives. While non-significant findings for the custody main effect seem discouraging at first glance, a discussion ensues speculating as to the utility of parental divorce as a useful sole independent variable in future studies. With divorce becoming commonplace in America today, it seems that studying parental styles may yield results more germane to current issues. *[Article copies available for a fee from The Haworth Document Delivery Service: 1-800-342-9678. E-mail address: getinfo@haworth.com]*

Steven T. Olivas, PhD, completed this study as his doctoral dissertation under the second author at the University of Oklahoma. He is presently on the faculty, Department of Psychology, Tennessee State University, 3500 John A. Merritt Boulevard, Nashville, TN 37209-1561. Cal D. Stoltenberg, PhD, is on the faculty, Department of Psychology, University of Oklahoma.

[Haworth co-indexing entry note]: "Post-Divorce Father Custody: Are Mothers the True Predictors of Adult Relationship Satisfaction?" Olivas, Steven T., and Cal D. Stoltenberg. Co-published simultaneously in *Journal of Divorce & Remarriage* (The Haworth Press, Inc.) Vol. 28, No. 1/2, 1997, pp. 119-137; and: *Child Custody: Legal Decisions and Family Outcomes* (ed: Craig A. Everett) The Haworth Press, Inc., 1997, pp. 119-137. Single or multiple copies of this article are available for a fee from The Haworth Document Delivery Service [1-800-342-9678, 9:00 a.m. - 5:00 p.m. (EST). E-mail address: getinfo@haworth.com].

Today, approximately one out of every two marriages ends in divorce (Paretti & diVitorrio, 1993). Consequently, at least two out of every five children in the United States will see their parents divorce during the course of their childhood (Cherlin, 1992; Cherlin et al., 1991; Levitin, 1983) and be subjected to all of the growing pains associated with family disruption. These pains include years of tension and stress prior to the final decision to divorce being made (Zeanah, 1983) and parental conflict, diminished contact with the noncustodial parent, residential change, and possible economic decline following the divorce (Cherlin, 1992; Furstenberg & Teitler, 1994). While it seems clear in the literature that divorce does have effects on children, there seems to be some question as to the nature and extent of those effects (Forehand, 1992).

There currently exists a notably large and somewhat controversial pool of research, going back approximately 15 years, evaluating the exact nature of the effects parental divorce has on children. Some studies have been weak, with serious flaws in their methodology. Weaknesses include improper causal attributions, inappropriate comparison groups (or inappropriate matching between groups), and ignoring differences within groups while searching for between groups differences (see Levitin, 1983 for complete review).

Researchers (Cherlin et al., 1991; Emery, 1982; Hetherington, Cox, & Cox, 1982; Lamb, 1986; Parker, Barrett, & Hickie, 1992; Zeanah, 1983), submit that it is the quality of parent-child interactions (relationships), and not the divorce per se, that is the most important factor in the emotional health and recovery of the children from divorce.

A pattern of poor parenting practices has been found to be especially true for divorced mothers with custody of their sons (Hetherington, 1986; Hetherington, Cox, & Cox, 1979). These mothers were found to be more restrictive, negative, and more demanding (Copeland, 1984; Levitin, 1983; Shaw, 1991; Zeanah, 1983), although relationships with daughters did not receive such negative ratings (Hetherington, 1989; Zaslow, 1988). Duffy (1994) explains that divorce can cause an inordinate number of changes in a woman's life, thereby leading to stress responsible for, among other symptoms, depression, low self-esteem, and reduced perception of social support.

It has also been found that single mothers spend less time with their children in conversation, reading, listening, helping with homework, or sharing an outing (Peters & Haldeman, 1987). While these problems will cause conflict in the mother-child dyad with either sex, boys seem to be particularly affected. Hetherington (1993), in an overview of the Virginia longitudinal study, also found that young boys showed more " . . . adverse and enduring responses to divorce and life in a home headed by a . . . custodial mother" (p. 49).

The most comprehensive study concerning effects of divorce on children has been conducted by Wallerstein and Kelly (1980). In their longitudinal qualitative study, they have followed the lives of many children whose parents divorced during the 1970s. Of these children, however, 90% were placed in the custody of their mothers following the breakup. For this longitudinal study, they interviewed the children at two, five, and ten year follow-up intervals.

In general, many children were found to be unhappy in their current relationships and showed marked concern about future relationships (Wallerstein, 1987). There were numerous relationship and/or personal troubles cited from all age groups (Wallerstein & Kelly, 1980), but some notable sex differences were also beginning to emerge. There was a widespread concern of betrayal and of being hurt or abandoned in relationships (both present and future), but girls were more likely to become involved in short-lived dating and sexual relationships (Wallerstein, 1985), while boys were far more likely to hold back in their relationships. Boys also had a somewhat unique concern about being unloved.

However, studies which are methodologically sound provide no conclusive, inevitable, immutable effects associated with divorce that are experienced by all children (Kulka & Weingarten, 1979; Levitin, 1983; Lopez, 1991). Relationships seem to be clearly affected, as the model of separation leads to cynicism toward the permanency of relationships and less intimate trust, but the exact effect has not been systematically pinpointed. Other researchers have taken this notion and developed theories of intimate relationships consistent with Bowlby's (1969) theory of attachment.

John Bowlby (1969; 1973) advanced his theory by noting that when an infant is separated from its mother, it shows a predictable series of emotional reactions, sometimes referred to as a fear response. This fear response is speculated to have an instinctive value designed to maintain the proximity of the caretaker and increase the chances for survival (Emery, 1982). Likewise, the knowledge that an attachment figure or caretaker is available and responsive will provide a strong sense of security (Bowlby, 1982).

The attachment figure, as described above, can be either a "good object" (perceived as trustworthy, loyal, friendly, accessible, and available); or a "bad object" (to whom attachment is uncertain, and who is either unwilling to respond, or will do so in a hostile manner; Bowlby, 1973). Based on experiences with the "object," the child constructs an internal working model of the attachment figure and the self, and will structure all subsequent interpersonal relationships within this framework (Schneider, 1991).

Ainsworth (1979) and her colleagues (Ainsworth, Blehar, Waters, & Wall, 1978) took this theory and began to apply it to adult functioning. Ainsworth developed the "Strange Situation" test, wherein the child's pattern of reacting would place him/her into one of three categories identified as "secure," "anxious," or "avoidant" (see Ainsworth et al., 1978 for complete description and review). This research yielded conclusions demonstrating that early patterns of infant-caregiver interaction related directly to attachment style.

Based on this body of literature, there has been increasing speculation that attachment style plays an important role in the formation of adult romantic relationships (Grossman & Grossman, 1990; Hazan & Shaver, 1987; Kotler, 1989; Levy & Davis, 1988; Shaver, Hazan, & Bradshaw, 1988). Collins and Read (1990) and Simpson (1990) wrote that attachment styles are related to trust, satisfaction, and commitment in the relationship. Even Bowlby (1979) suggested that there was a strong causal relationship between parent-child interactions and the adult capacity to make affectional bonds.

Hazan and Shaver (1987; Shaver & Hazan, 1987) have done extensive work in applying Bowlby's attachment theory to the development of adult romantic relationships. They report that secure subjects described themselves as easy to get to know, liked and understood by most people, and experience less self-doubt than insecurely attached adults. Insecure adults (anxious and avoidant), on the other hand, report self-doubt, low self-esteem, and fear that others would hurt or reject them if it suited their purposes (Shaver & Hazan, 1987; Strahan, 1991).

Bowlby felt that this attachment "system" persisted, given a stable family environment (Bowlby, 1980; 1988), in a continuous fashion throughout the life cycle. Several researchers have since discovered that attachment styles can be changed when the child is exposed to severe stress (Schneider, Braunwald, Carlson, & Cicchetti, 1985) which is apparent in cases of parental divorce (Bonkowski, 1989). Emery (1982) and Huntington (1982), in fact, state that there is an absence of environmental regularity/stability in disorganized families (especially when the parents are under stress or conflict), thereby giving way to attachment system restructuring.

There have been researchers interested in various other mitigating circumstances involved in parental divorce which may impact the children in a positive or a negative way (Cherlin et al., 1991; Emery, 1982; Wallerstein, 1987; Wallerstein & Kelly, 1980; Warshak, 1978; Weiss, 1988). Unfortunately, these results have also been conflictual as no definitive answers have emerged. One area of research which remains relatively untouched, however, is father custody situations.

As recently as 1980, the census bureau reported that 92% of children from divorced homes resided with their mothers (Black, 1982), although there has recently been a trend toward awarding fathers custody (Moore & Herlihy, 1994). However, Bender (1994) sums up current research by reporting, "Given the changes in the American family . . . , the current de-facto assumptions of maternal custody are clearly inadequate" (p. 121). For male children, then, it may be true that the father is the attachment figure who offers a more "secure" base than the mother (Lamb, 1979).

Perhaps the most complete discussion of father custody effects vs. mother custody effects can be found in the doctoral dissertation of War-shak (1978). Utilizing both quantitative and qualitative data, he found that fathers who had custody seemed more nurturing, supportive, and competent as parents than fathers from intact homes, seemingly mirroring the definition of a good attachment figure.

Warshak found that children living with the same sex parent (father custody sons and mother custody daughters) looked better adjusted and were rated more favorably than those living with the opposite sex parent. In a meta-analysis of the literature nearly 10 years later, Zaslow (1988) echoed these findings, concluding that same sex custody arrangements were optimal for boys and girls. Using attachment theory, these children were able to form and maintain secure attachment with the same sex parent, thereby not being forced to attach to another figure following the divorce (in other words, less stress would have been placed on the child's attachment system).

To conclude, Warshak (1986) summed up the scant research on father custody situations by stating " . . . data sources consistently revealed more favorable outcomes in children living with the same sex parent than children living with the opposite sex parent" (p. 195).

Problem Statement. In summary, the empirical and theoretical literature on the effects of divorce and the attachment process yields varied results. It appears the only consistent finding is that relationship difficulties are probable when the children reach adulthood. Their attachment styles, being somewhat malleable in the face of family discord, could possibly move from secure to insecure. Additionally, children from opposite sex custody arrangements appear to be less well adjusted than children from same sex custody situations. This study will specifically examine the following two areas: (1) the attachment status of adult children, and (2) the quality of intimate relationships of the adult children. Therefore, the following hypotheses are proposed:

1. Adult children from divorced households will show more instances of insecure attachment than children from intact families.
2. Adult males from divorced father custody households will show the highest incidence of secure attachment of all the divorced groups.
3. Adult children from divorced households will report lower satisfaction with intimate relationships than children from intact families.
4. Adult males from post-divorced father custody households will exhibit higher satisfaction with intimate relationships than any of the other divorced groups.

METHOD

Participants

The participants in this study were 72 undergraduates (36 female, 36 male) who were enrolled in a first-year psychology class at a major Southwestern University (age range 17-28, mean 20.03 years). Participants were selected from a general pool of psychology students on the basis of their responses to a demographic questionnaire administered during two large group general pretesting sessions for subject pool students on campus. Participants were then divided into six groups, dependent upon their status regarding the following characteristics: gender (male vs. female), and custody situation in family of origin (father custody, mother custody, or nondivorced parents) (see Table 1).

A power analysis (alpha set at .05, power set at .80) determined that there needed to be 12 members per group. Power was calculated at the

TABLE 1. Distribution of Participants Within Cells (N = 72)

	Father Custody	Mother Custody	Non-Divorced
Males	12	12	12
Females	12	12	12

Total: 72

univariate level utilizing effect size from four of the subscales on two of the instruments.

Effect size was calculated from previous studies using the Personal Assessment of Intimacy in Relationships inventory (PAIR; Johnson & Greenberg, 1985) and the Relationship Beliefs Inventory (RBI; Eidelson & Epstein, 1982). These studies designated two subscales for each instrument that best differentiated between control and experimental groups ("disagreement" and "cannot change" for the RBI; "intellectual intimacy" and "recreational intimacy" for the PAIR). Effect sizes for these subscales ranged from .5 to 1.05. Because there have been no published studies that have used the Attachment Styles Questionnaire (Feeney, Noller, & Hanrahan, 1994), a more conservative effect size (.40) was deemed appropriate for the purpose of power analysis. Control groups were then matched with target groups on the basis of the following demographic criteria: gender, type of family (divorced vs. intact), SES, parent's highest level of education completed, number of siblings, age at time of divorce, race, and custodial parent.

Instruments

Participants were initially presented with a follow-up brief demographic sheet containing questions pertaining to parents' marital status, age at time of divorce (if divorced family was indicated), gender of participant, current age, and number of siblings.

Satisfaction with intimacy in romantic relationships was measured using the PAIR (Schaefer & Olson, 1981). This inventory yields six subscale scores for measures of perceived relationship intimacy across six dimensions: emotional, social, sexual, intellectual, recreational, and conventionality. To make this scale more appropriate for this subject pool, the word "sexual" in items from the sexual subscale was replaced by the phrase "physically intimate" where applicable. Each individual filled out this questionnaire twice, once for the level of intimacy in their most intimate prior relationship, and once for the amount of intimacy they would desire in an ideal relationship. By subtracting actual intimacy from the desired score, a discrepancy measure is obtained that approximates their satisfaction with intimacy in personal/romantic relationships.

The development of the PAIR has included item and factor analysis. Split-half reliability coefficients for the subscales range from .70 to .82 (Schaeffer & Olson, 1981). Studies comparing the PAIR with the Locke-Wallace Marital Adjustment Scale (Locke & Wallace, 1959) yield Pearson correlation coefficients exceeding .30 (Scheaffer & Olson, 1981). Schaeffer and Olson have also correlated the PAIR with the Family Environment Scale (FES, Moos & Moos, 1976), and found positive correlation coefficients (ranging from .13 to .68) statistically significant at $p > .01$, indicating adequate concurrent validity.

Relationship quality is also measured via the RBI (Eidelson & Epstein, 1982). This instrument was developed to assess irrational beliefs about intimate relationships, assuming that these beliefs may adversely affect relationship quality. The instrument is a 40-item self-report scale consisting of five 8-item subscales: disagreement is destructive, partner cannot change, mind reading is expected, sexual perfectionism, and the sexes are different. The Cronbach alpha coefficients for the five RBI subscales range from .72 to .81, with all five subscales having been successfully correlated with marital adjustment scores (Eidelson & Epstein, 1982).

Finally, attachment style, drawing upon the research conducted by Hazan and Shaver (1987; Shaver & Hazan, 1987) was assessed using the Attachment Style Questionnaire (ASQ; Feeney, Noller, & Hanrahan, 1994). This instrument is a 40-item self-report questionnaire that numerically places the participant onto a continuum with "secure attachment" and "insecure attachment" styles at opposite poles. The "insecure" participants are further divided into "avoidant" and "anxious/ambivalent." Cronbach alphas for the three factors (Security, Avoidance, and Anxiety) were .83, .83, and .85, respectively. Test-retest reliability coefficients over a 10-week period with introductory psychology students were .74 (security), .75 (avoidance), and .80 (anxiety; Feeney, Noller, & Hanrahan, 1994).

Procedure

Following assignment to cells based on initial demographic data, participants were contacted by telephone and instructed where to meet the experimenter to complete participation. They were notified that the experimental session would last approximately 45 minutes, that they would receive research credit for participation, and that filling out questionnaires would be their major task.

Upon arrival at the testing location, participants were handed an experimental packet containing the instruments. All instruments were identified only by a unique number (from 1-200), and could not be traced to a particular participant in any way. Instruments were presented in random order behind the demographic sheet and an informed consent form to control for testing effects. Finally, participants were given brief but standardized instructions on how to complete their data sheet and instruments.

RESULTS

As indicated in the method section, all participants completed three questionnaires regarding previous relationship experience. Particular subscales or groups of subscales from these instruments were analyzed specific to the hypotheses.

The first hypothesis speculated that adult children from divorced backgrounds would show more instances of insecure intimate attachment than adults from non-divorced backgrounds. To answer this first question, four subscales from the ASQ (Relationships as Secondary and Discomfort indicating avoidant insecure attachment; Need for Approval and Preoccupation indicating anxious insecure attachment) were analyzed using a 2 (Sex) × 3 (Custody) MANOVA. Means and standard deviations for independent measures appear in Table 2, F and p values can be found in Table 3. There were no significant differences found for the Custody × Sex interaction or the Custody main effect, $Fs(8, 72) = 1.14$ and 1.23, n.s., respectively. Similarly, there was no consistent direction taken by the results, with the exception of the Relationships as Secondary subscale which yielded results opposite of the hypothesized direction (i.e., participants from non-divorced households were more likely to demonstrate symptoms consistent with avoidant attachment styles). The MANOVA did uncover a significant main effect for the Sex, $F(4, 72) = 2.79, p < .05$. Univariate tests, controlling alpha utilizing the Bonferoni adjustment, were conducted on individual subscales to better determine where actual differences existed. The only subscale to display significant differences was also Relationships as Secondary, $F(1, 72) = 8.99, p < .01$. This difference was found within the Sex main effect, indicating that the sexes significantly differ, with males more likely to place the relationship secondary to other outside interests.

The second hypothesis was that males from father custody households would show the highest incidence of secure attachment of the four divorced groups. Because the hypothesis addressed security in adult attachment, the Confidence subscale from the ASQ was analyzed with a simple ANOVA. Means for the subscale appear in Table 2. The Custody × Sex main effect yielded non-significant results, $F(2, 72) = 0.16$, n.s. To the contrary of the hypothesized direction, and although not statistically significant, males from divorced father custody households showed the least secure attachment style of any of the divorce groups. The Sex main effect approached significance, $F(1, 72) = 3.78, p = .0561$, with females scoring consistently higher than the males. This seems to indicate a tendency for females to feel more secure in romantic relationships than males, regardless of family history.

The final two hypotheses concern satisfaction in intimate romantic relationships, predicting that adults from intact backgrounds would report greater satisfaction with intimate relationships and that males from father

TABLE 2. Means and Standard Deviations for Independent Measures Sorted by Hypothesis Number

HYPOTHESIS #1

GENDER	INDEPENDENT MEASURE	FAMILY HISTORY/CUSTODY					
		NON-DIVORCED		DIVORCED/ FATHER		DIVORCED/ MOTHER	
MEN	Relationship as Secondary	19.33	5.33	17.50	5.66	18.83	3.59
	Need for Approval	22.67	5.96	21.33	3.45	21.58	3.37
	Discomfort	36.50	7.83	37.17	10.24	37.33	8.42
	Preoccupation	29.25	5.94	26.67	4.64	27.83	5.94
WOMEN	Relationship as Secondary	17.58	2.57	14.67	3.52	14.25	4.43
	Need for Approval	21.50	5.50	23.75	4.49	20.25	3.39
	Discomfort	35.67	7.48	40.08	6.78	34.50	10.56
	Preoccupation	25.00	4.92	31.25	6.66	27.00	5.46

HYPOTHESIS #2

GENDER	INDEPENDENT MEASURE	FAMILY HISTORY/CUSTODY					
		NON-DIVORCED		DIVORCED/ FATHER		DIVORCED/ MOTHER	
MEN	Confidence	31.67	6.69	32.42	5.84	33.08	4.03
WOMEN	Confidence	34.58	3.42	33.83	5.75	36.00	5.19

HYPOTHESES #3 AND #4

GENDER	INDEPENDENT MEASURE	FAMILY HISTORY/CUSTODY					
		NON-DIVORCED		DIVORCED/ FATHER		DIVORCED/ MOTHER	
MEN	Disagreement	**13.58**	6.53	**12.42**	3.87	**12.67**	6.56
	Cannot Change	**12.42**	4.21	**12.33**	3.37	**14.33**	4.94
	Intellectual Intimacy	**1.33**	11.61	**−7.00**	12.89	**−2.33**	11.11
	Recreational Intimacy	**−10.00**	11.50	**−11.33**	8.50	**−1.00**	8.72
WOMEN	Disagreement	**11.92**	4.44	**11.33**	5.30	**10.25**	5.89
	Cannot Change	**15.33**	3.82	**14.00**	6.25	**12.42**	4.56
	Intellectual Intimacy	**−1.00**	10.53	**0.67**	9.47	**−0.83**	11.79
	Recreational Intimacy	**−7.00**	15.46	**−4.00**	13.32	**−5.67**	7.33

Means are in bold type.
Standard deviations are in normal type.

TABLE 3. F and p Values for Independent Measures Sorted by Main Effect and Hypothesis Number

HYPOTHESIS #1

	Main Effect—Custody		Main Effect—Sex		Interaction—Custody × Sex	
MANOVA	$F = 1.23$	$p = .287$	$F = 2.79$	$p = .034*$	$F = 1.14$	$p = .345$
Relationship as Secondary	$F = 2.04$	$p = .138$	$F = 8.99$	$p = .004***$	$F = .66$	$p = .522$
Need for Approval	$F = .84$	$p = .437$	$F = 0.00$	$p = .979$	$F = 1.34$	$p = .269$
Discomfort	$F = .74$	$p = .483$	$F = .01$	$p = .903$	$F = .68$	$p = .501$
Preoccupation	$F = .73$	$p = .484$	$F = .02$	$p = .901$	$F = 3.75$	$p = .029$

HYPOTHESIS #2

	Main Effect—Custody		Main Effect—Sex		Interaction—Custody × Sex	
Confidence	$F = .58$	$p = .564$	$F = 3.78$	$p = .056**$	$F = .16$	$p = .851$

HYPOTHESIS #3

	Main Effect—Custody		Main Effect—Sex		Interaction—Custody × Sex	
MANOVA	$F = .576$	$p = .796$	$F = 1.11$	$p = .360$	$F = 1.18$	$p = .315$
Disagreement	$F = .34$	$p = .711$	$F = 1.75$	$p = .190$	$F = .09$	$p = .916$
Cannot Change	$F = .15$	$p = .862$	$F = .67$	$p = .417$	$F = 1.77$	$p = .178$
Intellectual Intimacy	$F = .62$	$p = .539$	$F = .34$	$p = .562$	$F = 1.32$	$p = .274$
Recreational Intimacy	$F = 1.48$	$p = .236$	$F = .51$	$p = .476$	$F = 1.77$	$p = .178$

* $p < .05$
** $p < .10$
*** $p < .05$ after Bonferoni Adjustment

custody backgrounds would report the highest satisfaction among the four divorced groups. The four subscales analyzed were determined by their authors to best differentiate between experimental and control groups on issues of relationship satisfaction (Disagreement and Partner Cannot Change from the RBI; Intellectual Intimacy and Recreational Intimacy from the PAIR). These subscales were analyzed at the multivariate level using identical main effects as above. Means and standard deviations for all independent measures appear in Table 2. Results across all three main effects yielded non-significant findings at the $p < .05$ level. All F and p values can be found in Table 3. The general direction of the results for hypothesis three was not consistently toward or against the hypothesized direction (i.e., there was no consensus regarding how custody arrangement affects relationship satisfaction). For hypothesis four, however, the results from three of the four subscales were in the direction of the hypothesis (i.e., males from father custody households did report the highest relationship satisfaction).

DISCUSSION

The purpose of this study was to conduct a preliminary examination of the effects of divorce and custodial arrangements on children's intimate/ romantic functioning during adulthood. It was hypothesized that children from intact family backgrounds would be more secure in their attachment patterns and more satisfied in romantic relationships than children from divorced backgrounds. Further, it was hypothesized that males from father custody post-divorce situations would be the most secure and most satisfied in romantic relationships of the four possible gender-by-parent custody arrangements.

Two MANOVAs and one ANOVA were computed with little support for the hypotheses found. No significant differences were discovered between divorced or intact groups regarding attachment style or relationship satisfaction, nor were significant differences detected between divorced groups.

The present study adds to a growing body of literature which discounts the "major negative" impact that growing up in a post-divorce household will have on the children. These non-significant between groups results were addressed directly in a recent paper written by Forehand (1992). In it, he states that while there do appear to be some differences between children from divorced vs. children from non-divorced backgrounds, ". . . the magnitude of the difference is quite small, and from a clinical perspective, of questionable importance" (p. 323). He cites work done by Forehand et al. (1991) and Amata and Keith (1991) as evidence of how statistical significance in and of itself does not necessarily translate into strong, pervasive differences between groups. It could be that we face a trend toward lesser differences in general in the literature, or that "real" differences did not exist in many previous studies.

While present attachment style results seem to run contradictory to selected previous findings (Bolgar, Zweig-Frank, & Paris, 1995; Davies & Cummings, 1994; Portes, Haas, & Brown, 1991, for example) whose conclusions indicate that the emotional security of children is contingent upon the parents' marital relationship, Parker, Barrett, and Hickie (1992) explain that parental separation per se does not necessarily predispose children toward conflict in adult relationships. They and other authors (Hazan & Shaver, 1987; Spigelman, Spigelman, & Engelsson, 1994) feel that there are too many intervening variables–including future intimate relationships–that could modify these children's relationship styles.

Despite controlling for many, it would appear extremely difficult to account for all of the possible intervening variables which may have affected these adults throughout their lifetimes. Examples of others not controlled in this study include contact with the non-custodial parent (Kurtz, 1994; Spigelman, Spigelman, & Engelsson, 1994), passage of time since the divorce (Spigelman, Spigelman, & Engelsson, 1994), and custodial parent's remarriage (Bolgar, Zweig-Frank, & Paris, 1995; Brennan & Shaver, 1993; Santrock, Warshak, Lindbergh, & Meadows, 1982; Spigelman & Spigelman, 1990).

Another possibility which was not controlled for was noted by Emery (1988) and Brennan and Shaver (1993). They found that hostility in the parental relationship may be more damaging (promoting insecurity) to the child than actual divorce. This could indicate that children face the possibility of living in an intact but stress-filled home, thereby increasing the incidence of insecure attachment in the non-divorced sample.

Rosen and Rothbaum (1993) also report inconsistent associations between parental behavior and attachment classifications. They go on to note that the "file drawer phenomenon" may exist, whereby many studies which fail to reject the null (i.e., find no significant ties between attachment style and parental behavior) may simply go unpublished and therefore unnoticed. The present study supports the notion that parental divorce does not significantly increase the likelihood of insecure adult attachment.

Satisfaction in interpersonal relationships also appears to be independent of family history or sex of the participant. This finding runs counter to the bulk of the literature which identifies same sex custody as promoting better adjustment than opposite sex custody (Fry & Leahey, 1983; Santrock, 1987;

Santrock & Warshak, 1979; Warshak, 1986), although participants may have responded to their most "stable" relationship rather than their "most intimate." As Kirkpatrick and Davis (1994) note, not all couples who stay together are in fact happy together. This selection phenomenon may account for results which counter the hypothesized direction.

A second possibility remains, and for this we return to the paper by Forehand (1992). It remains a possibility that the differences between groups have not historically been as great as the popular literature would have us believe. Or, as the divorce rate rises and it becomes more "normalized," it can logically be concluded that the qualities of divorcing families are looking more normal than in the past.

It could also be that as the incidence of children growing up in single parent households increases, the effects are tempered naturally through community resources created specifically to handle the stress, and the feeling of universality within peer groups. It stands to reason that as more investment is made across all of society to reduce the negative impact of divorce, the children are better able to take the disruption in stride. Finally, their peer groups have increased incidence of growing up in similar situations, thereby forming a de facto support group within which the children can learn to manage (Teja & Stolberg, 1993).

In conclusion, this study replicated findings that divorce was unrelated to attachment styles, but went one step further and indicated that custodial arrangement was also unrelated. Additionally, it found that custody may have a slight impact on the amount of security felt in romantic relationships, although the benefits of same sex arrangements yielded mixed results. Finally, neither sex of participant nor custodial arrangement was found to be related to overall romantic relationship satisfaction. With the growing body of work indicating a tempered impact of divorce per se, examination of the best custodial arrangements for the children–while not ignoring the importance of individual cases and circumstances–appears to be the area of research most germane to current issues.

Divorce in and of itself may be losing its importance as a useful independent variable for future study. It may be that the time has come to look beyond "divorce" and toward independent variables which will shed more light on the impact of parenting practices on children. Additional work will need to be done to ferret out custodial impact while controlling for familial variables such as parental conflict and the absence or presence of stepparents which may have acted as confounds to the present results.

REFERENCES

Ainsworth, M.D., Blehar, M., & Waters, E. (1978). *Patterns of Attachment: Observations in the Strange Situation at Home.* Hillsdale, NJ: Erlbaum.

Ainsworth, M.D. (1979). Infant-mother attachment. *American Psychologist, 34,* 932-937.

Amata, P.R., & Keith, B. (1991). Parental divorce and adult well-being: A meta-analysis. *Journal of Marriage and the Family, 53,* 43-58.

Bender, W.N. (1994). Joint custody: The option of choice. *Journal of Divorce & Remarriage, 21,* 115-131.

Black, K.N. (1982). Consequences for offspring of single-parent families. *Academic Psychology Bulletin, 4,* 527-534.

Bolgar, R., Zweig-Frank, H., & Paris, J. (1995). Childhood antecedents of interpersonal problems in young adult children of divorce. *Journal of the American Academy of Child and Adolescent Psychiatry, 34,* 143-151.

Bonkowski, S.E. (1989). Lingering sadness: Young adults' response to parental divorce. *The Journal of Contemporary Casework, 70(4),* 219-223.

Bowlby, J. (1969). *Attachment and Loss: Volume 1, Attachment.* New York, NY: Basic Books.

Bowlby, J. (1973). *Attachment and Loss: Volume 2, Separation: Anxiety and Anger.* New York, NY: Basic Books.

Bowlby, J. (1979). *The Making and Breaking of Affectional Bonds.* London: Tavistok.

Bowlby, J. (1980). *Attachment and Loss: Volume 3, Loss, Sadness, and Depression.* New York, NY: Basic Books.

Bowby, J. (1982). Attachment and loss: Retrospect and prospect. *American Journal of Orthopsychiatry, 52,* 664-678.

Bowlby, J. (1988). *A Secure Base.* New York, NY: Basic Books.

Brennan, K.A., & Shaver, P.A. (1993). Attachment styles and parental divorce. *Journal of Divorce & Remarriage, 21,* 161-175.

Cherlin, A.J. (1992). *Marriage, Divorce, Remarriage.* Cambridge, MA: Harvard University Press.

Cherlin, A.J., Furstenberg, F.F., Chase-Lansdale, P.L., Kiernan, K.E., Robins, P.K., Morrison, D.R., & Teitler, J.O. (1991). Longitudinal studies of effects of divorce on children in Great Britain and the United States. *Science, 252,* 1386-1389.

Collins, N.L., & Read, S.J. (1990). Adult attachment, working models, and relationship quality in dating couples. *Journal of Personality and Social Psychology, 58,* 644-663.

Copeland, A.P. (1984). An early look at divorce: Mother-child interactions in the first post-separation year. *Journal of Divorce, 8,* 17-30.

Davies, P.T., & Cummings, E.M. (1994). Marital conflict and child adjustment: An emotional security hypothesis. *Psychological Bulletin, 116,* 387-411.

Duffy, M.E. (1994). Testing the theory of transcending options: Health behaviors of single parents. *Scholarly Inquiry for Nursing Practice: An International Journal, 8,* 191-202.

Emery, R.E. (1982). Interparental conflict and the children of discord and divorce. *Psychological Bulletin, 92(2),* 310-330.

Emery, R.E. (1988). *Marriage, Divorce, and Children's Adjustment.* Newbury Park, CA: Sage.

Feeney, J.A., Noller, P., & Hanrahan, M. (1994). Assessing adult attachment. In M.D. Sperling & W.H. Berman (Eds.), *Attachment in Adults: Clinical and Developmental Perspectives.* New York, NY: Guilford Press.

Forehand, R. (1992). Parental divorce and adolescent maladjustment: Scientific inquiry vs. public information. *Behavioral Research and Therapy, 30,* 319-327.

Franklin, K.M., Janoff-Bulman, R., & Roberts, J.E. (1990). Long-term impact of parental divorce on optimism and trust: Changes in general assumptions or narrow beliefs? *Journal of Personal and Social Psychology, 59,* 743-755.

Fry, P.S., & Leahey, M. (1983). Children's perceptions of major positive and negative events and factors in single parent families. *Journal of Applied Developmental Psychology, 4,* 371-388.

Furstenberg, F.F., & Teitler, J.O. (1994). Reconsidering the effects of marital disruption. *Journal of Family Issues, 15(2),* 173-190.

Garber, R.J. (1991). Long-term effects of divorce on the self-esteem of young adults. *Journal of Divorce & Remarriage, 17,* 131-137.

Greenberg, E.F., & Nay, W.R. (1982). The intergenerational transmission of marital instability revisited. *Journal of Marriage and the Family, 44,* 335-347.

Grossman, K.E., & Grossman, K. (1990). The wider context of attachment in cross-cultural research. *Human Development, 33,* 31-47.

Hazan, C., & Shaver, P. (1987). Romantic love conceptualized as an attachment process. *Journal of Personality and Social Psychology, 52(3),* 511-524.

Hetherington, E.M. (1986). Family relations six years after divorce. In K. Palsey & M. Ihinger-Tallman (Eds.), *Remarriage and Stepparenting Today: Research and Theory.* New York, NY: Guilford.

Hetherington, E.M. (1993). An overview of the Virginia longitudinal study of divorce and remarriage with a focus on early adolescence. *Journal of Family Psychology, 7(1),* 39-56.

Hetherington, E., Cox, M., & Cox, R. (1979). The aftermath of divorce. In J.H. Stevens & M. Matthews (Eds.), *Mother-Child, Father-Child Relations.* Washington, DC: NAEYC.

Hetherington, E.M., Cox, M., & Cox, R. (1982). Effects of divorce on parents and children. In M. Lamb (Ed.), *Nontraditional Families.* New Jersey: Lawrence Erlbaum.

Huntington, D.S. (1982). Therapy with remarriage families: II. Attachment, loss, and divorce: A reconsideration of the concepts. *Family Therapy Collections, 2,* 17-29.

Johnson, S.M., & Greenberg, L.S. (1985). Emotionally focused couples therapy: An outcome study. *Journal of Marital and Family Therapy, 11(3),* 313-317.

Kirkpatrick, L.A., & Davis, K.E. (1994). Attachment style, gender, and relationship stability: A longitudinal analysis. *Journal of Personality and Social Psychology, 66,* 502-512.

Kotler, T. (1989). Patterns of change in marital partners. *Human Relations, 42(9),* 829-856.

Kulka, R.A., & Weingarten, H. (1979). The long-term effects of parental divorce in childhood on adult adjustment. *Journal of Social Issues, 35(4),* 50-78.

Lamb, M.E. (1979). The father's role in the infant's social world. In J.H. Stevens & M. Mathews (Eds.), *Mother-Child Father-Child Relationships.* Washington, DC: NAEYC.

Lamb, M.E. (1986). The changing role of fathers. In M.E. Lamb (Ed.), *The Father's Role: Applied Perspectives.* New York, NY: Wiley.

Levitin, T.E. (1983). An overview of research on the effects of divorce on children: Problems, questions & perspectives. *The Psychiatric Hospital, 14(3),* 145-151.

Levy, M.B., & Davis, K.E. (1988). Lovestyles and attachment styles compared: Their relations to each other and to various relationship characteristics. *Journal of Social and Personal Relationships, 5,* 439-471.

Lopez, F.G. (1991). The impact of parental divorce on college students. *New Directions for Student Services, 54,* 19-33.

Moore, J., & Herlihy, B. (1994). Groups for adolescent girls living in father-custody families. *Journal for Specialists in Group Work, 19,* 11-16.

Moos, R.H., & Moos, B.A. (1976). A typology of family social environments. *Family Process, 15,* 357-372.

Paretti, P.O., & diVitorrio, A. (1993). Effect of loss of father through divorce on personality of the preschool child. *Social Behavior and Personality, 21(1),* 33-38.

Parker, G.B., Barrett, E.A., & Hickie, I.B. (1992). From nurture to network: Examining links between perceptions of parenting received in childhood and social bonds in adulthood. *American Journal of Psychiatry, 149,* 877-885.

Peters, J.M., & Haldeman, V.A. (1987). Time used for household work: A study of school-aged children from single parent, two parent, one earner, and two earner families. *Journal of Family Issues, 8,* 212-225.

Portes, P.R., Haas, R., & Brown, J.H. (1991). Predicting children's adjustment to divorce. *Journal of Divorce, 15,* 87-103.

Rosen, K.S., & Rothbaum, F. (1993). Quality of caregiving and security of attachment. *Developmental Psychology, 29,* 358-367.

Santrock, J.W. (1987). The effects of divorce on adolescents: Needed research perspectives. *Family Therapy, 14(2),* 147-159.

Santrock, J.W., & Warshak, R.A. (1979). Father custody and social development in boys and girls. *Journal of Social Issues, 35(4),* 112-125.

Santrock, J.W., Warshak, R.A., Lindbergh, C., & Meadows, L. (1982). Childrens' and parents' observed social behavior in stepfather families. *Child Development, 53,* 472-480.

Schaefer, M.T., & Olson, D.H. (1981). Assessing Intimacy: The PAIR Inventory. *Journal of Marital and Family Therapy,* 47-61.

Schneider, E.L. (1991). Attachment theory and research: Review of the literature. *Clinical Social Work Journal, 19(3),* 251-266.

Schneider-Rosen, K., Braunwald, K.G., Carlson, V., & Cicchetti, D. (1985). Current perspectives in attachment theory: Illustration from the study of maltreated infants. *Monographs of the Society for Research in Child Development, 50(1-2)*, 194-210.

Shaver, P., & Hazan, C. (1987). Being lonely, falling in love: Perspectives from attachment theory. *Journal of Social Behavior and Personality, 2(2)*, 105-124.

Shaver, P., Hazan, C., & Bradshaw, D. (1988). Love as attachment: The integration of three behavioral systems. In R.J. Sternberg & M. Barnes (Eds.), *The Psychology of Love*. New Haven, CT: Yale University Press.

Shaw, D.S. (1991). The effects of divorce on children's adjustment: Review and implications. *Behavior Modification, 15(4)*, 456-485.

Simpson, J.A. (1990). Influence of attachment styles on romantic relationships. *Journal of Personality and Social Psychology, 59*, 971-980.

Spigelman, G., & Spigelman, A. (1990). A comparison of Egocentricity, Morbid, and Dependency scores between divorce and non-divorce Swedish children using Rorschach responses. *Psychological Research Bulletin, 30*, 1-20.

Spigelman, A., Spigelman, G., & Engelsson, I. (1994). The effects of divorce on children: Post-divorce adaptation of Swedish children to the family breakup: Assessed by interview data and Rorschach responses. *Journal of Divorce & Remarriage, 21*, 171-190.

Strahan, B.J. (1991). Attachment theory and family functioning: Explanations and congruencies. *Australian Journal of Marriage & Family, 12(1)*, 12-26.

Teja, S., & Stolberg, A.L. (1993). Peer support, divorce, and children's adjustment. *Journal of Divorce & Remarriage, 20(3/4)*, 45-64.

Wallerstein, J.S. (1985). Children of divorce: Preliminary report of a ten-year follow-up of older children and adolescents. *Journal of the American Academy of Child Psychiatry, 24*, 545-553.

Wallerstein, J.S. (1987). Children of Divorce: Report of a ten-year follow-up of early latency age children. *American Journal of Orthopsychiatry, 57(2)*, 199-211.

Wallerstein, J.S., & Kelly, J.B. (1980). *Surviving the Breakup: How Children and Parents Cope with Divorce*. New York, NY: Basic Books.

Warshak, R.A. (1978). The effects of father custody and mother custody on children's personality development. Unpublished Doctoral Dissertation. The University of Texas Health Sciences Center at Dallas.

Warshak, R.A. (1986). Father custody and child development: A review and analysis of psychological research. *Behavioral Sciences & the Law, 4(2)*, 185-202.

Weiss, M. (1988). Psychological development in adults who experienced parental divorce during adolescence. *Australian Journal of Sex, Marriage, & Family, 9(3)*, 144-149.

Zaslow, M.J. (1988). Sex differences in children's response to parental divorce: Research methodology and postdivorce family forms. *American Journal of Orthopsychiatry, 58*, 355-378.

Zeanah, P.D. (1983). Children of divorce. *Issues in Comprehensive Pediatric Nursing, 6*, 91-106.

Stigma, Identity Dissonance, and the Nonresidential Mother

Ginna M. Babcock

SUMMARY. Using an identity model, this study examines the dynamics of the parenting relationship nonresidential mothers have with their children following divorce. It explores the effect nonresidential status has on the salience of mother identity for women who live apart from their minor children. Mothers' perceptions of their altered position in the family and the attenuating effect nonresidential status has on their ability to fulfill roles associated with motherhood are examined. Results reveal coping strategies employed by respondents to reduce dissonance in the mother identity and to overcome negative stigma associated with being a nonresidential mother. Because nonresidential motherhood is becoming more common, policy implications are included. *[Article copies available for a fee from The Haworth Document Delivery Service: 1-800-342-9678. E-mail address: getinfo@haworth.com]*

INTRODUCTION

The high incidence of divorce–with an increase in paternal custody awards–accounts for a large part of the recent change in the structure of

Ginna Babcock, PhD, is Assistant Professor at the University of Idaho, Department of Sociology/Anthropology.

This study was supported by University of Idaho Research Office Seed Grant #KD Y600.

Address correspondence to: Ginna Babcock, Department of Sociology/Anthropology, University of Idaho, Moscow, ID 83844-1110, e-mail (gbabcock@uidaho.edu).

[Haworth co-indexing entry note]: "Stigma, Identity Dissonance, and the Nonresidential Mother." Babcock, Ginna M. Co-published simultaneously in *Journal of Divorce & Remarriage* (The Haworth Press, Inc.) Vol. 28, No. 1/2, 1997, pp. 139-156; and: *Child Custody: Legal Decisions and Family Outcomes* (ed: Craig A. Everett) The Haworth Press, Inc., 1997, pp. 139-156. Single or multiple copies of this article are available for a fee from The Haworth Document Delivery Service [1-800-342-9678, 9:00 a.m. - 5:00 p.m. (EST). E-mail address: getinfo@haworth.com].

American households. Between 1970 and 1995 the number of single-parent families maintained by fathers increased 317 percent (from 0.3 million to 1.4 million)–the fastest growing family form in the United States (Bryson, 1996). The resulting number of nonresidential mothers[1] represent an understudied population that should be incorporated into research, policy, and public awareness.

This study uncovers factors that influence a mother's decision to relinquish custody of her children after divorce. Consequences of that decision in terms of the quality and dynamics of the mothering relationship are examined. A major purpose of the research is to examine the causes, coping strategies, and outcomes of identity dissonance among nonresidential mothers. Specifically, the effect nonresidential status has on the salience of mothering identity and the general self-esteem for nonresidential mothers is explored.

Most of what is known about nonresidential parenting has been gained through studies of nonresidential fathers. These studies consistently find high levels of suffering, loneliness, and depression among respondents (Arditti, 1995; Arendell, 1992; Babcock, 1989). Babcock's (1989) study found that nonresidential fathers felt disconnected and out of control. They expressed grief and sadness over the loss of important roles in their lives caused by their nonresidential status (1989). In many ways, the experience of nonresidential mothers is similar to that of nonresidential fathers. Clearly, it is not easy for either parent to be absent from the daily life of a child. One notable difference exists between nonresidential fathers and mothers, however. For nonresidential fathers, the normative expectations associated with fatherhood (e.g., economic support and contact with children) can continue to be met. The nonresidential father appears to enjoy more acceptance than the nonresidential mother as long as he conforms to the central roles associated with fatherhood. If the divorced father fails to fulfill these roles, particularly the role of economic provider, he is often labeled a "deadbeat dad." He not only experiences stigmatization, but may expect to be legally sanctioned by state agencies (Drew, 1993). Fatherhood continues to be narrowly viewed, but motherhood is all-encompassing with myriad and amorphous interpersonal relationship roles.

Exploratory studies of the nonresidential mother status have uncovered prescribed roles associated with a traditional concept of motherhood that involve physical and emotional labor in the daily nurturing of children (Fischer and Cardea, 1981). Motherhood represents a position that is laden with societal expectations and ideological trappings. Enduring images of motherhood perpetuate the powerful belief that "motherhood is inevitable; every woman will or should be a mother. A woman's identity is tenuous and trivial without motherhood" (Thompson and Walker, 1991:91). As Glenn (1987) argues, the centrality of motherhood as the primary identity of women is taken for granted as a universal biological imperative. Given this pervasive view of motherhood in American society, a childless woman or a woman without her children living with her is often viewed as somehow less of a woman. These two categories of women are seen by some as defective, deviant, or even pathological (Bassin, Honey, and Kaplan, 1994).

The nonresidential mother challenges the beliefs underlying motherhood. There are few models for her in history, literature, or life (Rogak, 1987). While women's gender roles have been expanding since the 1960s into nontraditional occupations and alternative lifestyles, the nonresidential mother appears to be a status that remains far removed from social norms and beliefs (West and Kissman, 1991). Indeed, she represents a violation of societal expectations. By deviating from the traditional notions of motherhood, the nonresidential mother risks being stigmatized simply by virtue of her new status.

Structural elements such as the law and economics play important roles in determining the nature of nonresidential parenting relationships, although there are special implications for nonresidential mothering, as will be discussed below. Beyond structural elements, however, interpersonal and social psychological elements must be addressed as well. Studies suggest that motherhood continues to be an important identity for most nonresidential mothers (Greif and Pabst, 1988; Herrerias, 1995). Much of the distress reported by nonresidential mothers appears to be related to dissonance between their identity as mother and the inability to fulfill normative roles associated with motherhood. Virtually nothing is known about the strategies nonresidential mothers employ in dealing with this dissonance.

METHOD

While social scientists have risen to the challenge of studying the consequences of divorce, their research has focused primarily on single-parent mothers and their children (Arendell, 1986), remarriage and step-families (Pasley and Ihinger-Tallman, 1987), and non-custodial fathers (Babcock, 1989; Kruk, 1994; Umberson and Williams, 1993). There is a paucity of research on divorced women who relinquish physical custody of their minor children.

Notwithstanding a dramatic increase in maternal relinquishment of custody, few empirical studies have been conducted in this area. The dearth of research can be explained by methodological problems that continue to hamper study in this area. Although the number of nonresidential mothers is growing, this population remains small and difficult to locate (Herrerias, 1995). Extant studies tend to be exploratory in nature and utilize samples drawn exclusively from court records or from non-random convenience samples of white middle-class families. As much as possible, an effort was made in this study to avoid these problems.

The elements of this research design were developed in response to the multifaceted nature of nonresidential mothering. Because the issue itself tends to be subjective and personal, the incorporation of research approaches involving qualitative methods was appropriate. Qualitative data reveal the richness and diversity of women's mothering experiences and can provide insights into the dynamic nature of these varied phenomena. Qualitative methods arc cspccially uscful whcn attcmpting to undcrstand the meanings attributed to the parenting role by mothers themselves.

Feminist frameworks focus on the experience of women and other marginalized groups (Allen and Baber, 1992), and this study employs methodology using a feminist framework. The goal of the research is not to generalize findings but to understand how meaning is constructed by the individuals studied, and then to develop theory to explain these findings.

Sample

This study represents an in-depth analysis of the experience of nonresidential motherhood. By using a multi-pronged sampling frame, data more fully represent the experience of nonresidential mothers in a variety of settings. The population for the current study was women divorced between the years 1989 and 1994 who relinquished physical custody of at least one minor child either formally (through the courts), or informally (within the family setting). The decision was made to include respondents who experienced divorce as long ago as 1989 because longitudinal research suggests the presence of a great deal of internal shifting of custody within the first few years following divorce (Maccoby and Mnookin, 1992). It should be noted, however, that because of the high geographic mobility among nonresidential mothers, the probability of locating potential respondents still residing in the area is higher when sampling takes place soon after the divorce (Arditti, 1995; Herrerias, 1995).

In addition to addressing the problem of change over time, sampling in this study was guided by the need to address the ethnic, racial, and geographic homogeneity of a regional sample. In order to successfully reach design objectives, very specific sampling criteria were developed. The first phase in the procedure involved sampling public divorce records in four counties in Idaho, resulting in selection of thirty potential respondents with sixteen completed interviews.[2] While the selection of this geographical area represents a convenience sample, care was given to include respondents from rural and urban areas in counties throughout the state. An attempt also was made to sample minority populations including Native Americans.[3] The use of court dockets reduces the probability of self-selection bias and provides the opportunity for a potentially more diverse sample in terms of geographic location, socioeconomic status, and ethnicity.

Because of the variety of ways custody decisions are made, it is critical to sample cases involving informal custody arrangements as well as court-mandated arrangements. Court-ordered custody awards (e.g., in contested custody cases) represent a fraction of the population of interest because only about 10 percent of divorce cases with children involve litigation over custody issues (Buehler, 1995). In uncontested divorces, the court usually rubber-stamps the family's proposed custody arrangements (Mnookin and Kornhauser, 1979). It is possible that the dynamics of the mother-child relationship may differ for mothers whose custody decision was made informally compared to those who relinquished physical custody in court. A second sampling approach attempted to reach this part of the population by advertising in local newspapers and college Women's Centers in the four counties sampled in Idaho. This phase resulted in the recruitment of fifteen volunteer respondents, or about half of the final Idaho sample. In order to introduce geographic diversity to the study, questionnaires were sent to ten nonresidential mothers outside the state of Idaho.[4] This three-pronged sampling frame resulted in recruiting forty-one research participants.

Measurement

Primary data were collected through face-to-face interviews lasting from one to five hours. The general format of the interview was based on an instrument used in previous research (Babcock, 1989) conducted in 1988-1989 with nonresidential fathers. The interview explored several areas: respondent background, the children, and the respondent's attitude about her mothering role. This role was more extensively examined in terms of perceived competence, satisfaction, and esteem. Mother involvement was measured by nonphysical contact, financial support, and visitation. Finally, the extent of perceived negative social attitudes toward the nonresidential mother was explored.

All interviews were assigned identification numbers and audiotaped. Transcripts of interview tapes and field notes were made and stored on computer disks; back-up tapes and disks were made of all interviews, transcripts, mailed survey data, and field notes. All materials were secured to maintain confidentiality.

The bulk of analysis necessary for conceptualization incorporated a multi-stage process that utilized content analysis software developed for qualitative research (*HyperResearch,* 1994). The initial type of coding was *open* coding (Strauss, 1987:28). Close examination of transcripts resulted in the identification of provisional concepts and associated dimensions. The codes were entered into the software program and all relevant passages were marked. Data were sorted by code so that comparisons could be made, trends observed, and frequencies noted.

Primary analysis consisted of the *constant comparative method* (Glaser and Strauss, 1967:102). This approach involves making comparisons between multiple data sources in terms of key issues or themes that emerge from the data. Incidents of themes or key issues are collected and compared. In this manner, relationships between categories can be identified, leading to the generation of hypotheses and the development of theory.

RESULTS

While important in providing geographical diversity to the study, general characteristics of the self-selected sample of nonresidential mothers living outside the state of Idaho were quite similar to the Idaho sample. One dramatic difference between these populations involves the incidence of custody adjudication. Rates were much higher in the non-Idaho sample (60 percent of these mothers pursued physical custody in court, compared to 19 percent in the Idaho sample). It is possible that the mail survey sample experienced more conflicted divorces, therefore providing strong motivation to participate in a study of nonresidential mothers. In all cases of contested custody reported in the study, courts found for the father; however, the majority of mothers lost by default because they withdrew their petitions either before the case began or before a custody decision was formally reached by the judge.

To assess how willing respondents were about relinquishing custody, a number of measures were employed in the current study. Of particular interest is the finding that the majority of respondents (77 percent) reported being dissatisfied with their current custody arrangements while 53 percent indicated that they had relinquished custody voluntarily. While it is beyond the scope of the present paper to explore all issues related to custody relinquishment, the high correlation between these two indicators suggests a reticence on the part of a majority of respondents to formally pursue obtaining physical custody of their children even when they desire to do so. This finding warrants further study.

For the majority of mothers in this study the most powerful determining factor in custody relinquishment was related to a lack of economic resources, with almost 67 percent reporting the belief that the father was better able to provide for the children financially. From the initiation of divorce proceedings through the mothers' negotiation of post-divorce relationships with their children, economic resources played a central role. This finding is consistent with earlier studies where mothers reported relinquishing custody to fathers because of financial constraints (Fischer and Cardea, 1981; Greif and Pabst, 1988; Herrerias, 1995).

Only one mother in the study consistently reported feeling positive about her decision to relinquish custody, a striking contrast to all of the other respondents who expressed deep feelings of loss, pain, and sadness. For this mother, parenting caused emotional and economic strains that she sought to escape; custody relinquishment was a relief for her:

> I was never meant to be a mother. I married young and for all the wrong reasons. Since I'm not a very good mother and since I don't enjoy it very much, I guess we're just lucky he likes being a father. This way everybody wins. (K-01)

In only this case was the decision described as "a relief; a burden lifted" (K-01). When mothers in the study were asked to respond to the statement "when I became a non-custodial mother it was a very stressful time in my life," all but one indicated that they *strongly* agreed. Five mothers sought professional counseling during the post-divorce period specifically to deal with feelings associated with their nonresidential status.

A majority of the nonresidential mothers in this study pay child support to former spouses as well as maintaining close contact with their children through visitation, phone, letter, and electronic communication. Notwithstanding strong bonds between mothers and children, the physical separation associated with their nonresidential parent status appears to transform those relationships. For example, when the question "if you could change one thing about your relationship with the children, what would it be?" was asked, over half of the respondents (57 percent) answered without hesitation that they would like to have their children living with them or desired unlimited contact with the children. Responses to "what is the worst thing about your relationship with your children right now?" were highly correlated with the previous question. Over 66 percent of the responses indicated that the worst aspect of the mother-child relationship was missing the day-to-day activities in their children's lives. The following response attests to the sense of loss associated with the nonresidential parent status:

> I missed seeing my daughter in her first prom dress. I wasn't there when my son got his driver's license. I don't feel like a very good mother when my kids have to try and describe these really important events to me over the phone. I've missed so much, every day. (NP-02)

Satisfaction and competence in the mothering role identity were measured by adapting two parenting scales (Guidubaldi and Cleminshaw, 1989). Analysis of responses on the parent satisfaction scale indicates that the mothers in the study have very positive feelings toward their children and the relationships they have developed with them as nonresidential parents. Satisfaction in the mothering role is consistently high for respondents: almost 97 percent reported being happy as a parent.

Perceived maternal competence was measured by adapting the 10-item parent performance subscale of the Parent Satisfaction Scale (1989). The use of the parent performance subscale as a measurement of perceived competence in the mothering role may be somewhat less useful than the satisfaction scale. A number of mothers in the study could not respond to the statements because they felt that they were unable to perform basic parenting tasks due to their physical absence from the daily lives of their children.

The findings indicate that mother identity remains salient for all but one respondent: 60 percent indicated that motherhood was their most important identity, or master status. It was found that the mothers who experienced the most dissonance between mother identity and mother roles were the respondents who attempted to negotiate alternative roles when interacting with their children. In other words, in cases where emotional discomfort was intense, respondents altered the nature of their relationship with their children, creating one in which the mother could feel a sense of success. Conditions causing identity dissonance included: (1) the relinquishment of authority roles typically associated with residential parenthood (serving to minimize power differences between mothers and their children); (2) geographical distance and limited visitation time (increasing the novelty of visits); and (3) the practice of gift-buying and entertainment by nonresidential mothers ("Disneyland mom"). Under these conditions, relationships more closely approximated intimate and rewarding friendships than traditional mother-child interactions.

These findings suggest the presence of coping strategies nonresidential mothers may invoke when faced with varying levels of discomfort associated with failing to meet societal expectations of motherhood. Rather than to disassociate from the mothering role, respondents consciously changed the nature of relationships and were therefore able to continue to relate to their children without the guilt and recriminations they perceived to be associated with a nonresidential parent status. One respondent noted the changes in her parenting style caused by her nonresidential status:

> Sometimes it's actually easier being a noncustodial parent. You don't have to be the bad guy. You get to celebrate what time you have with them, which makes it always a good time. Parenting became more of a buddy thing than an authority figure. (L-06)

For many of the respondents, experiences were related that suggested the negotiation of a relationship with children that was highly intimate and enjoyable.

DISCUSSION

As noted previously, the number of nonresidential mothers is increasing and their number is challenging fundamental beliefs about the appropriate roles associated with the position of mother (Doudna, 1982). In the face of these fundamental beliefs it is not uncommon for the nonresidential mother to be labeled deviant and to experience condemnation and ostracism (Paskowicz, 1982). One of the more disconcerting findings in the present study relates to the strong and prevalent negative stigma experienced by respondents. Each respondent related at least one instance when she felt that she was being judged negatively because her children were not living with her; the judgments came from sources ranging from family members and neighbors to co-workers. Some respondents tended to self-stigmatize, judging themselves as failures because they felt unable to fulfill duties they associate with motherhood. One respondent discussed her feelings of embarrassment:

> I struggle with this a lot. I used to be a very open person, but now so many people automatically form an opinion of you if you don't have your kids with you all the time. They think you must be a terrible person. It always hurts. So, I'm more guarded now. I don't tell people that I'm a mother . . . at least, not until I know them. I can't stand to see how people look at me when they find out. (L-04)

At least 20 percent of the respondents indicated that discussion of these issues was avoided. The reason given most often had to do with the emotional distress caused by thinking about the loss of one's children. Respondents reported feelings that ranged from grief and sadness to anger, guilt, and loneliness. One of the most poignant descriptions of being a nonresidential mother came from a mother of two teen-aged sons:

> Being separated from your children is like having a limb cut off. No, it's worse. At least when you lose a leg, they can sew up the end and it will heal; the pain will eventually go away. People can look at you and understand why you're off balance; they see why you are in so much pain and empathize with you. But when you are a nonresidential mother, the pain never goes away, people don't understand your pain, and it takes years to regain your balance. (L-3)

The perception that the general public lacks an understanding of the nonresidential mother experience was a common finding in the present study. Respondents discussed the need for support groups and sympathetic counselors to help nonresidential mothers "get through" the divorce process and adjust to the nonresidential status. The second most common need reported by respondents related to increased education for divorcing mothers about their legal rights and financial matters related to divorce and custody.

On a cultural level, the power of ideology is demonstrated forcefully in the contemporary concept of motherhood (Hoffnung, 1995). Becoming a mother is viewed as an important rite of passage into adulthood and serves to prove womanhood. By implication, those who do not have their children with them are seen as less than complete or fulfilled women. Data from the current study reveal that our cultural, idealized conceptualization of motherhood is not supported by current social conditions. The overwhelming majority of respondents reported high levels of stress associated with their inability to meet societal demands made on them. Motherhood was seen as a permanent commitment by the respondents–and a highly salient identity. All but one respondent reported feeling depressed, sad, and disappointed in herself as a mother who is unable to fulfill the roles she perceives to be associated with that important identity.

On an interpersonal level, about 85 percent of the nonresidential mothers in this study reported altering role behaviors associated with mothering to something that represents a better combination of the expectations of motherhood and their real-life experience (including the constraints of geographic distance, lack of finances, etc.). Role change also occurred in response to perceived harsh judgment, stigmatization, and ridicule for not having their children with them, and in response to their own perceived failings as mothers. But a more dramatic finding suggests that in cases where behavioral change was inadequate in reducing the discomfort, respondents actually attempted to redefine motherhood. In these cases (about 65 percent), relationships are described that more closely resemble relationships such as aunt, sister, or friend, rather than the traditional notion of mother. The resultant relationships respondents developed with their children tended to be highly intimate and egalitarian. Respondents reported that the redefined relationship provided mutually satisfying interactions. Retrospective data from the current study demonstrate the ability of identity theory to explain this process.

IDENTITY MODEL

There are four elements in the identity theory formula: identity, behavior, identity standard, and commitment. Identities are meanings attributed to the self as object (Burke and Tully, 1977). Identities are seen as internal, reflexive designations that are tied to social positions such as mother (Burke, 1991b). Identities attributed to the self while in a role are referred to as role identities (Stets, 1995). Role identities have two components, an internal identity and an external role (Burke, 1991b). A role is a functional concept that is socially constructed. It denotes the "set of activities and attitudes intrinsic to a given status or social position" (Brown and Foye, 1982:316). As identities are tied to the cultural meanings of social positions with attendant behavioral expectations, the internalization of these expectations represents the basis of identities (Stryker, 1980). In other words, an identity is made up of a set of internalized meanings of the self in a social role (Burke, 1991b).

Identity salience refers to a set of identities organized into priorities. A salient identity has a "low threshold of invocation" and a high probability that it will be invoked in a given situation or across differing situations (McCall and Simmons, 1978:77). Behavior represents output in the identity model, or the performance of a specific role (Burke, 1991). Commitment is related to the degree to which an actor is willing to fulfill appropriate roles in the group, or to meet the expectations of the identity standard (Stryker, 1980).

Identity Standard

An identity standard represents a set of externally constructed cultural beliefs about a social position and its concomitant roles (Burke, 1989). It is external to the actor and is established and defined by social structure (1989). The mother identity standard embodies the idealized model of motherhood that has developed over time and in the context of patriarchy. It includes the beliefs that motherhood is natural, that all women should be mothers, and that all women have the desire and skills to be good mothers (Glenn, 1994).

One of the most dramatic findings in the current study is the high level of discomfort experienced by respondents when the reality of nonresidential mothering does not match their perception of the societal (identity) standard of motherhood. Because of a social perception that nonresidential mothers fail to meet the expectations of motherhood, respondents have had to cope with negative attitudes from myriad sources. These attitudes tend to isolate nonresidential mothers and put them at greater risk for feelings of guilt, low self-esteem, and depression (Chesler, 1986).

Insights from a growing body of social psychological research in the area of identity are helpful in understanding the strategies employed by respondents to cope with feelings of marginality and dissonance associated with their social position of nonresidential mother, a position that challenges the cultural standard of motherhood. As reported in this study, respondents attempted to alter behavior in order to meet the perceived expectations associated with the mothering identity standard. Such behavioral changes involved increased physical and nonphysical contact (as measured by visitation, correspondence through letters and cards, and phone conversations). For about 65 percent of the respondents, initial efforts to meet the expectations of the cultural ideal of motherhood by altering behavior proved to be inadequate in reducing the feelings of dissonance created by their nonresidential mother status. In response to continued discomfort in the nonresidential mothering role, yet with continued saliency of motherhood as an identity, respondents reported efforts to consciously redefine the motherhood standard.

According to identity theory, the identity process is a control system (Burke, 1991a; 1991b). As used in this study, the control system consists of four components: self-perceptions in the mothering role, an external identity standard of motherhood, behavior in the mothering role, and a comparator that compares the self-perceptions with the identity standard (Figure 1).

A feedback loop is established when a role identity is invoked by an actor (1991a). Mother identity is a role identity. Thus, while in the mother identity, a feedback process occurs where current perceptions of the self as mother are compared to an underlying mother identity standard that is socially constructed and external to the actor (Burke, 1991a). The

FIGURE 1. Identity Model

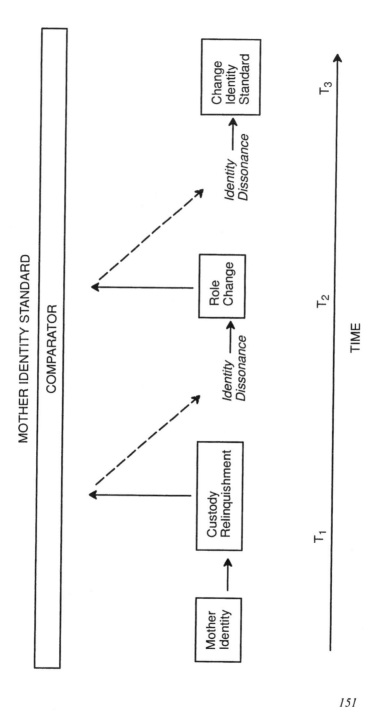

nonresidential mothers in the current study were aware of and initially embraced the identity standard, yet failed to successfully fulfill roles associated with that standard and thus experienced dissonance. Ninety-eight percent of the respondents continue to view mother identity as highly salient and were unwilling to remove themselves from the significant social networks associated with their children's lives or to forgo the motherhood status.

Identity theory proposes that the first coping strategy invoked to deal with dissonance between self-perceptions in the mothering role and the identity standard is behavior modification (role change). New behavior would thus be enacted that results in the best match between the self-perception and the identity standard. The goal of that behavior would then be to support and affirm one's identity as a mother. Indeed, in order to reduce the discrepancy between desired level of mother mastery and mother identity standard, the respondents altered, or modified, their role behavior. The most common strategies included attempts to increase closeness to children through phone conversation, letter-writing, gift-giving, and visitation.

Notably, however, efforts to reduce dissonance between self-perceptions of mother and the mother identity standard through behavior change were not effective for all respondents. The status of nonresidential mother involved dramatic disruptions of identity processes for the respondents in the current study. The life events of divorce and loss of custody physically separated respondents from daily participation in the nuclear family network. Thus, it was virtually impossible to fulfill roles prescribed by the mother identity standard. For the majority of respondents (65 percent), changing role behavior (output) did *not* restore homeostasis to the identity model, and a second coping strategy was invoked.

The experience of respondents in the current study reflects what Burke terms the *broken loop* (1991a:841). Life events, such as divorce and custody relinquishment, may serve to disrupt the system to such a degree that behavior change fails to ameliorate continued high levels of dissonance between self-perception and the identity standard, thus causing elevated levels of distress. In the current study, the first-order feedback loop was ineffective, and a move to a second-order feedback loop resulted, where attempts were made to alter the identity standard (1991a).

Findings suggest that in the process of moving to the second-order loop, mothers reported developing relationships with their children that might be more commonly associated with the position of aunt, sister, or even friend; however, this was not at the expense of their desire to maintain the centrality of their mother identity. In other words, while the roles and definition of the relationship between nonresidential mothers and children were consciously altered, respondents maintained the identity of mother; only the standard had changed.

The relationships that resulted from a changed identity standard were reported to be highly intimate and cherished. These were fairly egalitarian relationships and embodied a sense of urgency uncommon in mother-child relationships in intact families. Respondents reported that time spent in the mothering role was important and the desire to succeed was significant. An enhanced sense of kinship and closeness between mothers and children also was reported:

> We have a real closeness and we share an intimacy that is very rare in that we're able to share with a feeling of acceptance. My sons know that I unconditionally love them and I know that, even through all of this, that they love me. I'm proud of them as young men. They are real fine young men. (L-03)

Respondents in the current study made an effort to alter the meaning of motherhood to fit their lived experience; they attempted to change the identity standard. Because motherhood continues to be a highly salient identity, they chose to redefine the meanings associated with the status/ identity of mother rather than to forgo the mother identity and/or shift to another identity domain (i.e., focus on identity of worker, student, spouse). This finding reflects high commitment to the mother identity. As conceptualized by Burke and Reitzes (1991), commitment refers to the strength of a response an actor makes in restoring consonance between the identity standard and self-perceptions when a discrepancy exists between them (Burke, 1991:841). By redefining the mother identity standard, identity dissonance was reduced which resulted in reported lower stress levels and higher self-esteem.

Data in this study reveal efforts to deconstruct the idealized motherhood identity standard on a micro level. The data also suggest that the reconstruction of a more inclusive motherhood identity standard may come from marginalized groups such as nonresidential mothers rather than from more mainstream populations such as residential mothers or feminist scholars.

RECOMMENDATIONS

In an effort to eradicate a pattern of stigma and marginalization, increased education and public awareness about the nonresidential mother is warranted. By accurately describing the experience of nonresidential mothering, knowledge about this type of parenting will challenge many of the stereotypical beliefs about nonresidential motherhood, and thereby alleviate much of the stigma directed toward nonresidential mothers generally.

In addition to the general public, counselors and social workers need to be educated about the unique problems faced by this population. The findings suggest the need for increased resources and intervention services for women. Affordable and accessible mental health services for nonresidential mothers are essential. Support groups and self-help groups provide invaluable resources while having the potential to create change on an individual and community level.

It is important that the social definition of motherhood be expanded and changed. But, as the data in the current study reveal, such change is slow. In a small volume of anecdotes and insights on mothering, Dorothy Canfield Fisher cntreats mothers to "try to put aside our deeply ingrained traditions, to divest ourselves of our passionately held prejudices, and to look at the relations of the modern world to family life as they really are" (1914:263). Fisher's words are just as timely today as they were almost a century ago; in fact, her words have found a contemporary voice in feminist scholarship. For almost thirty years, feminist scholars have stressed the need to deconstruct the idealized model of motherhood in favor of a more inclusive, active, relational, woman-centered model. Scholars should continue to explore the variety of ways women experience mothering and move toward the development of a more inclusive and realistic motherhood model, a model where nonresidential mothers are not deviant, but simply represent a parenting style that takes place in an environment other than the family home. Policymakers must be advised to incorporate research findings into policy decisions and to cautiously move forward in the development of legislation to enhance the experience of all family forms.

NOTES

1. A nonresidential mother is defined as a divorced woman who currently lives apart from at least one of her minor children.

2. The four Idaho counties include Ada (SMSA, population 206,000); Kootenai (population 70,000); Latah (population 31,000); and Nez Perce (population 34,000).

3. The Coeur d'Alene Indian Reservation is located in Kootenai County. The Nez Perce Reservation is located in Nez Perce County. Interviews were completed with one Native American and two Hispanic respondents.

4. Respondents who participated in the study by filling out a mailed questionnaire were self-selected volunteers obtained through national advertising of the study. States represented include Texas, New Hampshire, Washington, Maine, Oregon, and New York.

REFERENCES

Allen, K. & Baber, K. (1992). Ethical and epistemological tensions in applying a postmodern perspective to feminist research. *Psychology of Women Quarterly 16*, 1-15.

Arditti, J. (1995). Noncustodial parents: Emergent issues of diversity and process. *Marriage & Family Review 20*, 283-304.

Arendell, T. (1992). After divorce: Investigations into father absence. *Gender & Society 6*, 562-586.

Babcock, G. (1989). *Fathers on the outside: Legal and social psychological aspects of post-divorce parenting.* Unpublished master's thesis, Washington State University, Pullman.

Bassin, D., Honey, M., & Kaplan, M. (1994). Introduction. In D. Bassin, M. Honey, & M. Kaplan (Eds.), *Representations of motherhood* (pp. 1-25). New Haven: Yale University Press.

Brown, B. & Foye, B. (1982). Divorce as a dual transition: Interpersonal loss and role restructuring. In V.L. Allen & E. van de Vliert (Eds.), *Role transition: Explorations and explanations* (pp. 315-329). NY: Plenum Press.

Bryson, K. (1996). Household and family characteristics. *Current Population Reports* (Census Bureau Series P20-488), Washington, DC: U.S. Government Printing Office.

Buehler, C. (1995). Divorce law in the United States. *Marriage & Family Review 21*, 99-120.

Burke, P. (1989). Gender identity, sex, and school performance. *Social Psychology Quarterly 52*, 159-169.

Burke, P. (1991a). Identity processes and social stress. *American Sociological Review 56*, 836-849.

Burke, P. (1991b). Attitudes, behavior, and the self. In J.A. Howard & P.L. Callero (Eds.), *The self society interface: Cognition, emotion and action* (pp. 189-208). Cambridge, MA: Cambridge University Press.

Burke, P. & Reitzes, D. (1981). The link between identity and role performance. *Social Psychology Quarterly 44*, 83-92.

Burke, P. & Tully, J. (1977). The measurement of role identity. *Social Forces 55*, 881-897.

Chesler, P. (1986). *Mothers on trial.* Seattle: Seal Press.

Doudna, C. (1982). The weekend mother. *The New York Times Magazine (10/3)*, 72-75.

Drew, S. (1993). Remedies for nonpayment. *Family Advocate 16*, 36-40.

Fischer, J. & Cardea, J. (1981). Mothers living apart from their children: A study in stress and coping. *Alternative Lifestyles 4*, 218-227.

Fisher, D. (1914). *Mothers and children.* NY: Henry Holt & Company.

Glaser, B. & Strauss, A. (1967). *The discovery of grounded theory: Strategies for qualitative research.* NY: Aldine.

Glenn, E. (1987). Gender and the family. In B. Hess & M. Ferree (Eds.), *Analyzing gender: A handbook of social science research* (pp. 348-380). Newbury Park: Sage.

Greif, G. & Pabst, M. (1988). *Mothers without custody.* Lexington, MA: D.C. Heath.

Guidubaldi, J. & Cleminshaw, H. (1989). Development and validation of the Cleminshaw Guidubaldi parent satisfaction scale. In M. Fine (Ed.), *The second handbook on parent education: Contemporary perspectives* (pp. 257-277). San Diego: Academic Press.

Herrerias, C. (1995). Noncustodial mothers following divorce. *Marriage & Family Review 20,* 233-255.

Hoffnung, M. (1995). Motherhood: Contemporary conflict for women. In J. Freeman (Ed.), *Women: A feminist perspective, fifth edition* (pp. 162-181). Mt. View, CA: Mayfield Publishing.

HyperResearch [Computer software]. (1994). Randolph, MA: ResearchWare, Inc.

Kruk, E. (1994). The disengaged noncustodial father: Implications for social work practice with the divorced family. *Social Work 39,* 15-25.

Maccoby, E. & Mnookin, R. (1992). *Dividing the child: Social and legal dilemmas of custody.* Cambridge: Harvard University Press.

McCall, G. & Simmons, J. (1968). *Identities and interaction.* NY: Free Press.

Mnookin, R. & Kornhauser, L. (1979). Bargaining in the shadow of the law: The case of divorce. *The Yale Law Journal 88,* 950-997.

Paskowicz, P. (1982). *Absentee mothers.* NY: Universe.

Pasley, K. & Ihinger-Tallman, M. (Eds.). (1987). *Remarriage & stepparenting: Current research & theory.* NY: Guilford Press.

Rogak, L. (1987). Mommy moves out. *New York Magazine 20,* 36-41.

Stets, J. (1995). Role identities and person identities: Gender identity, mastery identity, and controlling one's partner. *Sociological Perspectives 38,* 129-150.

Strauss, A. (1987). *Qualitative analysis for social scientists.* Cambridge: Cambridge University Press.

Stryker, S. (1980). *Symbolic interactionism: A social structural version.* Menlo Park, CA: Benjamin Cummings.

Thompson, L. & Walker, A. (1991). Gender in families. In A. Booth (Ed.), *Contemporary families: Looking forward, looking back* (pp. 76-102). Minneapolis, MN: NCFR.

Umberson, D. & Williams, C. (1993). Divorced fathers: Parental role strain and psychological distress. *Journal of Family Issues 14,* 378-400.

West, B. & Kissman, K. (1991). Mothers without custody: Treatment issues. In C. Everett (Ed.), *The Consequences of divorce: Economic and custodial impact on children and adults* (pp. 229-237). NY: The Haworth Press, Inc.

The Relation
of State-Anger to Self-Esteem,
Perceptions of Family Structure
and Attributions of Responsibility
for Divorce of Custodial Mothers
in the Stabilization Phase
of the Divorce Process

Solly Dreman
Charles Spielberger
Orly Darzi

SUMMARY. Research shows that divorced women usually experience high levels of anger even several years past the divorce event. The present research investigates the long-term influence of custodial mother's State-Anger (S-Anger, Spielberger, 1988) on divorced mothers' personal adjustment as measured in their ratings of self-es-

Solly Dreman, PhD, is Associate Professor, former Director of the Center for Family Life Research and of the Graduate Program in Clinical Psychology, Department of Behavioral Sciences at Ben Gurion University. Charles Spielberger, PhD, is Distinguished Research Professor and Director, Center for Research in Behavioral Medicine and Health Psychology, University of South Florida. Orly Darzi, MA, is a graduate student in Psychology, Department of Behavioral Sciences at Ben Gurion University.

Address correspondence to: Solly Dreman, PhD, Department of Behavioral Sciences, Ben Gurion University of the Negev, Beer Sheva 84105, Israel.

[Haworth co-indexing entry note]: "The Relation of State-Anger to Self-Esteem, Perceptions of Family Structure and Attributions of Responsibility for Divorce of Custodial Mothers in the Stabilization Phase of the Divorce Process." Dreman, Solly, Charles Spielberger, and Orly Darzi. Co-published simultaneously in *Journal of Divorce & Remarriage* (The Haworth Press, Inc.) Vol. 28, No. 1/2, 1997, pp. 157-170; and: *Child Custody: Legal Decisions and Family Outcomes* (ed: Craig A. Everett) The Haworth Press, Inc., 1997, pp. 157-170. Single or multiple copies of this article are available for a fee from The Haworth Document Delivery Service [1-800-342-9678, 9:00 a.m. - 5:00 p.m. (EST). E-mail address: getinfo@haworth.com].

157

teem, perceptions of cohesion and adaptability, and their attributions of responsibility for the divorce. S-Anger was chosen as the main independent variable in the present study since it is a situational variable that reflects more accurately the stressors of the postdivorce situation for divorced mothers such as increased parental responsibility, work overload and diminished quality of life due to lowered socioeconomic status. Mothers' S-Anger was found to be inversely related to their ratings of self-esteem, perceptions of cohesion and adaptability, as well as to attributions of personal responsibility for the divorce. Theoretical, research and interventive implications are discussed. *[Article copies available for a fee from The Haworth Document Delivery Service: 1-800-342-9678. E-mail address: getinfo@haworth.com]*

Although divorce research has investigated the effects of interpersonal parental conflict on postdivorce adjustment (Camara & Resnick, 1988, Emery, 1982; Hauser, 1985; Rutter, 1971; Wallerstein & Blakeslee, 1989), the effects of anger have been relatively ignored. Research shows that divorced women are characterized by more unresolved feelings of anger associated with their divorce and blame the ex-spouse for the marital failure, more than do divorced men, even several years after the divorce event (Dreman & Aldor, 1994a; Kitson & Sussman, 1982; Wallerstein, 1986). These higher anger levels may be related to harsher situational realities for divorced mothers compared to fathers postdivorce, such as increased parental responsibilities, work overload and poorer quality of life due to a diminishment of socioeconomic standing (Hartman, 1991; Herman, 1974; Katz, 1991, Katz & Pesach, 1985).

While it might be expected that parental anger would negatively affect adjustment, a recent review article notes that the role negative parental emotions play in adjustment has received little attention in the research literature (Dix, 1991). In one of the few studies which investigated the influence of parental anger on children's adjustment (Dreman & Aldor, 1994b), a higher level of state-anger (S-Anger: Spielberger, 1988) in divorced mothers was found to be related to poorer adjustment in children.

The present study investigates the relation between anger in divorced mothers in regard to their personal and family adjustment. Anger might result in lowered *self-esteem* in divorced mothers since it has been found to be associated with ineffective, insensitive and coercive parenting (Cowan & Cowan, in press) and may also cause difficulties in interpersonal relations in the social and work arenas. In addition, an angry divorced mother might perceive her family as less *cohesive* and as displaying less *adaptability*, processes which might result in poorer family adjustment. This follows since the angry parent may be less nurturing and flexible in their relationships with their children. In partial support of this contention is a recent study (Dreman & Ronen-Eliav, in press) which found that divorced custodial mothers, at least four years past divorce, who perceived their families as less cohesive and adaptable, rated their children's adjustment less positively than those with higher ratings.

Attribution of responsibility to the ex-spouse for the divorce has been found to be related to poor postdivorce coping and adjustment in divorced women (Peterson, 1980). Such attributions involving blame might not only prevent parental cooperation postdivorce, but may also diminish self-awareness, including the assumption of some personal responsibility and the implementation of behaviors designed to cope more effectively with the postdivorce situation. Since anger often results in externalization of responsibility and blame to others, angry divorced mothers may attribute more responsibility to the ex-spouse for the divorce, cooperate less and assume less responsibility than those who are less angry. These processes could ultimately contribute to poorer personal and family adjustment.

The present study investigates the relation between anger in divorced mothers, as expressed in situationally determined *S-Anger* (Spielberger, 1988), with *self-esteem* (Rosenberg, 1965), perceptions of *family cohesion* and *adaptability* (Olson, Portner, & Lavee, 1985), as well as *attributions of responsibility to the ex-spouse for the divorce* (Dreman & Aldor, 1988). State-anger was chosen as our measure of anger since it was felt to more accurately reflect ongoing situationally-related stressors, noted above, that divorced women experience in the one-parent household. In addition, S-Anger may reflect divorced-related memories that are evoked in a given situation. Such negative stressors, or memories of them, could result in elevated S-Anger levels which adversely affect adjustment. In this conceptual framework, the emotional component, S-Anger, serves as a mediating variable between ongoing divorce-related stressors and/or memories with postdivorce adjustment.

We predicted that the divorced custodial mothers with high levels of S-Anger would have lower levels of self-esteem, more negative perceptions of family cohesion and adaptability and would attribute more responsibility for the divorce to their ex-spouses than those with intermediate levels of anger. As for mothers with low levels of S-Anger, it might be hypothesized that they would have higher self-esteem, as well as more positive perceptions of family structure and of their ex-spouse, than those with higher anger levels. These mothers, however, could be suppressing or repressing anger, ultimately leading to poorer adjustment. Since we had no clear-cut prediction regarding the low anger group, the differences between them and mothers with higher anger levels were examined post hoc (see Method).

Clinical observations have noted that women, located three to four years past divorce, usually have undergone an "emotional divorce." Such emotional working through of the divorce experience enables them to adjust well in the personal, familial, work and social spheres in this "stabilization" phase of the divorce process (Hertz Brown, 1988). However, previously cited empirical research showed that divorced women's anger persists even several years after divorce. As a result, the divorced mothers, tested in the present study, were located at least four years past the divorce event, i.e., in the stabilization phase, in order to examine the long-term effects of anger on personal and family adjustment.

METHOD

Sample

Divorced mothers were randomly selected from an inclusive national computerized list of 14,000 divorced custodial mothers receiving child stipend payments from the National Insurance Institute in Israel. Of these, 2,500 mothers were approached by a letter from the Institute asking for their participation in a national study of divorced parents and their children. At this stage, many of the letters were returned because of the geographic mobility of this population group, though repeated attempts were made to locate them. Still, response rates were approximately 20% of letters delivered, which compares favorably with other survey research studies conducted in Israel that did not employ special techniques to increase these rates (Hornick & Maier, 1989).

The principal investigator subsequently sent letters to mothers of the Jewish faith (85% of all divorcees) who both answered and agreed to participate in the research (337 mothers). Jewish mothers were selected because this is the major ethnic denomination in Israel, as well as due to cultural and ethnic differences in divorce and custody arrangements between groups. This letter explained the purpose of the research, as well as ensuring confidentiality. A demographic questionnaire was sent along with this letter.

Mothers who had remarried or had been married and divorced more than once were excluded from the present study. This was due to the fact that we wished to focus on single-parent custodial households resulting from a first divorce in which the mother was living without an adult partner. Only mothers who were four or more years past the divorce event, i.e., in the "the stabilization phase," were selected. Another criterion was that mothers had to have at least one child between the ages of 6-18, in order to permit testing of children capable of filling out a pencil and paper questionnaire administered in a more comprehensive national study of divorce. These selection criteria, plus a 20% dropout between the first wave and the second wave of the study (see Procedure), resulted in a final sample of 172 custodial mothers. Sixty girls and 59 boys participated, one child selected from each household, with selection criteria including controls for gender, age and birth order.

Comparison of demographic characteristics showed that these mothers were similar in terms of ethnicity, number of children in custody, the age of the oldest child and other relevant variables to the total sample of divorced Jewish mothers. The population was skewed upwards in terms of age distribution (mothers' mean age 41.93 years) since mothers selected were at least four years past divorce. Mothers' mean time since divorce was eight years and nine months.

Measures

State-Trait Anger Expression Inventory (STAXI; Spielberger, 1988). The STAXI consists of 44 self-report items. Subjects are initially told that the questionnaire inquires about their feelings, attitudes and behaviors. Two scales measure *the experience of anger:* State-Anger (S-Anger) and Trait-Anger (T-Anger). Four scales measure *the expression of anger:* Anger-In, Anger-Out, Anger-Control and Anger-Expression. The S-Anger scale asks subjects to rate the *intensity* of their angry feelings "right now," on a 4-point Likert scale, ranging from "very much so" to "not at all." An example of such an item is "I feel angry."

Situationally-linked S-Anger was chosen as the main independent variable in the present study, because recent Israeli studies showed that of all the STAXI scales it most clearly differentiated divorced mothers from divorced fathers, as well as from mothers in two-parent families—divorced mothers displaying significantly higher S-Anger levels (Dreman & Aldor, in press). In addition, divorced mothers' S-Anger was found to be the only anger scale that significantly influences adjustment in the postdivorce family (Dreman, 1995; Dreman & Aldor, 1994b). Conceptually, S-Anger was felt to be most representative of the current situational stressors affecting mothers in the postdivorce family.

The STAXI has been extensively used in studies of stress and emotion and has proven reliabilities and validities (Spielberger, 1988). The Hebrew version of the STAXI (Dreman & Aldor, in press) was used in testing the Israeli sample of the present study.

Self-Esteem (Rosenberg, 1965). Parental self-esteem was measured by a 10-item Guttman scale which has satisfactory reproducibility and scalability. Subjects agree or disagree with five positively and five negatively worded items which openly dealt with this dimension and hence have face validity, e.g., "I take a positive attitude to myself"; or "At times I think I am no good at all." The scale has been shown to have external validity with depressed people and other clinical groups having lower self-esteem compared to non-clinical populations.

Family Adaptability and Cohesion Evaluation Scales (FACES; Olson, Portner & Lavee, 1985). This scale is a well-established instrument in family research with proven reliabilities and validities. Mothers were asked to evaluate their perceptions of family cohesion and adaptability on 20 items rated on a 5-point Likert scale. An example of an item that measures family cohesion is "Family members ask each other for help." An example of an item measuring perceived adaptability is "Different people act as leaders in our family." This instrument is based on a curvilinear circumplex model of family systems–extremely high or low levels of cohesion or adaptability found to be associated with less well-adjusted (unbalanced) family types. Olson notes that "normal" families tend to be more in the mid-range of the distribution for each of these orthogonal dimensions and behave in accordance with a linear model–with lower scores on these variables associated with poorer adjustment and higher scores with better adjustment in these families. Since contemporary views of divorced families perceive them as normal nonclinical families undergoing a life-crisis, it was expected that lower levels of perceived cohesion and adaptability would be related to high state-anger scores. The Hebrew version of FACES (Teichman & Navon, 1990) was used with Israeli subjects.

Parental Attributions of Responsibility (Dreman & Aldor, 1988). Divorced mothers' attributions of responsibility for the divorce were used as another measure of perceptions of the divorce situation. The question posed to mothers was "Who, in your opinion, is responsible for the divorce?", with the alternatives being: "myself," "my ex-husband," "the children," "other," each of which was rated on a five-point scale from "very responsible" to "not at all responsible." Construct validity of this measure was obtained, as evidenced by a negative correlation between frequency of paternal visits and attribution of responsibility for the divorce to the fathers by divorced mothers (Dreman & Aldor, 1988).

Procedure

This study examined the second wave of a longitudinal study designed to assess postdivorce adjustment in divorced families. Since the Self-Esteem Scale (Rosenberg, 1965) and FACES III (Olson, Portner & Lavee, 1985) were only introduced in this wave, tested on the average one-and-a-half years after the first testing, this was chosen as the period investigated. Another reason for selecting this wave was that a larger number of divorced mothers had reached the stabilization phase, i.e., at least four years past divorce, thus fulfilling this selection criterion. FACES III was administered as part of an initial divorce-related questionnaire sent by mail, while the STAXI and the Self-Esteem Scale were administered in a subsequent home visit by undergraduate students trained in testing and interview techniques by a graduate assistant.

RESULTS

S-Anger Means. Mean S-Anger scores were compared with the means of a comparison group of married mothers obtained in a Hebrew Standardization of the STAXI in Israel (Dreman & Aldor, in press). The mean S-Anger score obtained for these divorced mothers was significantly higher than that obtained for the comparison group, as expected (S-Anger Means [divorced versus married mothers]: 14.66 versus 12.48; $t(294) = 3.02$, $p < .003$).

Independent one-way analyses of variance (ANOVAS) were employed in which the relations of S-Anger with each of the dependent variables, self-esteem, family cohesion and adaptability, and attributions of responsibility, were examined separately. State-anger was divided into high, medium and low levels, since there were no clear-cut linear assumptions regarding how low levels of state-anger would be related to the dependent variables. Mothers with anger scores 1/2 standard deviation or more above the mean were classified as "high anger," those within plus or minus 1/2 standard deviation as "medium anger," and those 1/2 standard deviation or more below the mean as "low anger."

S-Anger and Self-Esteem. A significant relation was found between S-Anger and the divorced mothers' Self-Esteem ratings ($F(2,160) = 15.82$, $p < .0001$) with Self-Esteem levels decreasing in a linear fashion as S-Anger (SA) levels increased (Self-Esteem Means: low SA = 60.54; medium SA = 55.75; high SA = 51.42). These findings agreed with our predictions regarding the effects of high versus medium S-Anger levels on Self-Esteem. The fact that the lowest levels of S-Anger were related to the highest levels of self-esteem suggests that mothers with low state-anger are not suppressing or repressing anger, low anger levels contributing to good personal adjustment. In support of this was a planned comparison between mean Self-Esteem scores which showed that mothers with high and intermediate levels of S-Anger had significantly lower Self-Esteem scores than those with low levels of S-Anger (t(160) = -2.377, p < .021).

S-Anger and Family Cohesion and Adaptability. Examination of the relation between S-Anger with mothers' perceptions of Cohesion revealed a tendency for higher levels of S-Anger to be related to lower levels of Cohesion (Cohesion Means: low SA = 37.95; medium SA = 36.27; high SA = 35.37), though these results were not statistically significant. S-Anger was related to mothers' perceptions of Adaptability in a curvilinear fashion, with medium levels of S-Anger associated with the highest levels of Adaptability (adaptability means: low SA = 27.79; medium SA = 28.39; high SA = 27.42). While these results are consistent with our prediction that high levels of S-Anger will be related to lower levels of adaptability than intermediate levels, they did not reach statistically acceptable levels of significance.

Comparison of mean scores of the divorced mothers on Cohesion and Adaptability, with a population of mothers of similar age in two-parent families, revealed that divorced mothers had slightly lower scores on both these variables, though the differences were not significant (cohesion means [divorced versus married mothers]: 36.99 versus 37.44; adaptability means [divorced versus married mothers]: 27.96 versus 28.62). This adds support to the assumption that divorced women are a nonclinical population.

Since no significant relations were found between S-Anger with Cohesion and Adaptability on FACES III, a further analysis was done based on Olson's perception of these factors as curvilinear. According to this view, extreme levels on these factors, whether high or low, are related to poorer adjustment than more balanced perceptions, which lie more towards the midpoint of the continuum. Olson has devised a measure called "Distance From the Center" which combines both factors in one equation: *Distance From the Center* = $\sqrt{}$ *(Personal Cohesion − Normative Mean Score Cohesion)*^{2} + *(Personal Adaptability − Normative Mean Score Adaptability)*^{2}. Extreme scores on any factor or combination of factors, regardless of their direction, are indicative of poor adjustment in this equation. This results in a linear measure, in which greater distance from the center is indicative of maladaptive behavior.

Applying this conceptualization to the present study, we predicted that high levels of S-Anger in mothers would be related to greater distance from the center than medium levels of S-Anger on FACES III. Low levels of S-Anger were examined posthoc for reasons stated earlier. A significant main effect was found for S-Anger, mothers with high S-Anger displaying significantly greater distance from the center than those with medium or low levels (Distance From the Center Means: low SA = 36.45; medium SA = 32.05; high SA = 94.38, $t(160) = 3.51$, $p < .001$), confirming our predictions. Mothers with medium levels of S-Anger displayed the smallest distance from the center, although their scores did not differ significantly from mothers with low levels.

S-Anger and Attribution of Responsibility to the Ex-Spouse. A positive linear trend was observed for S-Anger–mothers, with higher S-Anger, attributing more responsibility for the divorce to the ex-spouse than those with lower levels (Attribution of Responsibility to the Ex-Spouse: low SA = 3.62; medium SA = 3.75; high SA = 3.91). While these trends are in agreement with our predictions with regard to high and medium levels of S-Anger, they did not reach statistical levels of significance.

An additional analysis of variance of S-Anger with self-attributions of responsibility for the divorce revealed a close to significant negative relationship–mothers' self-attributions decreasing as their S-Anger levels increased (Attribution of Responsibility to the Self: low SA = 3.20; medium SA = 2.90; high SA = 2.32, $F(2,161) = 2.87$, $p < .059$). Planned comparisons of the means revealed that the only significant difference was that obtained between high S-Anger versus the medium and low levels combined ($t(161) = 2.08$, $p < .004$).

DISCUSSION

Anger and Postdivorce Adjustment

The results of the present study, conducted in Israel, show that divorced mothers still have high levels of S-Anger, even though they are located, on the average, eight years and nine months past the divorce event. These findings add cross-cultural validity to American findings (Kitson & Sussman, 1982; Wallerstein, 1986) on the persistence of anger and blame in divorced women even several years past the divorce event.

While clinical observations suggest that divorced women attain emotional resolution that allows them to adjust well in this "stabilization phase" of the divorce process (Hertz Brown, 1988, Wallerstein, 1986), the present study casts doubt on this contention. This follows, since mothers with high S-Anger levels were found to have lower self-esteem, less balanced perceptions of family structure and diminished attributions of personal responsibility in the postdivorce context.

Anger not only adversely affects appraisals of one's postdivorce plight, as well as adjustment after divorce, but this process may be circular since poorer adjustment and more negative appraisals may exacerbate anger. Such circular "first-order" processes (Watzlawick, Weakland, & Fisch, 1974) may explain the persistent nature of anger and anger-related behaviors in women, postdivorce.

Anger and Gender

S-Anger has been defined as situationally-dependent–varying "as a function of perceived injustice, attack or unfair treatment by others, and frustration resulting from barriers to goal directed behavior" (Spielberger, 1988, p. 1). Relatedly, a recent review of gender differences in anger noted that women report anger as resulting from unjust and/or insulting behavior from others, whereas men's anger is more a reaction to verbal or physical provocation (Johnson, 1990). Negative societal attitudes towards divorced women (Katz & Pesach, 1985), difficulties in limit-setting with sons in the absence of a disciplining father (Hetherington, Stanley-Hagan, & Anderson, 1989), work and domestic overload (Hartman, 1991), as well as lowered quality of life related to diminished socioeconomic status (Katz, 1991), may all contribute to women's perceptions of injustice, insult and frustration, resulting in elevated levels of S-Anger.

Another contributing factor to increased *experience* of anger, as expressed in S-Anger levels, is related to social sanctions which prohibit anger *expression* by women. Johnson (1990), in a review of gender differences in anger, found that while women report more anger experience than men, they express less overt anger. Combined, these findings suggest that the high levels of S-Anger reported by custodial mothers in the present and other studies (e.g., Dreman & Aldor, 1994a, 1994b; Kitson & Sussman, 1982; Wallerstein, 1986) may reflect their more intense experience of injustice, frustration and insult in the postdivorce situation.

It should be noted that the testing situation of the present study may also contribute to higher S-Anger levels in our divorced women. This follows, since they underwent extensive psychometric testing and interviewing concerning divorce-related topics which may have evoked stressful memories related to the divorce, in turn increasing their levels of S-Anger.

Theoretical Implications

The present study has shown that divorced mothers' S-Anger experience affects both appraisal of the divorce situation, expressed in their perceptions of family structure and attributions of responsibility, as well as their adjustment as expressed in self-esteem ratings. Conceptually, our findings suggest that an emotional component, S-Anger, mediates between ongoing postdivorce stressors in their impact on both cognitive appraisals and adjustment postdivorce.

While there are stress management theories which claim that *cognitive* appraisals of crisis events, as well as available coping resources, mediate between stressors and ultimate adjustment (e.g., McCubbin & Patterson, 1983; Lazarus and Folkman, 1984; Olson, 1993; Olson, in press), the results of the present study suggest that there is also a need to take into account the role that *emotions* play as a mediating variable in this causal chain.

Research Implications

Future studies should devote more attention to the role of emotions in mediating between stressors, cognitive appraisals, coping resources and ultimately adjustment of families in crisis. Illustrative of such an approach is a study which elicited anger in mothers under stressful circumstances, with elicited anger resulting in harsher appraisals of children than those exhibited by mothers in a happy or neutral mood (Dix, Reinhold, & Zambarano, 1990). Such negative, emotion-mediated appraisal processes might ultimately lead to poorer adjustment in children by evoking more negative parent-child interactions.

An unexpected finding in the present study was that mothers with high S-Anger did not attribute significantly more blame and responsibility for the divorce to ex-spouses. It might be contended that these women, in the stabilization phase, are more cognizant of *current* adverse situational factors affecting them than of the past and their failed marriage. As a result they may attribute more blame for their present divorce plight to these factors than they attribute to their ex-spouse. Future research might investigate how much responsibility divorced women attribute to such contingencies in the present postdivorce environment, as opposed to factors related to their prior marriage.

Another avenue of research concerns cross-cultural differences in the experience and expression of anger. A recent study showed that a normative population of Israeli women, married and single, displayed less Anger-Out, as well as more Anger-In and Anger-Control on the STAXI, than a comparison group of American women (Dreman & Aldor, in press). This stronger tendency to suppress *expression* of anger amongst Israeli women in general, may help explain the high S-Anger *experience* of the divorced women in the present study. In the future, we intend to compare Israeli and

American *divorced* women on measures of S-Anger, Anger-Out, Anger-In and Anger-Control, in order to investigate cross-cultural differences in both the experience and expression of anger in these populations.

Interventive Implications

As for interventive implications, since maternal S-Anger may be influenced by objective postdivorce difficulties, societal remedies, such as improved child care facilities, more flexible work schedules, economic benefits to the single-parent mother and educational programs reducing stigma towards single-parent families may reduce maternal anger elicited by such situational contingencies. As for anger related to more subjective distress, therapeutic intervention might be needed to help these women attain emotional resolution which enables them to accept the positive, in addition to the negative aspects and "injustices" of their past marital relationship. Such interventions might serve to decrease anger, promoting more parental cooperation and ultimately better postdivorce adjustment (Camara & Resnick, 1988). In addition, such "working through" might help these women get on with their lives by helping them establish relationships with significant others, less tainted by anger related to past disappointments.

REFERENCES

Camara, K.A., & Resnick, G. (1988). Interparental conflict and cooperation: Factors moderating children's post-divorce adjustment. In E.M. Hetherington & J.D. Arasteh (Eds.), *Impact of divorce, single-parenting, and stepparenting on children* (pp. 169-195). Hillsdale, NJ: Erlbaum.

Cowan, C.P., & Cowan, P.A. (in press). Working with couples during stressful transitions. In S. Dreman (Ed.), *The family on the threshold of the 21st century: Trends and implications.* Mahwah, NJ: Lawrence Erlbaum.

Dix, T. (1991). The affective organization of parenting: Adaptive and maladaptive processes. *Psychological Bulletin, 110,* 3-25.

Dix, T., Reinhold, D.P., & Zambarano, R.J. (1990). Mothers' judgments in moments of anger. *Merrill-Palmer Quarterly, 36,* 465-486.

Dreman, S. (1995). The experience and expression of anger in divorced mothers: Effects on postdivorce adjustment in children. In C. Spielberger & I. Sarason (Eds.), *Stress and emotion: Anger, anxiety and curiosity, Volume 15* (pp. 75-79). New York: Taylor & Francis.

Dreman, S., & Aldor, R. (1988). *An inventory for measuring coping and adjustment in divorced families.* Unpublished manuscript.

Dreman, S., & Aldor, R. (1994a). A comparative study of custodial mothers and fathers in the stabilization phase of the divorce process. *Journal of Divorce & Remarriage, 21,* 59-79.

Dreman, S., & Aldor, R. (1994b). Work or marriage? Competence in custodial mothers in the stabilization phase of the divorce process. *Journal of Divorce & Remarriage, 22,* 3-22.

Dreman, S., & Aldor, R. (in press). *The experience and expression of anger in a stressful society: Standardization of the STAXI in Israel.* Tel Aviv: Ramot Press, Tel-Aviv University (in Hebrew).

Dreman, S., & Ronen-Eliav, H. (in press). The relation of divorced mothers' perceptions of family cohesion and adaptability to behavior problems in children: A cross-respondent analysis. *Journal of Marriage and the Family.*

Emery, R.E. (1982). Interparental conflict and the children of discord and divorce. *Psychological Bulletin, 92,* 310-330.

Hartman, H. (1991). The division of labor in Israeli families. In L. Shamgar-Handleman & R. Bar-Yosef (Eds.), *Families in Israel.* Jerusalem: Academon-The Hebrew University (in Hebrew).

Hauser, B.B. (1985). Custody in dispute: Legal and psychological profiles of contesting families. *Journal of the American Academy of Child Psychiatry, 24,* 575-582.

Herman, S.J. (1974). Divorce: A grief process. *Perspectives in Psychiatric Care, 12,* 108-112.

Hertz Brown, J. (1988). The postdivorce family. In B. Carter & M. McGoldrick (Eds.), *The changing family life cycle: A framework for family therapy* (pp. 398). New York: Gardner.

Hetherington, E.M., Stanley-Hagan, M., & Anderson, E.R. (1989). Marital transitions: A child's perspective. *The American Psychologist, 44,* 303-312.

Hornick, Y., & Maier, N. (1989). An analysis of non-respondents in a mail survey. *Megamot, 32,* 386-400 (in Hebrew).

Johnson, E.H. (1990). *The deadly emotions: Anger, hostility and aggression.* New York: Praeger Publications.

Katz, R. (1991). "Marital status and well-being." A comparison of widowed, divorced, and married women in Israel. *Journal of Divorce & Remarriage, 14,* 203-218.

Katz, R., & Pesach, N. (1985). Adjustment to divorce in Israel: A comparison between divorced men and women. *Journal of Marriage and the Family, 47,* 765-772.

Kitson, G.C., & Sussman, M.B. (1982). Marital complaints, demographic characteristics and symptoms of mental distress in divorce. *Journal of Marriage and the Family, 44,* 87-101.

Lazarus, R.S., & Folkman, S. (1984). *Stress, appraisal and coping.* New York: Springer Publishing Company.

McCubbin, H.I., & Patterson, J.M. (1983). The family stress process: The Double ABCX model of adjustment and adaptation. In H.I. McCubbin, M.B. Sussman, & J.M. Patterson (Eds.), *Social stress and the family: Advances and developments in family stress theory and research* (pp. 7-37). New York: The Haworth Press, Inc.

Olson, D.H. (1993). Circumplex model of marital and family systems: Assessing family functioning. In F. Walsh (Ed.) (2nd edition), *Normal family processes* (pp. 104-137). New York: Guilford Press.

Olson, D.H. (in press). Family stress and coping: A multi-system perspective. In S. Dreman (Ed.), *The family on the threshold of the 21st century: Trends and implications*. New York: Lawrence Erlbaum.

Olson, D.H., Portner, J., & Lavee, Y. (1985). *Family adaptability and cohesion evaluation scales (FACES III)*. St. Paul, MN: Family Social Sciences, University of Minnesota.

Peterson, L.C. (1980). *Guilt, attributions of responsibility, and resolution of the divorce crisis*. Paper presented at the Fourth Biennial Eastern Conference on Nursing Research, Boston University, Boston.

Rosenberg, M. (1965). *Society and adolescent self-image*. Princeton: Princeton University Press.

Rutter, M. (1971). Parent-child separation: Psychological effects on the children. *Journal of Child Psychology and Psychiatry, 12,* 233-260.

Spielberger, C.D. (1988). *Manual for the state-trait anger inventory (STAXI)*. Odessa, FL: Psychological Resources.

Teichman, Y., & Navon, S. (1990). Family assessment: The circumplex model—Translation and standardization of FACES III to Hebrew. *Psychologia, 2,* 36-46 (in Hebrew).

Wallerstein, J.S. (1986). Women after divorce: Preliminary report from a ten-year follow-up. *American Journal of Orthopsychiatry, 56,* 65-77.

Wallerstein, J.S., & Blakeslee (1989). *Second chances: Men, women, and children a decade after divorce*. New York: Taylor and Fields.

Watzlawick, P., Weakland, J., & Fisch, R. (1974). *Change: Principles of Problem Formation and Problem Resolution*. New York: W.W. Norton & Co.

Tendency to Stigmatize Lesbian Mothers in Custody Cases

Kelly A. Causey
Candan Duran-Aydintug

SUMMARY. Using Goffman's stigma framework, in this study we measured the general public's tendency to stigmatize lesbian mothers and correlated their responses to a custody decision they had to make when the mother was presented as a lesbian. Results indicated no difference between urban and rural residents' responses in terms of their tendency to stigmatize and their custody decisions. Respondents overwhelmingly preferred joint custody. Males had a higher tendency to stigmatize the lesbian mothers. Religiosity was an effective factor, whereas education was not. *[Article copies available for a fee from The Haworth Document Delivery Service: 1-800-342-9678. E-mail address: getinfo@haworth.com]*

Current laws regarding the custody rights of gays[1] and lesbians indicate a movement away from a "per se classification" of unfitness toward a "nexus" approach, requiring evidence that the parent's sexual orientation

Kelly A. Causey obtained her MA degree from the University of Colorado at Denver, Department of Sociology in 1995. Candan Duran-Aydintug, PhD, is Professor at the University of Colorado at Denver, Department of Sociology.

The authors wish to thank to Professor Richard Anderson for his help on previous versions of this manuscript.

Address correspondence to: Candan Duran-Aydintug, Department of Sociology, University of Colorado at Denver, CB 105, POB 173364, Denver, CO 80217-3364, e-mail (cduranaydint@castle.cudenver.edu).

[Haworth co-indexing entry note]: "Tendency to Stigmatize Lesbian Mothers in Custody Cases." Causey, Kelly A., and Candan Duran-Aydintug. Co-published simultaneously in *Journal of Divorce & Remarriage* (The Haworth Press, Inc.) Vol. 28, No. 1/2, 1997, pp. 171-182; and: *Child Custody: Legal Decisions and Family Outcomes* (ed: Craig A. Everett) The Haworth Press, Inc., 1997, pp. 171-182. Single or multiple copies of this article are available for a fee from The Haworth Document Delivery Service [1-800-342-9678, 9:00 a.m. - 5:00 p.m. (EST). E-mail address: getinfo@haworth.com].

171

demonstrates a detriment to the child (see Duran-Aydintug and Causey, 1995 for further information and for a review of the existing literature). Still, a lesbian mother's likelihood for gaining the custody rights is usually not more than 50%, considerably low compared to the standard maternal custody award of almost 90% (Bozett, 1987).

In the court decisions the most widely used assumption is the one that children will be stigmatized by their peers and otherwise harmed by society at large; they will be hurt because of the stigma attached to the parent's homosexuality (Duran-Aydintug and Causey, 1995; Weston, 1991). When judges refer to "stigma" attached to the parent, what is it exactly that warrants consideration? To answer this, the concept of stigma must first be addressed.

STIGMA

Erving Goffman defines stigma as an "undesired differentness from what we had anticipated" (1963, p. 5). The anticipation comes from categorizing people on the basis of certain attributes appropriate to their category. This is considered one's "social identity." Once the attributes have been assigned, people begin to have expectations and to formulate demands of this person. This is the person's "virtual identity." If the person is able to meet these demands and fulfill the expectations, then he/she has acquired an "actual identity." Those who do not meet the demands, and offer, instead, evidence to challenge our expectations, become stigmatized. They have shown a discrepancy between their "virtual identity" and their "actual identity." Goffman categorized three forms of stigma: physical deformities, blemishes of character, and tribal. According to these categories, homosexuality is considered a blemish of character.

Using Goffman's framework for stigma, the discrepancy between "virtual" and "actual" identity is inevitable for the lesbian mother. Initially, a woman with her child(ren) is given the attributes of a mother. She is expected to be the primary caretaker and to love her children above all else. She is expected to behave in a way that *all* mothers should behave. However, once a woman is known to be a lesbian, she has then offered evidence to challenge the expectations. The discrepancy is that lesbians are not supposed to be mothers and lesbians are not capable of behaving in the same way as other mothers behave.

When the discrepancy is exposed, Goffman suggests that four actions are taken by those who stigmatize, in this case, heterosexuals. The first action is that a stigma theory is constructed to explain why the stigmatized person is inferior to all others. This accounts for the danger this person represents. An example of this is the assumption that all homosexuals are mentally ill and therefore should not raise children. The second action is the use of stigma terms to ensure the awareness of the person's uniqueness. This action is witnessed when heterosexuals use the derogatory terms such as "faggot" or "dyke" to describe a homosexual. The third action is imputing a wide range of imperfections on the basis of the original one. A lesbian mother is assumed to be less maternal and of poor moral character because of her original "imperfection," being homosexual. The fourth action is supporting a standard of judgment that does not apply to them. An example of this approach is how judges look unfavorably upon mothers who "incite" prejudice because they are activists within the gay community and/or they are openly affectionate with their partners. Even when the affection is displayed exclusively within the home, courts still believe the community at large will harm the child. Bottoms v. Bottoms' 1993 case (cited in Pershing, 1994) is a recent example of this where, initially, the mother was denied custody because she and her partner displayed affection in front of the child which the court found inappropriate. The unlikeness of a lesbian mother to gain custody when her homosexual lifestyle is indiscreet suggests that some courts do support anti-gay mores. Lesbian mothers are asked by the courts to refrain from affection, withhold participation in community organizations, and sever relationships with loved ones in order to gain custody. Heterosexual mothers, on the other hand, are not forced into this type of predicament.

Although the specific biases used against lesbian mothers are refuted by scientific research (Patterson, 1992; Patterson, 1994; Paul, 1986), the conclusion that children will be stigmatized by society is still accepted by many. The stigma factor also enables the judge to avoid exposing personal bias by deferring to the "intolerant" society as being responsible for perpetuating homophobia (Kraft, 1983).

The assumption that the child with a homosexual mother will be stigmatized is dangerous because it is not linked to parental fitness or the parent-child relationship. It is based on anticipated fear which, in many cases, goes unverified. In such cases, judges assume the teasing exists, that the teasing is in fact harmful, and that teasing based on a parent's sexual orientation is more serious than teasing based on other attributes such as physical characteristics, intelligence, or ethnicity.

According to research (Green et al., 1986; Golombok et al., 1983) no differences were found in terms of popularity between children of heterosexual mothers and lesbian mothers and the quality of peer relations was rated good.

The purpose of this research is to examine the tendency to stigmatize homosexual mothers who are seeking child custody and the effects of stigmatization on child custody decisions. Several hypotheses were generated from the review of the literature, the legal opinions from custody cases involving lesbian mothers and the in-depth interviews conducted with legal professionals (Duran-Aydintug and Causey, 1995). Two of the hypotheses came from these interviews with legal professionals (district court judges, attorneys, guardian ad litems, and court evaluators) and from the previous studies. According to the legal professionals the location in which the case is tried impacts the decision of the judge. They asserted that rural counties, assumed to be more conservative and religious, would pressure the judge to decide against the mother. The judge was also thought to be influenced by simply living in a rural community and supporting the commonly held assumptions about lesbian mothers. Previous research shows also that negative attitudes toward homosexuals are positively related to conservative religious values, intolerance of ambiguity, cognitive rigidity, and conservative values (Delvin and Cowan, 1985; Herek, 1984; Kite and Deaux, 1986; Kurdek, 1988; MacDonald and Games, 1974). These two hypotheses are that respondents residing in rural areas will indicate a higher tendency to stigmatize than the ones residing in urban areas and that the higher the level of religiosity, the higher the tendency to stigmatize the lesbian mothers. These corresponded to a third hypothesis which stated that the lower the tendency to stigmatize, the greater the likelihood of recommending custody to the mother.

Two other hypotheses were derived from several court cases, the concerns of legal professionals interviewed, and from former research. Court opinions have cited the need for men to be considered of equal merit to women to parent their children. Additionally, trends in child custody are moving to support a presumption of joint custody, which supports having both parents involved in raising the child. Legal professionals claimed that the publicity of men's rights groups, indicating a trend toward acknowledging fatherhood, encourages judges and others to consider the father more than they have in the past and that putting more emphasis on this would hurt a lesbian mother because her homosexuality would be perceived as a weakness and the father would benefit from that. Given the proportion of judges who are male, legal respondents were also concerned that they would favor the father in a case involving a lesbian mother. Additionally, earlier studies indicated that negative attitudes toward lesbians are more prevalent in males than in females (Kite, 1984; Kurdek, 1988). These hypotheses stated that men will indicate a higher tendency to stigmatize lesbian mothers than women and also men will be more likely than women to award the custody of the child to the father if the mother is a lesbian.

The final hypothesis responds to demographic information in relationship to the characteristics of stigma. Legal respondents thought that urban areas were less conservative and religious (which is targeted in a previously stated hypothesis) and that people in that area are perceived as more educated and therefore less likely to stigmatize a lesbian mother. This hypothesis aimed at assessing this claim is, as shown in Herek's (1984) study, the tendency to stigmatize is inversely related to level of education.

METHOD

Sample. In order to test the hypotheses stated above, a sample of rural and urban residents of Colorado was surveyed. To obtain a representative sample, the 63 counties in Colorado were initially stratified according to population size based on data from the 1990 Census. Counties with a population size of 35,001 and above were defined as urban and counties with a population size of 35,000 and below were defined as rural. This yielded 11 urban and 52 rural counties. Next, from each group one county was selected randomly. Arapahoe County represented the urban group, whereas Crowley County represented the rural group.

Voter registration lists from each county were selected as the sampling frame because they are fairly comprehensive, accessible, and the cost involved is modest. These lists do not contain citizens of the county who are younger than 18, citizens who did not register to vote, citizens who had not voted in the last two general elections, and residents who legally cannot vote. Residents living in rural areas of Arapahoe County (Bennett, Deer Trail, Strasburg, Watkins, and Byers) were also discarded if their number was generated. Once the 400 individuals (200 from each county) were selected randomly, respondents of Arapahoe County were sent questionnaires on standard white bond paper and respondents of Crowley County were sent questionnaires on colored paper.

Sample Characteristics. Twenty people of the 400 total were not able to be reached because the addresses given from the voter registration list were incorrect. Eleven of those names were from Crowley County and eight were from Arapahoe County. Eight individuals, four from Arapahoe and four from Crowley County, declined participation by phone. Seven of the respondents had died previously, three being from Arapahoe County and the other four from Crowley County. Thus, the total number in the sample was reduced to 365 of which 109 people completed the questionnaire, giving a 30% response rate. Fifty of those respondents were from

Crowley County and 59 were from Arapahoe County. Forty percent of all respondents were men, while 60% were women. The mean age of the respondents was 59. Ninety-five percent considered themselves Caucasian/European American, whereas 5% of the respondents considered themselves Native American, Hispanic, or Indian.

Procedure. After permission had been obtained from the Human Subjects Research Committee at the University of Colorado-Denver, a cover letter was attached to each questionnaire explaining the respondents' rights by participating in the research, directions for completion of the questionnaire, how to submit it for inclusion into the study, and the responsibilities of the researchers to maintain confidentiality.

The questionnaires were mailed to the respondents with self-addressed and stamped envelopes which were sent along to make it as effortless as possible for the respondents to return the questionnaire by the given deadline. The estimated time for completion of the questionnaire was about 20 minutes. Respondents were given two weeks to complete and return the questionnaire. Because of time and cost limitations, no follow-up strategy was used. Upon receipt of a questionnaire, an identification number was assigned to it. Each questionnaire was coded as described in the following section.

Measurement. The questionnaire[2] consisted of four sections. In section A, respondents were asked in forced choice items to state their personal history of child custody. If relevant, they were asked questions related to their involvement in the child custody case, the year it occurred, and their relationship to the child. Section B listed twelve Likert scale items ranging from strongly agree to strongly disagree. The items were designed to measure "the tendency to stigmatize" related to common assumptions regarding lesbians and parenthood either based on the literature or emerging from the interviews conducted with legal professionals (Duran-Aydintug and Causey, 1995). Tendency to stigmatize was measured by a score ranging from one to five with one indicating the lowest tendency to stigmatize on a particular item and five indicating the greatest tendency to stigmatize based on a particular item. An example is the item, "Gay parents tend to raise gay children." Given the options of strongly agree to strongly disagree, the item was coded such that "strongly agree" received a score of five and "strongly disagree" received a score of one. A respondent who chose "strongly agree" would therefore have a higher tendency to stigmatize for that item than a respondent who chose any of the other options. All twelve of the items were coded and totaled so that each respondent received a total score from which a mean "tendency to stigmatize" score was calculated. Here forward, this mean score will be referred to as "mean stigma score." In section C a vignette was presented describing a custody case involving a lesbian mother. Respondents were asked to make the custody decision. Four choices were offered: the father should get sole custody, the mother should get sole custody, they should have joint custody, and other, where respondents could explain any other choice they would prefer. The choice of custody was used as a cross-reference with mean stigma score in the data analysis. Respondents were then asked to explain their decision. Explanations for the custody decisions were analyzed separately.

The final section focused on demographics. Respondents were asked to state their sex, date of birth, ethnicity, occupation, level of education, measured as number of years in school, and religiosity. Religiosity was measured on a scale of one to ten, with one being not religious at all and ten being very religious.

RESULTS

To test the first hypothesis, which states that residents in a rural area will have a greater tendency to stigmatize than residents in an urban area, a t-test was conducted using mean stigma scores. The mean stigma score for the rural group was 2.98 (from a scale of 1-5). The mean stigma score for the urban group was 3.05. The difference between the means for the two categories was not statistically significant ($p > .05$)

The second hypothesis states that the higher the level of religiosity, the greater the tendency to stigmatize. An ANOVA test was conducted using mean stigma scores by level of religiosity. $F = 3.9109$, ($p < .05$) indicated significance and support for the hypothesis.

The third hypothesis states the lower the tendency to stigmatize, the greater the likelihood of recommending custody to the lesbian mother. Seventy-nine percent of respondents selected joint custody. Fourteen percent of respondents chose the father having sole custody of the child. Six percent of respondents selected "other" by explaining that they did not have enough facts to make a proper decision or that they would not consider either parent because they claimed that both divorce and homosexuality are morally wrong. One of the respondents thought the mother should get sole custody. Respondents were grouped by selection each made for custody, then a mean stigma score was calculated. Respondents who decided that the father should have sole custody of the child had a mean stigma score of 3.6. Respondents who decided that the mother should get sole custody had a mean stigma score of 2.4. Respondents selecting joint custody had a mean stigma score of 2.87, and the ones selecting "other" had a mean score of 3.5. This indicates support for the hypothesis that the lower the tendency to stigmatize, the more likely the lesbian mother will get custody. More importantly, these scores may also indicate that the lower the tendency to stigmatize, the more likely the mother will not be denied custody, as indicated by a mean stigma score 2.87 for those who preferred joint custody.

To test the fourth hypothesis, which states that men indicate a greater tendency to stigmatize than women, a t-test was conducted using mean stigma scores to compare men to women. A t-score of 3.11, (p < .001) indicated significance for men having a higher tendency to stigmatize than women. This supported the hypothesis.

The fifth hypothesis, which states that tendency to stigmatize is inversely related to level of education, was tested by calculating mean stigma scores by educational level to compare means. Respondents with a middle school education level had a mean stigma score of 2.9. Respondents with a high school education level had a mean stigma score of 3.0, one to two years of college experience had a mean stigma score of 3.1, three or more years of college had a mean stigma score of 2.9, a graduate level education had a mean stigma score of 3.0, and respondents who indicated "other" had a mean stigma score of 3.4. Based on these mean scores, no significant difference was found (p > .05) to support the hypothesis that tendency to stigmatize is influenced by educational level of the respondents.

DISCUSSION

A divorce situation inspires a myriad of personal challenges and competing demands. The greatest anxiety may be about the custody process itself. During this proceeding the multi-faceted lives of those involved with the child are scrutinized to determine with whom the child will live. Everyone involved must ask the same important question when faced with a custody proceeding: What factors must be considered to make the best determination for the child? The major factors of interest for this research study were sexual orientation of the mother and society's perspective about that.

Some judges claim that it is appropriate to bring up the sexual orientation of the mother as it possibly may adversely affect the child. A majority of the respondents supported the judges' reasoning. Giving a mean score of (4), respondents disagreed with the item "Custody of the child should be decided without knowledge of the parent's sexual orientation." Why would respondents want to know the sexual orientation, in this case, of the mother? They stated that "When deciding custody, it is important to ask the child with whom he/she wants to live" and that sexual orientation may influence that decision.

This study also indicates that region does not have an effect on stigma. This may be due to the situation of stigma being created out of perception, not fact. Arapahoe County, for example, may be equally as conservative as Crowley County and may have a similar tendency to stigmatize a lesbian mother. The perception, however, is that Arapahoe County is liberal and more open-minded given the diversity of an urban setting and therefore would not be as likely to stigmatize a lesbian mother compared to Crowley County. Given that no difference was shown between the two counties, the perception that Arapahoe County would be more supportive of a lesbian mother may have been incorrect.

Education level did not make a difference either. The mean stigma score for the respondents in both the urban and rural areas was (3). Given the options of the Likert scale items, this represents a "neutral" score. It is also important to note that respondents were neutral about some of the most common assumptions regarding lesbians and their children. Survey respondents scored a (3) on the following items: gay parents raise gay children, a lesbian mother puts her lover first, and children of lesbian mothers have a difficult time figuring out their sexual identity.

If optimistic, one may interpret that neutral scores for these items are a sign that false perceptions regarding homosexuals are dissipating. Neutral scores from both the urban and rural counties may also be a product of statewide attention garnered through a ballot initiative from two years ago. This initiative sought approval for excluding sexual orientation from equal protection ordinances. Further research should examine whether judges would respond differently based on the outcome or the existence of the initiative. However, a neutral score may also indicate that the items presented were not compelling enough to incite a stronger position. If a particular community is only compelled to respond to a case that happens locally, then a neutral score may be warranted and perceptions from legal professionals that community pressures vary may be substantiated.

The custody decision, offered in the vignette, demonstrated a preference for joint custody (79%). A majority of the respondents agreed with the statement that "a father can be as good a parent as a mother" and they were neutral about the statement "children belong with their mothers." Perhaps the survey respondents are open-minded given willingness to consider the father. With men's rights groups receiving more attention, this heightened awareness may have influenced respondents to consider the father equally as competent as the mother.

Joint custody decision favors the lesbian mother because it indicates that sexual orientation is not as important compared to the desire to have both parents involved with the child. While the respondents claimed they wanted to know the orientation and agreed that children of lesbian mothers are harassed by peers, they still chose joint custody, thereby validating the mother's involvement with her child. Joint custody also ensures that the father can have continued involvement with his child(ren). This is consistent with the survey respondents strongly agreeing that an ideal family is a mother, father and child. In fact, while men revealed a significantly higher tendency to stigmatize than women, they, too, preferred joint custody over sole custody of the father. More important than the preference for joint custody is the decision not to deny the mother custody, which in some communities is a viable threat.

The preference for joint custody does warrant further research into the effects of stigma. Does the particular stigma matter? If the mother had been a criminal or possessed some sort of disability would joint custody still be preferred? If both parents possessed a stigma, would joint custody have been preferred?

The "best interest of the child" standard does not specify which "clearcut factors" are to be considered and how much weight each of them should be given. There is growing concern about the wide discretion judges possess in these cases and that their decisions may be tarnished due to political, religious, and personal pressures and stereotypes. Giving the custody of the child to the lesbian mother may be in the child's best interest when she is proven to be the better parent and the one who has bonded with the child. Lesbian mothers, however, may face legal obstacles stemming from unsubstantiated assumptions which prevent them from getting custody. Some legal opinions indicate support for rulings based solely on sexual orientation, while some research indicates no support for the assumptions used to deny custody to the lesbian mother.

RECOMMENDATIONS

Courts should rely more heavily on the expert testimonies that are informed from the social sciences and suggest ways to deal with results of societal stigma, in particular, peer harassment. Family researchers are encouraged to redefine "family" so those new structures, which do not perpetuate the "ideal norms," are included in the legal definitions of "family." As recently suggested by Allen and Demo (1995), existing knowledge regarding gay and lesbian families needs to be expanded. Toward this aim, legal professionals may also support efforts to legalize marriage for gays and lesbians which would legally validate this family structure while further broadening society's view on what defines a family.

Further research is essential to better understand the implications of court decisions concerning lesbian mothers pursuing custody. Additionally, research is needed to establish and solidify communication between social researchers and the legal system so that other stigmatized populations do not experience similar inequalities. It is also strongly suggested that legal professionals maintain their focus on the quality of the relationships among family members rather than the structure of the family.

In this study the response rate was lower than desirable. Dealing with a sensitive issue like lesbian mothers, stigma, and child custody decisions, it is highly reasonable to assume that response bias had an effect on the response rate. We recommend that researchers in this area start with a much larger sample than ours, understand the possibility of response bias, and try to find ways to reduce it as effectively as possible.

NOTES

1. While gay fathers may experience bias in child custody suits, given the scope of this research, the focus will be on lesbian mothers.
2. The questionnaire is available from the authors upon request.

REFERENCES

Allen, K. R., and Demo, D. H. (1995). The families of lesbians and gay men: A new frontier in family research. *Journal of Marriage and the Family, 57,* 111-127.

Boozed, F. W. (1987). Gay fathers. In F. W. Boozed (Ed.), *Gay and Lesbian Parents.* New York: Praetor.

Delving, P. K., and Cowman, G. A. (1985). Homophobia, perceived fathering, and male intimate relationships. *Journal of Personality Assessment, 49,* 467-473.

Duran-Aydintug, C., and Causey, K. (1995). Child custody determination: Implications for lesbian mothers. *Journal of Divorce & Remarriage, 25,* in press.

Goffman, E. (1963). *Stigma.* New York: Simon & Schuster, Inc.

Golombok, G., Spencer, A., and Rutter, M. (1983). Children in lesbian and single-parent households: Psychosexual and psychiatric appraisal. *Journal of Child Psychology and Psychiatry, 24,* 551-572.

Green, R., Mandel, J. B., Hotvedt, M. E., Gray, J., and Smith, L. (1986). Lesbian mothers and their children: A comparison with solo parent heterosexual mothers and their children. *Archives of Sexual Behavior, 15,* 167-184.

Herek, G. M. (1984). Beyond "homophobia": A Social psychological perspective on attitudes toward lesbians and gay men. *Journal of Homosexuality, 10,* 1-22.

Kite, M. E. (1984). Sex differences in attitudes toward homosexuals: A meta-analytic review. *Journal of Homosexuality, 10,* 69-82.

Kite, M. E., and Deaux, K. (1987). Gender belief systems: Homosexuality and the implicit inversion theory. *Psychology of Women Quarterly, 11,* 83-96.

Kraft, P. (1983). Recent developments: Lesbian child custody. *Harvard Women's Law Journal, 6,* 183-192.

Kurdek, L. A. (1988). Correlates of negative attitudes toward homosexuals in heterosexual college students. *Sex Roles, 18,* 727-738.

MacDonald, A. P., Jr., and Games, R. G. (1974). Some characteristics of those who hold positive and negative attitudes toward homosexuals. *Journal of Homosexuality, 1,* 9-27.

Patterson, C. J. (1992). Children of lesbian and gay parents. *Child Development, 63,* 1025-1042.

Patterson, C. J. (1994). Children of the lesbian baby boom: Behavioral adjustment, self-concepts, and sex-role identity. In B. Greene and G. M. Herek (Eds.), *Lesbian and Gay Psychology: Theory, Research, and Clinical Applications* (pp. 156-175). Thousands Oaks, CA: Sage.

Paul, J. P. (1986). *Growing up with a gay, lesbian, or bisexual parent: An exploratory study of experiences and perceptions.* Unpublished doctoral dissertation, University of California at Berkeley, Berkeley, CA.

Pershing, S. B. (1994). Entreat me not to leave thee: Bottoms v. Bottoms and the custody rights of gay and lesbian parents. *William and Mary Bill of Rights Journal, 3,* 289-325.

Weston, Kath. 1991. *Families We Choose.* New York: Columbia University Press.

Young People's Attitudes
Toward Living in a Lesbian Family:
A Longitudinal Study of Children Raised
by Post-Divorce Lesbian Mothers

Fiona Tasker
Susan Golombok

SUMMARY. The present investigation explored the factors associated with the diversity of children's attitudes toward growing up with their mother in a lesbian-led family after the end of their mother and father's relationship. Twenty-five young adults from lesbian families and a comparison group of 21 young adults raised by single heterosexual mothers first participated in the study in 1976-77, and again in 1991-92. No differences were observed between young people from lesbian and heterosexual post-divorce families in their acceptance of their family identity during adolescence. However, in comparison with those from heterosexual post-divorce families, young people from lesbian backgrounds were more positive about their nonconventional family of origin in early adulthood. The findings show that acceptance of their les-

Fiona Tasker, PhD, is affiliated with the Department of Psychology, Birkbeck College, Malet Street, London WC1E 7HX, UK. Susan Golombok, PhD, is associated with Family & Child Psychology Research Centre, City University, Northampton Square, London EC1V 0HB, UK.

The authors would like to thank the Welcome Trust for funding this research and the staff of the National Health Service Central Register for their assistance with tracing families. The authors are grateful to Michael Rutter for his advice and encouragement at the early stages of the follow-up study.

[Haworth co-indexing entry note]: "Young People's Attitudes Toward Living in a Lesbian Family: A Longitudinal Study of Children Raised by Post-Divorce Lesbian Mothers." Tasker, Fiona, and Susan Golombok. Co-published simultaneously in *Journal of Divorce & Remarriage* (The Haworth Press, Inc.) Vol. 28, No. 1/2, 1997, pp. 183-202; and: *Child Custody: Legal Decisions and Family Outcomes* (ed: Craig A. Everett) The Haworth Press, Inc., 1997, pp. 183-202. Single or multiple copies of this article are available for a fee from The Haworth Document Delivery Service [1-800-342-9678, 9:00 a.m. - 5:00 p.m. (EST). E-mail address: getinfo@haworth.com].

bian family identity during adolescence was associated with close and stable family relationships, the absence of peer stigma, and the sensitivity of their family in relating their identity to others outside the home. *[Article copies available for a fee from The Haworth Document Delivery Service: 1-800-342-9678. E-mail address: getinfo@haworth.com]*

The majority of empirical research studies on the well-being of children in lesbian families have focused on the issues raised in post-divorce custody disputes between lesbian mothers and their ex-husbands. These issues have been considered again recently in public debates concerning adoption rights and access to assisted reproduction procedures (for example, donor insemination) for lesbian women. In custody disputes lesbian women are often deemed unsuitable as parents on the grounds that their children would develop behavioral or emotional problems, would show atypical gender development, and would develop difficulties in peer relationships (for recent reviews of the legal issues see Arnup, 1995; Duran-Aydintug & Causey, 1996). However, none of these contentions has been supported by empirical studies of children raised by lesbian mothers (see reviews by Belcastro, Gramlich, Nicholson, Price & Wilson, 1993; Falk, 1989; Patterson, 1992, 1995; Golombok & Tasker, 1994). Research that has reported on family relationships has shown that lesbian mothers are just as child-centered as heterosexual mothers (Kirkpatrick, 1987; Miller et al., 1981; Pagelow, 1980) and just as positive and nurturant toward their children (Golombok et al., 1983; Mucklow & Phelan, 1979).

Existing research on children's relationships with stepparents has examined heterosexual stepfamilies only. Studying lesbian stepfamilies, where the mother forms a new relationship with a female partner, provides an opportunity for the influence of the gender of the stepparent to be explored. Data from a longitudinal study of young adults raised by lesbian mothers (Tasker & Golombok, 1995) showed that young men and women generally reported a close relationship with their mother, and a more positive relationship with her new female partner than that reported by a comparison group of young adults raised in heterosexual stepfamilies who were asked about the quality of their relationship with their mother's new male partner.

Valuable as previous research has been in establishing that lesbian women make just as good mothers as heterosexual women, little research has explored the diversity and variations of lesbian family lifestyles (Belcastro et al., 1993; Patterson, 1992), in particular the experiences that contribute to young people's acceptance or rejection of their family, and the factors associated with changes in acceptance/rejection during the transition from adolescence to adult life.

Uncontrolled studies of children raised by lesbian mothers suggest that children may have initial problems in accepting their mother's lesbian identity (Lewis, 1980), although adolescents appear to be more accepting of their mother's sexual orientation if they had learned of her lesbian identity early in childhood (Huggins, 1989; Pennington, 1987). Lewis (1980) also showed that the children of mothers who found it difficult to communicate and answer questions as they arose, had most difficulty in coming to terms with their mother's lesbian relationships. Whereas the majority of children studied by Lewis came to admire their mother for her stance against convention, some appeared to be ambivalent about her identity in that they expressed a disproportionate fear of social stigma, intense anger at a particular aspect of household arrangements, a reluctance to discuss negative incidents, or seemed to act out their rejection through leaving home.

It has been suggested that the absence of a father may affect sons more than daughters in lesbian families, and that adolescent boys may be particularly negative about their mother's new lesbian relationships (Hall, 1978; Lewis, 1980). However, research on heterosexual stepfamilies has generally concluded that it is girls who experience more problems in forming a positive relationship with a new stepfather, or a new stepmother (Bray & Berger, 1993; Hetherington & Clingempeel, 1992; Pasley & Ihinger-Tallman, 1987), although both boys and girls may find it particularly difficult to adjust to the arrival of a new stepfather during early adolescence (Hetherington, 1993). One of the few studies of adolescents in lesbian families found that daughters with low self-esteem tended to be more negative than those with high self-esteem about their mother's lesbian lifestyle (Huggins, 1989). Huggins also reported that girls from single-parent lesbian families tended to have lower self-esteem than those who lived with their mother and her female partner, and that adolescent girls from lesbian single-parent families and stepfamilies had a more positive self-concept if family relationships were good, and the response of others outside the home (including their father) was not hostile to the new family set-up.

A study of the well-being of lesbian mothers themselves has found that those who were "out" about their sexual identity tended to have higher self-esteem, and that their psychological health was positively associated with involvement in the lesbian community and feminist politics (Rand, Graham & Rawlings, 1982). Whereas it has been suggested that children fare best in lesbian homes where mothers have a strong positive identity, good parenting skills, and are well integrated in a supportive social network that includes other lesbian families (Pennington, 1987), public concern is often expressed that children may be more likely to be stigmatized by peers if their mother is open about being lesbian and active in lesbian politics (B v B, 1991). The potentially hostile response of peers is, not surprisingly, a major concern of children brought up in lesbian families (Lewis, 1980; Pennington, 1987), and of their mothers (Lesbian Mothers Group, 1989).

Using data from a longitudinal study of adults raised as children in lesbian families (Tasker & Golombok, 1995; Golombok & Tasker, 1996), the aim of the present investigation was to elucidate the reasons why some young people from lesbian households may be resentful or embarrassed about their family, and to identify factors which contribute to a positive family image both during adolescence and later in adult life. It was expected that acceptance of their post-divorce lesbian family identity would be associated with positive and stable family relationships, the mother's acceptance of her lesbian identity, the mother's discretion in relation to others outside the family (particularly the child's friends), the father's acceptance of the new family structure, and the absence of peer group stigma.

METHODS

Subjects

In 1976-1977 a group of lesbian mothers, and a comparison group of single heterosexual mothers, were first interviewed for the study. The mothers were recruited through advertisements in lesbian and single-parent publications, and through contacts with lesbian and single-parent organizations. The criteria for inclusion were that the lesbian mothers regarded themselves as predominantly or wholly lesbian in their sexual orientation, and that their current or most recent sexual relationship was with a woman. The single-parent group was defined in terms of mothers whose most recent sexual relationship had been heterosexual, but who did not have a male partner living with them at the time of the study. Each group comprised 27 mothers and their 39 children.[1]

At the time of the initial study, the average age of the children was 9.5 years. Therefore, ethical considerations meant that in order to re-contact children fourteen years later, it was first necessary to locate the mothers

---

1. The data from two children age 4 years and one child age 19 at the time of the original study are included at follow-up. This increased the pool of potential participants from 75 (Golombok et al., 1983) to 78.

and request permission to interview their children. For the follow-up study, conducted in 1991-1992, 51 of the 54 mothers who participated in the initial study were traced, mostly with the aid of the U.K. National Health Service Central Register. Therefore, three children in the original sample could not be traced. Furthermore, one daughter had died prior to the follow-up study. From the remaining 74 potential recruits, 46 young adults aged 17-35 years were interviewed, representing a response rate of 62%. For 11/12 of the non-interviewees amongst children from lesbian backgrounds, and 13/16 of the non-interviewees from single-parent heterosexual backgrounds, mothers declined to allow their children to participate further in the research. In the four remaining cases, the children were contacted but did not wish to take part.

The average age of the interviewees at the time of follow-up was 23.5 years with no age difference between young adults from the two types of family background. The groups consisted of eight men and 17 women raised by lesbian mothers and 12 men and nine women raised by heterosexual mothers (Fisher's Exact Test; p = 0.078). No statistically significant differences were identified when the proportions of young adults from lesbian and heterosexual single-parent homes were compared in terms of ethnicity and educational qualifications. Furthermore, there was no difference between groups in terms of mother's social class as assessed in the original study, although significantly more of the lesbian mothers had received further education (13/18 vs. 5/16 Fisher's Exact Test; p = 0.020).

Data from the initial study were examined to ascertain the characteristics of the follow-up sample and possible reasons for sample attrition. There were no differences between follow-up participants and non-participants on the following key variables: age and gender of children, mother's social class, mother's psychiatric history, quality of the mother-child relationship, quality of children's peer relationships, children's gender role behaviour, and the presence of emotional or behavioral problems in the children.

However, non-participants tended to be more likely than participants to have experienced a period of separation from their mother prior to the original study (Fisher's Exact Test; p = 0.086). As children were contacted via their mother for the follow-up, it is possible that those who had previously been separated from their mother were less in contact with her as young adults. Within the lesbian mother group, children whose mother reported greater inter-personal conflict with her cohabitee were also less likely to contribute to the follow-up study (t = 3.87; df = 19; p < 0.01). However, children who were aware of their mother's lesbian identity at the time of the original study tended to be more likely to participate (t =

− 1.77; df = 37; p < 0.10). Indeed, only one child in the follow-up group remained in ignorance of her mother's lesbian relationships.

Measures

Initial study. Data on family functioning and on children's well-being were obtained from the lesbian mothers in the original study using an adaptation of a standardized interview previously designed to assess family functioning (Brown & Rutter, 1966; Rutter & Brown, 1966). The variables from the original study that are relevant to the follow-up investigation of young adults' feelings about their family identity were: (i) mother's warmth to child (a rating which took into account the mother's tone of voice, facial expressions and spontaneous comments when talking about the child) (rating made on a 6-point scale ranging from "0" none to "5" very warm) (ii) mother's relationship history ("0" four partners or less to "1" five or more partners or concurrent relationships) (iii) quality of mother's relationship with her female partner ("1" fully harmonious to "5" serious conflict) (iv) extent to which mother and partner share child care ("0" mother and partner share child care to "1" mother main caregiver) (v) child's contact with father ("0" none to "2" at least weekly contact) (vi) number of years child spent in a heterosexual home (years) (vii) child's awareness of mother's lesbian identity ("0" none to "2" fully aware) (viii) mother's contentment with her sexual identity ("1" prefer to be heterosexual to "5" positive about lesbian identity) (ix) mother's political involvement ("0" no involvement in lesbian/gay politics to "3" frequent involvement) (x) mother's openness in showing physical affection in front of child ("0" none to "2" kiss or caress) (xi) extent to which mother is "out" in local community ("0" not out to "2" public knowledge) (xii) extent to which mother is "out" to child's school teachers ("0" not out to "2" discussed with teachers) (xiii) mother's attitude towards men ("1" negative to "5" some sexual feelings toward men) and (xiv) quality of child's peer relationships ("0" good to "2" definite difficulties).

Follow-up study. The main source of data for the follow-up study was provided by individual interviews with the young adults. Interviews took place either at the subject's home or at the university. The interviews lasted for two-and-a-half hours on average, and were conducted by a female interviewer (FT). A semi-structured interview with a standardized coding scheme was developed for the study. The flexibility of the semi-structured approach allowed respondents to recount their own experiences and feelings, increasing the validity of the data collected in this previously uncharted research area, whilst the standardized coding procedure ensured that each variable was rated according to fixed criteria. The interested reader is referred to Tasker and Golombok (1997) for an overview of the entire interview and a detailed description of the anchor points and coding criteria for each variable. The variables that are examined in the present paper are described below.

Overall ratings of the interviewee's acceptance of his or her familial identity, either as a lesbian family or as a post-divorce heterosexual family, were assigned (excluding data relating to the quality of his/her family relationships). Interviewees from both the lesbian mother and the heterosexual mother groups were rated on their feelings about coming from a nontraditional family and how they presented this to others outside the family in addition to their personal acceptance of their mother's identity and lifestyle.

Following Lewis's (1980) description of responses to growing-up in a lesbian family, a four-point rating scale was constructed on which interviewees were classified as feeling "1" opposed/resentful, "2" embarrassed, "3" accepting, or "4" proud of their family identity. Anchor points for this scale were as follows: "opposed/resentful" (angry with mother or completely refuse to acknowledge mother's relationships, n = 12 and n = 3 subjects for adolescent and adult ratings), "embarrassed" (secretive about mother's relationships but no resentment or personal denial, n = 9 and n = 3 subjects for adolescent and adult ratings), "accepting" (pleased that mother is happy with her identity, no attempt to keep mother's relationships secret from friends, n = 23 and n = 28 subjects for adolescent and adult ratings), "proud" (very positive about mother's relationships, acknowledged mother's relationships to a wider audience than just close friends, n = 0 and n = 9 subjects for adolescent and adult ratings). Two ratings were made for each respondent, the first focused on acceptance of family identity whilst in high school, and the second concerned acceptance of family identity as young adults. Fourteen randomly selected interviews were coded by a second rater in order to calculate inter-rater reliability. Inter-rater reliabilities for these two variables were 0.80 and 0.87 respectively.

Ratings were also made on the following variables: (i) current relationship with mother ("1" very negative to "4" very positive) (ii) mother's relationship style ("1" exclusive to "4" non-exclusive) (iii) mother's satisfaction with her primary relationship ("1" very unhappy to "4" very happy) (iv) conflict in mother's primary relationship ("1" regular episodes of conflict to "4" no serious episodes of conflict) (v) adolescent relationship with mother's partner ("1" very negative to "4" very positive) (vi) current relationship with mother's partner ("1" very negative to "4" very positive) (vii) closeness of current relationship with father ("1" very negative to "4" very positive) (viii) father's attitude towards mother's relationships ("1" opposed/upset to "3" expressed support) (ix) mother's contentment with her identity ("1" prefer to be heterosexual to "3" very positive) (x) mother's involvement in feminist politics ("0" not involved to "1" feminist) (xi) mother's involvement in lesbian/gay rights politics ("0" not involved to "1" involvement) (xii) mother's openness in showing physical affection in front of child ("0" interviewee not embarrassed to "1" some embarrassment felt) (xiii) mother's openness about her lifestyle in front of child's school friends ("0" discreet to "1" interviewee felt mother was too open) (xiv) mother's response to school friends visiting home ("1" very unwelcoming to "3" welcoming) (xv) mother's attitude towards men ("0" negative to "1" neutral or positive) (xvi) mother's response to young adult's own relationship partners ("1" disapproving to "3" welcoming) (xvii) teasing about mother's lifestyle ("0" not teased to "1" teased about mother), and (xviii) teasing about own sexuality ("0" not teased to "1" teased about sexuality). Inter-rater reliability Pearson's product-moment correlation coefficients ranged from 0.68 to 1.00 on the above variables. Thirteen of the 18 variables (72%) measured at follow-up attained an inter-rater reliability of over 0.75.

RESULTS

Acceptance of Family Identity in Postdivorce Lesbian and Nontraditional Postdivorce Heterosexual Families

No difference was found between young adults from lesbian and heterosexual backgrounds in their retrospective reports of how positive they felt as an adolescent about their family identity ($t = -1.41$; $df = 42$; ns), either as a member of a lesbian family (mean = 2.08; s.d. = 0.83) or of a post-divorce heterosexual family (mean = 2.45; s.d. = 0.89). Young men and women from heterosexual (mean = 2.74; s.d. = 0.65) and lesbian families (mean = 3.21; s.d. = 0.78) became more positive about their family identity as they reached young adulthood, and this was especially so for those from lesbian families ($t = 2.11$; $df = 41$; $p < 0.05$). Within the lesbian family group, no gender or social class differences were found with respect to acceptance/rejection of family identity.

Acceptance of Lesbian Family Identity During Adolescence

Among participants from lesbian families, Pearson product-moment correlation coefficients were conducted between the dependent variables (acceptance of lesbian family identity during adolescence and acceptance of lesbian family identity in adulthood) and the variables from both the initial study and the follow-up study (see Table 1).[2]

Only one variable from the initial study was significantly correlated with feelings about lesbian family identity in adolescence. Young adults whose mothers reported a relationship history of short-term relationships or affairs were more likely to be negative about their family identity during adolescence ($r = -0.415$, $p < 0.05$). Similarly, the equivalent variable, mother's relationship style, assessed retrospectively in the follow-up study, was associated with more negative feelings during adolescence about their mother's lesbian identity ($r = -0.662$, $p < 0.001$).

Two other variables measuring family relationships at follow-up were associated with young adults' retrospective reports of acceptance of their family during adolescence. Young adults who felt closer to their mother at the time of the follow-up interview reported greater acceptance of their lesbian family identity as adolescents ($r = 0.503$, $p < 0.05$). While a nonsignificant trend in the data indicated that those who described a good relationship with their mother's partner at the time of the follow-up interview also tended to report greater acceptance of their family identity as adolescents ($r = 0.371$, $p < 0.10$).

A number of variables measured at follow-up relating to whether or not the mother had been open about her lesbian relationships were correlated with young adults' retrospective reports of acceptance of their family identity during adolescence. Those who felt that their mother had been too open about her lifestyle in front of their school friends were more likely to report that they had negative feelings about their family identity during their high school years ($r = -0.596$, $p < 0.01$). Similarly there was also a nonsignificant trend in the data suggesting that those who had been embarrassed by their mother showing affection to her partner tended to be less accepting of their family identity during adolescence ($r = -0.412$, $p < 0.10$). On the other hand, those who felt that their mother had been accepting of their own boyfriends or girlfriends were more likely to hold a favourable view of their family identity ($r = 0.547$, $p < 0.01$). Two other nonsignificant trends in the data are congruent with these associations. Firstly, young adults who reported that their mother held a positive view of men also tended to be more accepting of their family identity during adolescence ($r = 0.428$, $p < 0.10$).

---

2. A similar set of investigations were attempted on the data from young adults brought up by heterosexual mothers. However, as there was little variation among this group of young people in terms of their acceptance of family identity, further analyses were abandoned.

TABLE 1. Correlations Between Family Characteristics and Acceptance of Family Identity During Adolescence

FAMILY RELATIONSHIPS (INITIAL STUDY)	ACCEPTANCE IN ADOLESCENCE	FAMILY RELATIONSHIPS (FOLLOW-UP)	ACCEPTANCE IN ADOLESCENCE
Mother's expressed warmth to child	−.214 (n = 23)	Current relationship with mother	.503* (n = 24)
Mother's relationship history	−.415* (n = 24)	Mother's relationship style	−.662*** (n = 24)
Quality of mother's relationship with her female partner	.128 (n = 13)	Mother's satisfaction with her primary relationship	.005 (n = 23)
Mother and her partner share child care	.128 (n = 13)	Conflict in mother's primary relationship	.046 (n = 22)
Child's contact with father	−.190 (n = 24)	Adolescent relationship with mother's partner	.311 (n = 24)
Number of years child raised in heterosexual home	.116 (n = 24)	Current relationship with mother's partner	.371+ (n = 24)
Child's awareness of mother's lesbian identity	.204 (n = 24)	Closeness of current relationship with father	.064 (n = 18)
		Father's attitude towards mother's relationships	.196 (n = 17)
MOTHER'S IDENTITY (INITIAL STUDY)	ACCEPTANCE IN ADOLESCENCE	MOTHER'S IDENTITY (FOLLOW-UP)	ACCEPTANCE IN ADOLESCENCE
Mother's contentment with her sexual identity	−.020 (n = 24)	Mother's contentment with her sexual identity	−.285 (n = 23)
Mother's political involvement	−.183 (n = 24)	Mother's involvement in feminist politics	−.164 (n = 23)
		Mother's involvement in lesbian/gay rights politics	.052 (n = 23)

192

MOTHER'S OPENNESS ABOUT LESBIAN IDENTITY (INITIAL STUDY)	ACCEPTANCE IN ADOLESCENCE	MOTHER'S OPENNESS ABOUT LESBIAN IDENTITY (FOLLOW-UP)	ACCEPTANCE IN ADOLESCENCE
Mother's openness in showing affection in front of child	−.189 (n = 18)	Mother's openness in showing physical affection in front of child	−.412+ (n = 19)
Mother "out" in local community	.050 (n = 24)	Mother's openness about lifestyle in front of child's school friends	−.596** (n = 23)
Mother "out" to child's school teachers	−.068 (n = 24)	Mother's response to child's school friends visiting home	.402+ (n = 24)
Mother's attitude towards men	−.086 (n = 24)	Mother's attitude towards men	.428+ (n = 21)
		Mother's response to young adult's own relationship partners	.547** (n = 24)
PEERS RESPONSE (INITIAL STUDY)	ACCEPTANCE IN ADOLESCENCE	PEERS RESPONSE (FOLLOW-UP)	ACCEPTANCE IN ADOLESCENCE
Quality child's peer relationships	.239 (n = 18)	Teased about mother's lifestyle	−.397+ (n = 24)
		Teased about own sexuality	−.609** (n = 24)

+p < .10; *p < .05; **p < .01; ***p < .001

Secondly, those who felt their mother had welcomed school friends' visits to the house tended to be more positive about their lesbian family background during adolescence (r = 0.402, p < 0.10).

The negative response of peers during high school also appears to be strongly associated with a more negative view of family identity during adolescence. Interviewees who recalled being teased about their own sexuality (r = −0.609, p < 0.01), reported less acceptance of their family identity during their high school years. Similarly a further nonsignificant trend in the data indicates that those who remembered being teased about their mother's lifestyle were also less accepting as adolescents of their family identity (r = −0.397, p < 0.10).

Acceptance of Lesbian Family Identity in Adulthood

When the variables associated with interviewees' current feelings in adulthood about their family identity are examined, the picture changes (see Table 2). The majority of variables that related to acceptance or rejection of their lesbian family background during adolescence were no longer significantly associated with young adults' current feelings about their mother's identity. However, there was a nonsignificant trend indicating that those who remembered having been teased about their own sexuality during their schooldays tended to remain opposed to, or embarrassed about, their family identity as young adults (r = −0.361, p < 0.10).

Four nonsignificant trends in the data suggest that other factors may be associated with young adults' feelings about coming from a lesbian family background. Firstly, there was a nonsignificant trend indicating that young people who were most positive about their lesbian family identity tended to have mothers who, at the time of the first study, were open about being a lesbian mother to their son or daughter's school (r = 0.400, p < 0.10). Secondly, those whose mothers reported having had a greater number of relationships prior to the original study, tended to have a more positive view of their family identity as young adults (r = 0.347, p < 0.10). Finally, data from the follow-up study suggests that young adults who reported that their mother had been involved in the gay rights movement tended to be more positive about their lesbian family identity (r = 0.380, p < 0.10), as did those who reported that their mother had been involved in feminist politics (r = 0.380, p < 0.10).

DISCUSSION

In early adulthood young men and women brought up by lesbian mothers were generally more positive about their family identity than were those brought up in post-divorce heterosexual families and no differences on average were observed between young people from lesbian and non-traditional heterosexual families in their acceptance of their family identity during adolescence. However, feelings of hostility or embarrassment during adolescence about coming from a lesbian family were expressed by young people who recollected experiences of peer group stigma, especially if they remembered being teased during high school about their own sexual identity. By adulthood, those who had been teased about their own sexual identity appeared to remain rejecting, although the association was somewhat diminished. The negative response of others, therefore, may have had a corresponding negative effect on children's own attitudes towards their family.

Congruent with these findings, young people who felt that their mother had been too open about her lesbian identity in front of their school friends were less accepting of their lesbian family identity during adolescence. In contrast, those who felt that their mother was sensitive to their need for discretion felt more positive, perhaps because they were reassured that only trusted friends would learn about their family background. It is important to point out, however, that it is not possible to determine the direction of influence in these associations within the data from the follow-up study. This finding is in line with that of Bozett (1988) who, in his research on children of gay fathers, highlighted the importance for young people of feeling in control of the information that peers receive about their family circumstances.

Other trends in the data also support the suggestion that how the family relates to those outside the home contributes to the adolescent's feelings about coming from a post-divorce lesbian-led family. Young people who felt that their mother had not welcomed their school friends at home tended to be rejecting of their mother's lesbian identity during adolescence. Furthermore, young adults who felt that their mother tended to disapprove of their own boyfriends or girlfriends, and those who reported that their mother tended to have a negative attitude towards men, were least accepting of their lesbian family background during adolescence.

Two separate aspects of relationships within the young person's family were shown to be associated with acceptance of coming from a lesbian family background. Firstly, interviewees who reported that their mother had long-term stable relationships were more likely to report being positive about their family background during adolescence. A possible explanation is that mothers who have a greater number of relationships appear more openly lesbian, and that this raises the profile of the mother's lesbian lifestyle in a more direct way than is experienced by those whose

TABLE 2. Correlations Between Family Characteristics and Acceptance of Family Identity During Adulthood

FAMILY RELATIONSHIPS (INITIAL STUDY)	ACCEPTANCE IN ADULTHOOD	FAMILY RELATIONSHIPS (FOLLOW-UP)	ACCEPTANCE IN ADULTHOOD
Mother's expressed warmth to child	-.182 (n = 23)	Current relationship with mother	.305 (n = 24)
Mother's relationship history	.347+ (n = 24)	Mother's relationship style	-.002 (n = 24)
Quality of mother's relationship with her female partner	.224 (n = 13)	Mother's satisfaction with her primary relationship	-.141 (n = 23)
Mother and her partner share child care	.416 (n = 13)	Conflict in mother's primary relationship	-.220 (n = 22)
Child's contact with father	.222 (n= 24)	Adolescent relationship with mother's partner	.142 (n = 24)
Number of years child raised in heterosexual home	.044 (n = 24)	Current relationship with mother's partner	-.117 (n = 24)
Child's awareness of mother's lesbian identity	.059 (n = 24)	Closeness of current relationship with father	-.064 (n = 18)
		Father's attitude towards mother's relationships	.030 (n = 17)
MOTHER'S IDENTITY (INITIAL STUDY)	ACCEPTANCE IN ADULTHOOD	MOTHER'S IDENTITY (FOLLOW-UP)	ACCEPTANCE IN ADULTHOOD
Mother's contentment with her sexual identity	-.270 (n = 24)	Mother's contentment with her sexual identity	-.170 (n = 23)
Mother's political involvement	.044 (n = 24)	Mother's involvement in feminist politics	.380+ (n = 23)
		Mother's involvement in lesbian/gay rights politics	.380+ (n = 23)

MOTHER'S OPENNESS ABOUT LESBIAN IDENTITY (INITIAL STUDY)	ACCEPTANCE IN ADULTHOOD	MOTHER'S OPENNESS ABOUT LESBIAN IDENTITY (FOLLOW-UP)	ACCEPTANCE IN ADULTHOOD
Mother's openness in showing affection in front of child	.358 (n = 18)	Mother's openness in showing physical affection in front of child	.070 (n = 19)
Mother "out" in local community	.133 (n = 24)	Mother's openness about lifestyle in front of child's school friends	−.110 (n = 23)
Mother "out" to child's school teachers	.400+ (n = 24)	Mother's response to child's school friends visiting home	.181 (n = 24)
Mother's attitude towards men	−.018 (n = 24)	Mother's attitude towards men	.229 (n = 21)
		Mother's response to young adult's own relationship partners	.106 (n = 24)
PEERS RESPONSE (INITIAL STUDY)	ACCEPTANCE IN ADULTHOOD	PEERS RESPONSE (FOLLOW-UP)	ACCEPTANCE IN ADULTHOOD
Quality child's peer relationships	.331 (n = 18)	Teased about mother's lifestyle	−.099 (n = 24)
		Teased about own sexuality	−.361+ (n = 24)

+p < .10; *p < .05; **p < .01; ***p < .001

mothers have long-term relationships with a special partner. Perhaps with each of their mother's new relationships children once again need time to come to terms with changes in family composition. Furthermore, it has been observed that children in postdivorce heterosexual families can become extremely upset when their mother or father experiments with a series of new heterosexual relationships (Wallerstein & Blakeslee, 1989). However, when interviewees reported on their views as adults of belonging to a lesbian family this association was almost reversed; those whose mothers reported a greater number of relationships at the time of the initial study tended instead to report being proud of being brought up by a lesbian mother.

Secondly, young adults who reported closer relationships with their mother and her partner at the time of the follow-up study reported greater acceptance of their lesbian family during adolescence. Adolescents who felt most positively about their mother's identity may have developed closer relationships with their mother and her female partner. Alternatively, those who have closer relationships currently may have forgotten earlier difficulties.

Neither the quality of the mother's primary relationship, nor the quality of children's relationship with their mother's female partner during their adolescent years, appear to be central to how children feel about having a lesbian mother, either during adolescence or early adulthood. Children who had a poor relationship with one or more of their mother's partners could still feel positively about their mother's lesbian identity. Conversely, one of the few participants who remained extremely negative in adulthood about having a lesbian mother, had experienced fairly good relationships with all of her mother's female partners (in contrast to her stormy relationship with her mother).

Contrary to the findings of Huggins (1989), there is no evidence from this study that fathers' opposition or support for mothers' lesbian relationships had any effect on children's acceptance or rejection of their mothers' lesbian identity. Young adults often did not discuss their mother's relationships with their father, or if they did so, were not necessarily swayed by his opinions.

It is also interesting to note that neither the child's gender, socioeconomic status of the family, nor the child's age when the mother identified as lesbian were significantly associated with acceptance of lesbian family identity. This suggests that these variables were less important than mother's sensitivity to the situation, and how peers outside the family responded. However, the small sample size may have meant that more subtle effects remained undetected.

Whether their mother is positive about her own identity, or politically active, seemingly makes little difference to adolescents' acceptance of their lesbian family background. However, there were a couple of nonsignificant trends in the data suggesting that interviewees whose mothers expressed feminist or pro-gay rights views, or who previously had been open to the child's school, tended to be those young adults who were unafraid to be public about their lesbian family background, if an appropriate opportunity arose.

The research was conducted with a self-selected volunteer group of lesbian mothers and their children, which has implications for the generalizability of the findings. It is not possible to recruit a representative sample of lesbian mothers since many do not declare their sexual identity. Thus the study may have sampled lesbian families that were functioning well, particularly in view of the attrition of families where mothers reported greater conflict with their partner at the time of the original study. In addition, the young adults who participated at follow-up tended to be those who were more aware of their mother's lesbian identity initially. Those who grow up with the knowledge may be more accepting in the long-term than those who make a dramatic discovery of a prior family secret. Nevertheless, there was sufficient variation among the young people in terms of their acceptance/rejection of family identity for associated factors to be explored.

Interview data are always open to bias owing to self-presentation effects. It is, of course, possible that lesbian mothers would wish to portray a particularly positive picture of family life to counteract the discrimination they so often face. However, these motivations may apply less to young adults who have grown up in lesbian families. Steps were taken to minimize this potential source of bias. The flexible semi-structured interview procedure allowed the interviewer to probe any apparently contradictory answers, and the in-depth open-ended approach was used to enable interviewees to tell their own life-story. Any major negative or positive effects of upbringing in a lesbian household therefore should have been identified, although it is conceivable that more subtle effects may have been missed because of the relatively small sample size. Limitations of sample size also meant that multivariate statistical analyses were inappropriate, thus the connections between the variables remain statistically unexplored.

The mothers in the present study all gave birth to their children in the context of a heterosexual relationship and identified as lesbian later in the child's life. Uncontrolled studies have found that the extent to which children have come to terms with their parents' divorce is a key factor in determining their willingness to accept their mother's lesbian identity

(Lewis, 1980). However, there were few indications of divorce concerns for the interviewees in the present study, perhaps because of the length of time that had elapsed since this had occurred. Nevertheless, in comparison with children born into lesbian families headed either by a single mother or a lesbian couple, the issues faced in accepting their family identity by these young people who had experienced their father's departure from the home, and the resultant family transitions, may be very different indeed.

This study demonstrates the importance of examining the diversity of experience of children in lesbian families, an area of research that has been largely neglected (Patterson, 1992). The different pattern of variables associated with acceptance of family identity during adolescence and early adulthood point to the importance of assessing the changing influences on acceptance of family identity as children from lesbian families grow up. Young adults from lesbian families were generally positive about their family relationships and their family identity. However, adolescence appeared to be a time when some young people remembered feeling negative or embarrassed about coming from a lesbian family. Findings from the present study on acceptance of family identity during adolescence point to the role of close and stable family relationships, the absence of peer stigma, and the ways in which their mother and her partner help the adolescent to bridge the gap between peers and their family environment. After leaving home as young adults these factors become less important and many young people begin to take a pride in their lesbian family background.

REFERENCES

Arnup, K. (1995) Living in the margins: Lesbian families and the law. In K. Arnup (Ed.), *Lesbian parenting: Living with pride and prejudice* (pp. 378-398). Charlottetown, Canada: Gynergy.

B v B (1991) *Family Law, 21,* 174.

Belcastro, P.A.; Gramlich, T.; Nicholson, T.; Price, J. & Wilson, R. (1993) A Review of data based studies addressing the affects of homosexual parenting on children's sexual and social functioning. *Journal of Divorce & Remarriage, 20,* 105-122.

Bozett, F.W. (1988) Social control of identity by children of gay fathers. *Western Journal of Nursing Research, 10,* 550-565.

Bray, J.H. & Berger, S.H. (1993) Developmental issues in stepfamilies research project: Family relationships and parent-child interactions. *Journal of Family Psychology, 7,* 76-90.

Brown, G.W. & Rutter, M.L. (1966) The measurement of family activities and relationships: A methodological study. *Human Relations, 19,* 241-263.

Duran-Aydintug, C. & Causey, K.A. (1996) Child custody determination: Implications for lesbian mothers. *Journal of Divorce & Remarriage, 25,* 55-74.

Falk, P.J. (1989) Lesbian mothers: Psychosocial assumptions in family law. *American Psychologist, 44,* 941-947.

Golombok, S., Spencer, A. & Rutter, M. (1983) Children in lesbian and single-parent households: Psychosexual and psychiatric appraisal. *Journal of Child Psychology & Psychiatry, 24,* 551-572.

Golombok, S. & Tasker, F. (1994) Children in lesbian and gay families: Theories and evidence. *Annual Review of Sex Research, 5,* 73-100.

Golombok, S. & Tasker, F. (1996) Do parents influence the sexual orientation of their children? Findings from a longitudinal study of children raised by lesbian mothers. *Developmental Psychology, 32,* 3-11.

Hall, M. (1978) Lesbian families: Cultural and clinical issues. *Social Work, 23,* 380-385.

Hetherington, E.M. (1993) An overview of the Virginia Longitudinal Study of Divorce and Remarriage with a focus on early adolescence. *Journal of Family Psychology, 7,* 39-56.

Hetherington, E.M. & Clingempeel, W.G. (1992) Coping with marital transitions: A family systems perspective. *Monographs of the Society for Research in Child Development, 57* (2-3, Serial No. 227).

Huggins, S.L. (1989) A comparative study of self-esteem of adolescent children of divorced lesbian mothers and divorced heterosexual mothers. In F. Bozett (Ed.), *Homosexuality and the family* (pp. 123-135). New York: Harrington Park Press.

Kirkpatrick, M. (1987) Clinical implications of lesbian mother studies. *Journal of Homosexuality, 13,* 201-211.

Kirkpatrick, M., Smith, C. & Roy, R. (1981) Lesbian mothers and their children: A comparative survey. *American Journal of Orthopsychiatry, 51,* 545-551.

Lesbian Mothers Group (1989) "A word might slip and that would be it." Lesbian mothers and their children. In L. Holly (Ed.), *Girls and sexuality: Teaching and learning* (pp. 122-129). Milton Keynes: Open University Press.

Lewis, K.G. (1980) Children of lesbians: Their point of view. *Social Work, 25,* 198-203.

Miller, J.A., Jacobsen, R.B. & Bigner, J.J. (1981) The child's home environment for lesbian vs. heterosexual mothers: A neglected area of research. *Journal of Homosexuality, 7,* 49-56.

Mucklow, B.M. & Phelan, G.K. (1979) Lesbian and traditional mothers' responses to child behavior and self-concept. *Psychological Reports, 44,* 880-882.

Pagelow, M.D. (1980) Heterosexual and lesbian single mothers: A comparison of problems, coping and solutions. *Journal of Homosexuality, 5,* 198-204.

Pasley, K. & Ihinger-Tallman, M. (1987) The evolution of a field of investigation: Issues and concerns. In K. Pasley & M. Ihinger-Tallman (Eds.), *Remarriage and stepparenting: Current research and theory* (pp. 303-313). New York: Guilford Press.

Patterson, C.J. (1992) Children of lesbian and gay parents. *Child Development,* *63,* 1025-1042.

Patterson, C.J. (1995) Lesbian mothers, gay fathers and their children. In A.R. D'Augelli & C.J. Patterson (Eds.), *Lesbian, gay and bisexual identities over the lifespan: Psychological perspectives* (pp. 262-290). Oxford: Oxford University Press.

Pennington, S.B. (1987) Children of lesbian mothers. In F.W. Bozett (Ed.), *Gay and lesbian parents* (pp. 58-74). New York: Praeger.

Rand, C., Graham, D.L.R. & Rawlings, E.I. (1982) Psychological health and factors the court seeks to control in lesbian mother custody trials. *Journal of Homosexuality, 8,* 27-39.

Rutter, M. & Brown, G.W. (1966) The reliability and validity of measures of family life and relationships in families containing a psychiatric patient. *Social Psychiatry, 1,* 38-53.

Tasker, F. & Golombok, S. (1995) Adults raised as children in lesbian families. *American Journal of Orthopsychiatry, 65,* 203-215.

Tasker, F. & Golombok, S. (1997) *Growing up in a lesbian family: Effects on child development.* New York: Guilford Press.

Wallerstein, J.S. & Blakeslee, S. (1989) *Second chances: Men, women and children a decade after divorce.* London: Bantam Press.

Grandparent Involvement Following Divorce: A Comparison in Single-Mother and Single-Father Families

Jeanne M. Hilton
Daniel P. Macari

SUMMARY. Although the value of the grandparent role has been widely documented, researchers rarely have examined the specific activities shared by grandparents and grandchildren, nor have comparisons been made of the involvement of grandparents in single-mother and single-father families. In this study, data on the involvement of grandparents with a school-aged grandchild were gathered from custodial parents in 30 single-mother and 30 single-father families during a two-hour interview. A self-report questionnaire on grandparenting was used to evaluate how gender of grandparent, kin position, and gender of custodial parent influenced the amount of contact, types of activities, and overall level of involvement between grandparents and grandchildren. Using analysis of covariance, significant effects on the dependent variables were found for both the covariate (geographic

Jeanne M. Hilton, PhD, is affiliated with the Department of Human Development and Family Studies and Daniel P. Macari, PhD, is affiliated with the Department of Counseling and Educational Psychology, University of Nevada.

This research was funded by Nevada Agricultural Experiment Station, NAES Project 948, "School-Aged Youth at Risk in Single-Parent Families."

Address correspondence to: Jeanne M. Hilton, Department of Human Development and Family Studies, University of Nevada, Reno, NV 89557-0131. Electronic mail may be sent via internet to (hilton@hdfs.unr.edu).

[Haworth co-indexing entry note]: "Grandparent Involvement Following Divorce: A Comparison in Single-Mother and Single-Father Families." Hilton, Jeanne M., and Daniel P. Macari. Co-published simultaneously in *Journal of Divorce & Remarriage* (The Haworth Press, Inc.) Vol. 28, No. 1/2, 1997, pp. 203-224; and: *Child Custody: Legal Decisions and Family Outcomes* (ed: Craig A. Everett) The Haworth Press, Inc., 1997, pp. 203-224. Single or multiple copies of this article are available for a fee from The Haworth Document Delivery Service [1-800-342-9678, 9:00 a.m. - 5:00 p.m. (EST). E-mail address: getinfo@haworth.com].

proximity) and the independent variables. Grandparents were found to be more involved with their grandchildren when they lived close-by, had an adult child with custodial status, were grandmothers, or had a grandchild living in a single-father family. These results challenge many gender-based assumptions that have driven previous research and shaped grandparents' legal rights. Professionals working with families, including family lawyers, can use this information to promote practice and policy that enhances intergenerational relationships in single-parent families. *[Article copies available for a fee from The Haworth Document Delivery Service: 1-800-342-9678. E-mail address: getinfo@haworth.com]*

Grandparents play an important role in the lives of their grandchildren. The bond between grandparents and grandchildren begins with the birth of a child and continues throughout life, giving children a sense of continuity, identity, and family history (Creasey, 1993). In addition, grandparents provide children with novel stimulation and are usually more tolerant of children's behavior than are parents. These factors color children's view of life (Conroy & Fahey, 1985), encourage risk taking (Wilcoxon, 1987), and help children resolve problems more successfully (Blau, 1984).

Grandparents may have an even greater influence on children when parents are divorced. They offer support and nurturance to the family, often providing financial assistance (Johnson, 1988) and child care (Myers & Perrin, 1993). They also serve as a stabilizing force and a stress buffer by providing children with a trustworthy and stable relationship (Clingempeel, Colyar, Brand, & Hetherington, 1992; Kennedy & Kennedy, 1993; Kivett, 1991). In particular, grandparents ease tensions by providing children with attention and activities away from their parents (Blau, 1984). They also negotiate between parents and children, helping them to understand one another (Barranti, 1985).

In examining the possible roles of grandparents in the lives of grandchildren following divorce, family scholars agree that the support grandparents have to offer during times of family distress can benefit children (Kennedy, 1990, 1992; Kornhaber & Woodward, 1981; McCrimmon & Howell, 1989; Wallerstein, 1986). They also report that grandparents can make significant contributions to the lives of children, even when the relationship between grandparent and grandchild is not intense (Derdeyn, 1985; McCrimmon & Howell, 1989).

Despite these observations, researchers rarely have discussed the extent to which grandparents actually enact these roles, nor have comparisons been made of the involvement of grandparents in single-mother and single-father families. Therefore, three dimensions central to an examination of involvement of grandparents in the lives of grandchildren following divorce were assessed in this study: (1) amount of contact, (2) types of activities, and (3) frequency of involvement in these activities.

FACTORS THAT INFLUENCE AMOUNT OF CONTACT

Factors that have been found to mediate amount of contact between grandparents and grandchildren following divorce include: geographic proximity, sex of grandparent, relationship of the grandparents to the parents, and sex of the custodial parent.

Geographic Proximity

When grandparents live more than a day's drive away from their grandchildren, contact is bound to be affected. The extent to which this happens, however, has been debated. Kivett (1985) reported that living in close geographic proximity was the single most important factor affecting grandparent-grandchild visits. On the other hand, Thompson and his colleagues found that geographic proximity was not necessarily a major barrier to contact between the generations (Thompson, Scalora, Limber, & Castrianno, 1991). They reported that although changes in the transportation and communications industries increase the probability that grandparents will live some distance from their grandchildren, these same changes make it easier to maintain contact.

Sex of Grandparent

Amount of contact with grandchildren also has been reported to vary depending on whether the grandparent is male or female. Generally, the grandmother role is reported to be more involved than that of the grandfather (Thomas, 1986). According to researchers, grandmothers are more likely than grandfathers to perform basic childrearing functions and have warmer, more expressive relationships with their grandchildren (Eisenberg, 1988). They have more contact with grandchildren, especially following divorce (Eisenberg, 1988; Gladstone, 1987, 1991; Kivett, 1991), engage in a greater number of activities than grandfathers, and these activities are both instrumental and expressive in nature (Thomas, 1986; Eisenberg, 1988). In contrast, the activities of grandfathers have been found to be somewhat limited and primarily instrumental (Hagestad, 1985; Cherlin & Furstenberg, 1986).

Although these studies suggest that grandfathers are less involved and give less priority to the grandparent role than grandmothers, other research indicates that the importance of grandfather role may have been greatly underestimated (Baranowski, 1990; Kivett, 1991). For example, there is some disagreement regarding what grandfathers do based on the generation of the person reporting the data. Grandfathers emphasize their instrumental activities (Hagestad, 1985) whereas grandchildren report that grandfathers provide both instrumental and expressive experiences (Baranowski, 1985, 1990). This difference in perception may be due to cohort differences in role definition.

Another indication that the grandfather role may be broader than previously thought is the recent observation that most researchers have been insensitive to gender differences in the measurement of intergenerational exchanges (Baranowski, 1990; Kivett, 1991). According to Baranowski (1990), when the grandparent role is evaluated it is usually in the context of a maternal role consisting of activities that are of little importance to men.

Finally, it has been suggested that grandfathers become more involved in activities as their grandchildren grow older (Hagestad & Speicher, 1981; Hagestad, 1985). Since most of the research on grandparenting has focused on young grandchildren, the full range of activities engaged in by grandfathers has probably been underestimated.

Kin Position of Parents and Grandparents

Another factor influencing amount of intergenerational contact is based on the ways in which grandparents and parents are related to one another, or their kin position. Parents tend to control the amount of contact between grandparents and grandchildren, and degree of control depends on: (1) whether the grandparents are maternal or paternal, (2) blood relatives or in-laws, and (3) whether the grandparents are related to the custodial or noncustodial parent.

Maternal versus paternal kin position. Maternal/paternal kin position has been most commonly used to explain changes in contact with grandchildren following divorce. Researchers consistently have reported that contact decreases for paternal grandparents and increases for maternal grandparents (Johnson, 1988; Creasey, 1993; Thompson et al., 1991; Myers & Perrin, 1993). However, this observation may be misleading as mothers are more likely than fathers to retain custody of children after divorce and most studies fail to control for custodial status of the divorced parent (Kruk & Hall, 1995; Creasy, 1993). As a result, maternal grandparents are more likely to be related to custodial parents while paternal grandparents are related to noncustodial parents.

Within this body of literature, researchers report that conflict between custodial and noncustodial parents often leads to diminished contact for paternal grandparents (Johnson, 1988; Kivett; 1991; Gladstone, 1991). Furthermore, when a noncustodial parent is absent, paternal grandparents are likely to reduce or lose contact with their grandchildren (Kruk & Hall, 1995). Whether the same holds true for maternal grandparents in single-father families has not been examined.

A more serious problem was identified by Kruk and Hall (1995) who believe that the critical variable determining grandparent involvement following divorce is parental custody, not maternal/paternal kin position. Myers and Perrin (1993) came to the same conclusion and created a new status for grandparents: those whose adult child has custody are "custodial grandparents" and those whose adult child does not have custody are "noncustodial grandparents." These observations underscore a different (and probably more relevant) type of kin position that is created by divorce. Although the issue has been raised by researchers, no studies have been done evaluating the effects of custodial/noncustodial status of grandparents on their involvement with grandchildren.

In-laws versus blood relationships. Grandparents' relationships with both their own child and the former daughter- or son-in-law are also relevant. Matthews and Sprey (1984) found that paternal grandparents are most likely to maintain contact when they nurture a friendly relationship with a former daughter-in-law, while remaining somewhat detached from the day-to-day functioning of the family. Sometimes this alignment with a former daughter-in-law is maintained at the expense of the relationship with the son. This is most likely to occur when the son abdicates his paternal role (Johnson & Barer, 1987).

Although troubled relationships among in-laws are an obvious deterrent to intergenerational contact, the relationship between grandparents and an adult child is also an important predictor of contact with grandchildren. In fact, the legacy of the earlier parent-child relationship seems to be more important in determining intergenerational contact than are age, health, or geographical proximity of the grandparent (Thompson et al., 1991). In general, grandparents who have a good relationship with an adult child are more likely to have access to their grandchildren (Nahemow, 1985). Conversely, when grandparent-adult child relationships are strained, especially in the context of divorce, the grandparent-grandchild relationship is likely to be disrupted or terminated (Gladstone, 1987, 1991; Johnson & Barer, 1987; Nahemow, 1985; Thompson et al., 1991).

Sex of Custodial Parent

As mediators between the generations, both custodial and noncustodial parents may either encourage or discourage contact, which in turn influences both the quality and quantity of grandparent-grandchild interaction (Robertson, 1976). Of course, custodial parents are positioned to have the most control in setting the pace for these interactions. Therefore, although the number and proportion of custodial fathers is growing rapidly, almost all of the literature on intergenerational relationships following divorce is limited to families with custodial mothers.

Within this body of literature, researchers have reported that custodial mothers who lose their marital identity often want a clean break from their former husbands and in-laws (Williams, 1986; Kruk & Hall, 1995). As a result, paternal grandparents are less likely to maintain contact with their grandchildren when the former daughter-in-law has custody (Cherlin & Furstenberg, 1986; Johnson, 1988). They live further away from their grandchildren, see them less often, and provide less financial support than do maternal grandparents (Cherlin & Furstenberg, 1986). Ironically, paternal grandparents who are most involved with their grandchildren prior to divorce are most at risk of losing contact because custodial mothers see them as a threat to the restructured family unit (Williams, 1986).

Little is known about intergenerational relationships in families where fathers have custody and the amount of contact between grandparents and grandchildren in these families is virtually unknown. Researchers report that noncustodial fathers rely on family support during the crisis of divorce but then back off when the crisis subsides (Ahrons & Bowman, 1982). Custodial fathers, on the other hand, rely on the grandparent generation for support and advice long after the divorce is granted (Ahrons & Bowman, 1982; Hanson, 1986). This suggests that level of contact between paternal grandparents and grandchildren may be greater when a father has custody, but does not address the issue of contact with maternal grandparents in single-father families, or how contact in single-father families compares to contact in single-mother families.

FACTORS THAT INFLUENCE TYPES OF ACTIVITIES AND LEVEL OF INVOLVEMENT

Amount of contact is only one dimension of involvement. The types of activities shared by grandparents and grandchildren and the amount of time spent in various activities are also important. Generally, there is very little detail in the literature regarding what grandparents and grandchildren actually do together (Eisenberg, 1988). For the most part, researchers have categorized interactions between grandparents and grandchildren as either instrumental or expressive along traditional gender lines, and differences among grandparents and their interactions with grandchildren have not been addressed (Eisenberg, 1988).

The few studies examining specific shared activities generally have relied on retrospective data gathered from college students about interactions with a most-close grandparent. In two of these studies, researchers assessed 29 activities, including family celebrations, spending the night, taking vacations, recreational activities and hobbies, chores, child care, teaching skills, telling stories, and communicating by phone and letter (Kennedy, 1992; Kennedy & Kennedy, 1993). They concluded that social types of activities probably are the most characteristic of grandparent/ grandchild interactions.

In other studies, shared activities that adult grandchildren recall most frequently included gift-giving, shared outings, family celebrations, and telling family stories (Robertson, 1976; Baranowski, 1990). Thomas and Datan (1982) found that the amount of involvement in activities was related to age of the child. Recreational activities increased as children reached school age and children became more helpful to grandparents as they got older.

Geographic Proximity

Although grandparents may be able to maintain contact when they live great distances from their grandchildren, their interactions with grandchildren, at least in some activities, are bound to be limited. Grandparents who live within daily driving distance have more frequent opportunities to interact with children, which they apparently use to their advantage (Eisenberg, 1988; Thompson et al., 1991). Kennedy (1992) reported that about half of the activities he examined were influenced by geographic proximity, but exactly what these activities were was not specified, other than that writing letters was more frequent when grandparents lived away from their grandchildren.

Sex of Grandparent

Sex of grandparent is more influential in determining types of activities shared than amount of contact. Specific activities most often associated with grandfathers include crafts, outdoor recreation, community events, financial assistance, sharing information, and teaching skills (Kennedy, 1990, 1992; Kennedy & Kennedy, 1993). Activities involving family caring, socializing, and communication are more characteristic of grandmothers (Johnson, 1983; Kennedy, 1990, 1992; Thompson et al., 1991).

Kin Position of Parents and Grandparents

For divorced families, age of the parents is the only factor in the grandparent-parent relationship that has been linked to the type of activities and level of involvement shared in the grandparent/grandchild relationship. Younger single parents are more likely to need assistance from their parents such as financial help (Myers & Perrin, 1993; Cherlin & Furstenberg, 1986), emotional support (Kivett, 1991; Clingempeel et al., 1992), and child care (Gladstone, 1987; Kennedy, 1992). When this occurs, the grandparent and grandchild are more likely to share time and activities with one another. No studies were found evaluating the effects of kin position or custodial status of the parent on shared activities between grandparents and grandchildren.

Sex of Custodial Parent

Two studies were found with reference to shared activities of grandparents and grandchildren in single-parent families, but sex of the custodial parent was not considered in either study (Kennedy, 1992; Kennedy & Kennedy, 1993). Furthermore, methodological problems somewhat limit the usefulness of these studies. For example, no attempt was made to control for factors that might influence activities shared by grandparents and grandchildren such as whether the single parent was divorced, never married, or cohabiting. In addition, the analysis of shared activities in single-parent families was restricted to a brief descriptive summary of the data (Kennedy, 1992; Kennedy & Kennedy, 1993).

To summarize, most studies of the role of grandparents in divorced families have compared grandmothers with grandfathers in terms of the frequency of interaction and quality of the grandparent/grandchild relationship. It is also common to find studies on the role of grandparents from the perspective of maternal/paternal kin position. A few studies have considered the grandparent role within the context of custody status ("custodial" grandparents versus "noncustodial" grandparents), and very few have looked at grandparenting in single-mother versus single-father families (Ahrons & Bowman, 1982). Nothing has been written, however, comparing grandparents across all three dimensions: (1) grandmothers versus grandfathers, (2) custodial versus noncustodial grandparents, and (3) grandparents in single-mother versus single-father families.

In spite of limitations in previous research on the grandparent role in divorced families, there is ample evidence that grandparents have a strong influence on the development and functioning of grandchildren (Kruk & Hall, 1995; Kennedy, 1993; McCrimmon & Howell, 1989). Therefore, the purpose of this study was to determine, more specifically, how gender of grandparents, kin position, and gender of custodial parents affect the amount of contact, types of activities, and level of involvement shared by grandparents and grandchildren in divorced families. Data were gathered from single-mother and single-father families and analyses were done comparing: (1) custodial and noncustodial grandparents, (2) grandmothers and grandfathers, and (3) grandparents in single-mother versus single-father families.

METHODOLOGY

Sample

The data for this study were collected from the parent in 30 single-mother and 30 single-father families. Most of the families were recruited through public schools, but a few single-father families were referred by word-of-mouth. The schools participating in the study were randomly selected from a list of all public schools in two metropolitan school districts in the state of Nevada. From the target schools, classrooms in grades one through four with at least one child from a single-father family were identified. Teachers in these classrooms were contacted and asked to help identify potential respondents from single-mother and single-father families.

Criteria for participation in the study were: (1) the single parent lived with a child (age 6-10) in a household with no other adults, (2) the child resided with the single parent an average of at least 20 nights per month, and (3) the single parent was divorced or separated with no history of remarriage. Families with school-aged children were targeted for two reasons: grandmothers are more likely than grandfathers to share activities with preschoolers, and shared activities with both grandmothers and grandfathers drop off in adolescence. The time requirement was used to establish that the single parent had primary physical custody, and the restrictions on remarriage and cohabiting were used to avoid confounding the effects of divorce on the grandparent-grandchild relationship.

Potential respondents were screened by telephone and a two-hour interview was scheduled with those who qualified and were willing to participate. During the interview, the parent filled out a consent form and completed a set of self-administered questionnaires. The interviewer answered questions about the study, checked for missing and inconsistent responses on the questionnaires, and gave the respondents ten dollars as a token of appreciation for their participation in the study.

Telephone screenings were attempted with 62 single mothers (30 participated; 23 disqualified; 9 refused) and 49 single fathers (30 participated; 18 disqualified; 1 refused). The response rate was calculated by dividing the number of families who refused by the number contacted who qualified. Using this method, the response rates were 77 percent for single mothers and 97 percent for single fathers.

Description of the Instrument

Demographic information on the sample was collected using a questionnaire developed for the study. Age and sex of children, parents and grandparents, and education of parents were reported as individual variables. Marital history, household characteristics, and income were reported as family variables. Income was computed using annual household income from all sources, such as wages, child support, and public assistance.

Amount of contact between grandparents and grandchildren was assessed for each grandparent using one question: "How often does the child visit each of his/her grandparents?" Responses ranged from 1 (rarely or never) to 5 (daily).

The types of activities and overall level of interaction between grandparents and grandchildren were evaluated using a measure developed for the study. Questions were adapted from items previously used by Kennedy (1992). Parents were asked a series of questions about the maternal grandmother and grandfather and the paternal grandmother and grandfather, including which grandparents were alive and deceased, whether a grandparent had no contact with a grandchild and if so, what the reasons were for the lack of interaction. In addition, number of miles each grandparent lived from the family (geographic proximity) was assessed for each living grandparent.

Eleven activities engaged in by grandparents and the focal child were evaluated (see Table 1). How frequently grandparents engaged in each of the activities was assessed separately for each grandparent who was not deceased. A four-point scale ranging from 1 (rarely or never) to 4 (frequently) was used for each question. The types of activities shared by grandparents and grandchildren were evaluated using individual item scores. Overall level of interaction was evaluated by adding the scores on

TABLE 1. Characteristics of the Sample

Variables	Single-Mother Families (n = 30)	Single-Father Families (n = 30)
Individual Variables:		
Age of Parent (mean)	35.6	37.5
Years of Education (mean)	13.3	15.1
Ethnicity		
Anglo-American	93%	86%
African-American	7%	10%
Hispanic	0%	4%
Family Variables:		
Years Married	7.5	6.9
Years Since Divorce/Separation	4.3	3.4
Annual Family Income (median)	$15-20,000	$35-40,000
Household Size	2.9	2.8
Number of Children	1.9	1.8
Age of Children		
Oldest Child	9.3	9.6
Youngest Child	7.5	7.3

each of the 11 items to produce a total score. Reliability and validity of the total score, using Cronbach's alpha coefficient (Cronbach, 1951), was .95.

Analyses

Data on grandparents were collected from the parents who participated in the study. In the case of single-mother families, the maternal grandparents were designated as custodial grandparents and the paternal grandparents were designated noncustodial. In single-father families, the paternal grandparents were considered custodial and the maternal grandparents were considered noncustodial.

Out of the 240 grandparents of the children in the study, 48 were deceased, which resulted in 192 persons whose grandparenting was evaluated. Of these, 15 had little or no contact with their grandchildren. The most frequently cited reason for lack of contact was a poor relationship with the son-in-law or daughter-in-law. Other reasons that were reported included: geographic distance, health of the grandparent, and lack of interest of the parent/grandparent.

For purposes of the analyses grandparents were grouped into eight categories. Four groups consisted of custodial grandparents: single-father custodial grandmothers (n = 28), single-father custodial grandfathers (n = 25), single-mother custodial grandmothers (n = 24), and single-mother custodial grandfathers (n = 23). The remaining four groups consisted of noncustodial grandparents: single-father noncustodial grandmothers (n = 23), single-father noncustodial grandfathers (23), single-mother noncustodial grandmothers (22), and single-mother noncustodial grandfathers (n = 24).

A series of 2 × 2 × 2 analyses of covariance compared custodial/noncustodial grandparents, grandmothers/grandfathers, and grandparents in single-mother/single-father families. In the first analysis, amount of contact was the dependent variable. In the second set of analyses, comparisons were made using grandparent involvement with the focal child in 11 separate activities as dependent variables. The last analysis was run using a total involvement score (summed score over the 11 activities) as the dependent variable. For all analyses, geographic proximity was used as the covariate and a probability level of .05 was used to indicate significance.

RESULTS

Description of the Sample

The sample of single parents was primarily Anglo-American with a small percentage of African-Americans and Hispanics (Table 1). Although this was not a completely random sample, the ethnicity of the respondents was fairly representative of the ethnic composition of individuals living in Nevada when the data were collected in 1994. At that time 84 percent were Anglo-American, 6 percent were African-American, and 10 percent were Hispanic (U.S. Bureau of the Census, 1990).

On average, the single fathers were about two years older than the single mothers and had an additional two years of education. Greater contrasts were found between the two groups in median household income, with single mothers reporting about half the income of the single fathers. The pattern of these findings is consistent with those reported by other researchers regarding single-parent families (Eggebeen, Snyder, & Manning, 1996).

Marital history was similar for the two groups, although both years of marriage and length of time since divorce/separation were slightly higher for the single mothers than for the single fathers. Household characteristics, including household size, number of children, and age of oldest and youngest child were nearly identical for both groups.

Amount of Contact

The covariate, geographic proximity, had a significant effect on the amount of contact between grandparents and their grandchildren. After the effects of the covariate were removed, significant main effects were found between custodial and noncustodial grandparents and between grandmothers and grandfathers (Table 2). Custodial grandparents had more contact than noncustodial grandparents, and grandmothers had more contact than grandfathers. There were no differences in amount of contact for grandparents in single-mother and single-father families, and there were no interaction effects among the variables.

Types of Activities and Level of Involvement

When types of activities and level of involvement were examined, a significant effect was found for the covariate, geographic proximity or how close the grandparent lived to the child, for all activities except "grandparent and child communicate by letters, phone calls or cards" and "grandparent takes child on vacation." After the effects of the covariate were removed, significant main effects were found for comparisons between custodial and noncustodial grandparents, grandmothers and grandfathers, and grandparents in single-mother and single-father families for both the activities, and the overall involvement score (Table 3). The pattern of findings was consistent, and there were no interaction effects in any of the analyses.

For the comparison between custodial and noncustodial grandparents, a significant main effect was found across all 11 activities and in overall involvement. In both single-mother and single-father families, custodial grandparents were significantly more involved than noncustodial grandparents.

The comparison between grandmothers and grandfathers produced a significant main effect for four activities: "Grandparent helps child with personal problems," "Grandparent teaches child a skill . . . ," "Grandparent and child go on outings," and "Grandparent has special treats for the child." For each of these activities, and in overall involvement, grandmothers scored higher than grandfathers.

The comparison between grandparents in single-mother and single-father families produced a significant main effect for four of the activities: "Child stays overnight," "Child helps grandparent with chores," "Grandparent helps child with personal problems," and "Grandparent tells child stories about things that have happened in the family." Grandparents in single-father families engaged in these activities more often and had a

TABLE 2. Means Scores for Amount of Contact, Activities, and Overall Involvement of Grandparents

Variable:	Custodial	Noncustodial	Grandmothers	Grandfathers	Single-Father	Single-Mother
CONTACT	3.02	1.87	2.64	2.24	2.44	2.49
ACTIVITIES						
Child stays overnight	2.40	1.58	2.13	1.85	2.15	1.85
Letters/phone calls	3.07	2.22	2.75	2.54	2.67	2.63
Child helps with chores	2.30	1.38	2.00	1.68	1.98	1.72
Celebrations	3.17	2.03	2.77	2.42	2.62	2.61
Child care	2.28	1.43	2.06	1.63	1.90	1.83
Shared vacations	1.84	1.31	1.65	1.51	1.65	1.52
Help child with problems	2.36	1.36	2.05	1.65	2.06	1.68
Teach child a skill	2.48	1.58	2.21	1.84	2.11	1.97
Shared outings	2.57	1.53	2.26	1.83	2.12	2.00
Special treats for child	2.93	2.06	2.72	2.25	2.51	2.51
Family stories	2.90	1.92	2.58	2.23	2.60	2.24
OVERALL	28.29	18.42	25.18	21.41	24.36	22.55

TABLE 3. Effects of Geographic Proximity, Custody Status of Grandparent, Sex of Grandparent, and Sex of Custodial Parent on Amount of Contact and Activities Shared by Grandparents and Grandchildren

Variable:	Geographic Proximity $F(1, 8)$	Custodial/ Noncustodial $F(1, 8)$	Grandmothers/ Grandfathers $F(1, 8)$	Single-Mother/ Single-Father $F(1, 8)$
AMOUNT OF CONTACT	54.532****	43.953****	4.720*	.335
ACTIVITIES				
Child stays overnight	18.339****	24.807****	2.241	7.817**
Letters/phone calls	3.301	24.503****	1.110	.251
Child helps with chores	9.685**	33.657****	3.359	4.938*
Celebrations	29.298****	44.481****	3.643	.937
Child care	10.387**	28.279****	7.330**	.866
Shared vacations	2.419	13.408****	.548	1.509
Help child with problems	8.169**	41.033****	5.333*	9.164**
Teach child a skill	11.806***	31.813****	4.850*	2.339
Shared outings	9.358**	40.096****	6.371*	1.513
Special treats for child	13.796****	23.467****	6.986**	.294
Family stories	10.765***	32.030****	3.362	7.617**
OVERALL	18.595****	52.640****	6.557*	4.464*

```
   *  p < .05
  **  p < .01
 ***  p < .001
****  p < .000
```
Note: There were no significant interaction effects in any of the analyses

significantly higher overall involvement score than grandparents in single-mother families.

DISCUSSION

As expected, living close to a grandchild affected amount of contact and limited all activities except communicating by letter, phone calls, and cards, and taking vacations together. However, after adjusting for the distance grandparents lived from their grandchildren, significant differences still were found for each of the factors examined in the study. Overall, grandparents maintained greater contact when they lived close to their grandchildren, had custodial status, and were grandmothers. Grand-parents were more involved with their grandchildren when they lived close-by, had custodial status, were grandmothers, and their grandchildren lived in a single-father family.

Probably the most striking finding was that custodial grandparents were more involved than noncustodial grandparents across all activities, even after adjusting for the covariate. This finding challenges earlier allegations that grandparent involvement is linked to maternal/paternal kin position and supports the previously untested observation that custody status is the more relevant variable.

Grandmothers were more involved than grandfathers in child care, help with personal problems, teaching skills, going on outings, and providing treats, but there were no differences between grandmothers and grandfa-thers in staying overnight, communicating, sharing chores, celebrating holidays, taking vacations, or telling family stories. Although the pattern for greater involvement by grandmothers than grandfathers is not surpris-ing, it is important to recognize that these differences were limited to five activities. It is noteworthy that grandfathers are just as involved as grand-mothers with over half of the activities and that they engage in both instrumental and expressive types of interactions. This supports previous findings that grandfathers are involved, take their role seriously, and par-ticipate in both instrumental and expressive activities (Baranowski, 1990; Thomas, 1986).

Because so little research has been done on grandparenting in single-parent families, and comparisons between custodial single-mother and single-father families have not been done, the types of activities engaged in by grandparents in these families were of particular interest. Grandpar-ents in single-father families were more involved than grandparents in single-mother families in staying overnight, sharing chores, helping with personal problems, and telling family stories. There were no differences in communicating, celebrating holidays, providing child care, taking vaca-tions, teaching skills, going on outings, or providing treats. These findings indicate that there is not much difference in grandparent involvement for most activities among single-mother and single-father families. The differ-ences that do exist favor greater involvement by grandparents in single-fa-ther rather than single-mother families.

The findings of this study challenge many of the assumptions that have driven previous research on the grandparent role, especially those based on gender stereotypes. For example, one assumption has been that tradi-tional differences in gender roles would be expected to carry over to grandparenting from the parenting role and that men and women will function as grandparents much as they did as parents earlier in adulthood (Baranowski, 1985; Kivett, 1991). Based on this assumption, activities of grandparents are commonly categorized as instrumental (male) or expressive (female) in nature (Hagestad, 1985; Cherlin & Furstenberg, 1986). Women are assumed to function as kin-keepers, forging stronger bonds among their own bloodline, which allows maternal grandparents to have closer ties to grandchildren than paternal grandparents (Eisenberg, 1988; Hagestad, 1985).

An alternative view might be that the demands on grandparents are different than those on parents and the context within which grandparents function is very diverse. This is especially true when parents divorce; grandparents' roles are affected dramatically. They may be called upon to provide support to the family at levels that would have been considered interference prior to the divorce.

The results of this study support this view. Our research concurs with an ever-increasing body of knowledge showing decreased relations between *paternal* grandparents and grandchildren following divorce . . . when mothers have custody. When fathers have custody *maternal* grandparents are less involved. There is no support for previous claims that paternal grandparents are less involved because women maintain a unique role as intergenerational kin-keepers, leading to more involvement from grandmothers and maternal grandparents than grandfathers and paternal grandparents.

In fact, there was no evidence in the findings of this study to suggest that gender dominates grandparent involvement in any way. Instead, it appears to be the context in which grandparenting occurs that is the critical element shaping interactions with grandchildren. The importance of considering context was underscored by the finding that paternal grandparents are not disengaged or disinterested . . . they are disadvantaged by a legal system that disproportionately awards custody to mothers.

The assumptions that have driven research also have shaped grandparents' legal rights following divorce and promoted inequities in the law. The need for this issue to be addressed is evident in the growing number of grandparents' rights groups that have successfully pushed for the right to continue a relationship with grandchildren following divorce.

Currently all 50 states have some form of grandparent rights legislation. The main consideration in determining how these rights will be implemented is reported to be the best interests of the child. In reality, parental rights prevail. For example, if a divorced parent has had parental rights terminated or gives up a child for adoption, grandparent rights are terminated, too (McCrimmon & Howell, 1989). Activists are currently stressing the need for grandparents' rights to be independent of those of parents. This study documents that noncustodial grandparents are disadvantaged by the current system, which compromises the rights of both grandparents and grandchildren.

When grandparents are denied visitation, grandchildren lose the nurturance, leniency, and historical context that can only be provided by a grandparent. Grandparents, in turn, often experience dissatisfaction and difficulty in resolving developmental issues related to the void created by severed family relationships. These findings can be used to identify grandparents and grandchildren most at risk for this type of loss. For example, if after the marital separation, grandfathers are more likely to lose contact with grandchildren than grandmothers, and if noncustodial grandparents interact less with grandchildren than custodial grandparents, the relationship between grandchildren and noncustodial grandfathers may be particularly vulnerable.

Similarly, an understanding of the activities associated with each type of grandparent-grandchild relationship is critical for an accurate assessment of the frequency and quality of the particular intergenerational bond. It is hardly fair to measure a grandfather-grandchild relationship by asking about activities typical of a grandmother-grandchild relationship, or to evaluate the role of paternal grandparents without considering custody status.

Marriage and family therapists, grandparents' rights advocates, family mediation specialists and others working with families in transition need to be cognizant of the wealth of potential resources available through grandparents as well as the potential difficulties for all parties concerned if contact with grandparents is denied. Increased knowledge of the roles associated with various grandparent-grandchild relationships as well as an understanding of the changes in grandparenting following divorce can help these professionals optimally serve clients. Documenting the implications of loss of contact between grandparents and grandchildren following divorce provides family professionals with objective data to guide their efforts to reduce intergenerational conflict during this troubled time.

Practicing family lawyers can also benefit from this information. Grandparents' rights laws have served the dual purpose of providing a framework for both legal and out-of-court resolutions. In other words, in addition to the power of the actual law, the mere existence of legislation protecting grandparents' rights provides this population with a tool to strengthen their position during family negotiations. While the "best interests of the child" are still of paramount consideration when determining visitation rights, parents are most likely to try to avoid an additional lawsuit during this time of economic and emotional upheaval, preferring to work out a mutually agreeable solution out of court (Thompson et al., 1991). Stressing the legal position of grandparents while pointing out the negative effects that decreased contact with the noncustodial grandparents might have on grandchildren may help the parents see the salience of considering grandparents' visitation rights during the divorce process.

One of the problems in studying the contributions of grandparents following divorce is the tremendous amount of diversity in how grandparents perceive and carry out their roles. Although researchers have tried to define and conceptualize the grandparent role using typologies (Neugarten & Weinstein, 1964; Robertson, 1976; Kivnick, 1983; Cherlin & Furstenberg, 1986), the most current research indicates that the grandparent role is complex, depending on numerous factors, including the unique characteristics of the individuals involved (Sanders & Trygstad, 1993). Although this study contributes to a greater understanding of some of these complexities, limitations of the study need to be addressed in future research.

One of the main limitations is the size of the sample, which was restricted by the difficulty in finding divorced fathers with primary custody of a school-aged child, living independently from other adults. Although such families are relatively scarce, their numbers are growing rapidly and data from these families is invaluable in helping to sort out the effects of gender and custody status on intergenerational relationships in single-parent families.

Another limitation that will be easier to resolve in future research is the need to collect data on grandparents from multiple sources, including both grandparents and grandchildren. As indicated in earlier studies, there may be strong generational effects on perceptions of role behavior. By gathering data from each generation, a clearer picture of the role of grandparents and its relevance to each generation should emerge.

Finally, data were collected in a single state. Larger studies that are nationally representative and include longitudinal data are needed. Divorce is a life transition. Tracking changes in grandparent/grandchild relationships over time and examining how these changes evolve in divorced and intact families would provide a major breakthrough in reconceptualizing the role of grandparents.

REFERENCES

Ahrons, C. R., & Bowman, M. E. (1982). Changes in family relationships following divorce of adult child: Grandmother's perceptions. *Journal of Divorce, 5,* 49-68.

Baranowski, M. D. (1985). Men as grandfathers. In S. M. H. Hanson & F. W. Bozett (Eds.), *Dimensions of fatherhood* (pp. 217-238). Beverly Hills, CA: Sage Pub.

Baranowski, M. D. (1990). The grandfathers-grandchild relationship: Meaning and exchange. *Family Perspective, 24,* 201-215.

Barranti, C. C. R. (1985). The grandparent/grandchild relationship: Family resource in an era of voluntary bonds. *Family Relations, 34,* 343-352.

Blau, T. H. (1984). An evaluative study of the role of the grandparent in the best interests of the child. *American Journal of Family Therapy, 12,* 46-50.

Cherlin, A., & Furstenberg, F. (1986). *American grandparenthood.* New York: Basic Books.

Clingempeel, Colyar, Brand, & Hetherington. (1992). Children's relationships with maternal grandparents: A longitudinal study of family structure and pubertal status effect. *Child Development, 63,* 1404-1422.

Conroy, D. B., & Fahey, C. J. (1985). Christian perspective on the role of grandparents. In V. L. Bengtson & J. F. Robertson (Eds.), *Grandparenthood* (pp. 195-207). Beverly Hills: Sage Pub.

Creasey, G. L. (1993). The association between divorce and late adolescent grandchildren's relations with grandparents. *Journal of Youth and Adolescence, 22,* 513-529.

Cronbach, L. J. (1951). Coefficient alpha and the internal structure of tests. *Psychometrika, 16,* 297-334.

Derdeyn, P. P. (1985). Grandparent visitation rights: Rendering family dissension more pronounced? *American Journal of Orthopsychiatry, 55,* 277-287.

Eggebeen, D. J., Snyder, A. R., & Manning, W. D. (1996). Children in single-father families in demographic perspective. *Journal of Family Issues, 17,* 441-465.

Eisenberg, A. R. (1988). Grandchildren's perspectives on relationships with grandparents: The influence of gender across generations. *Sex Roles, 19,* 205-217.

Gladstone, J. W. (1987). Factors associated with changes in visiting between grandmothers and grandchildren following an adult child's marriage breakdown. *Canadian Journal on Aging, 6,* 117-127.

Gladstone, J. W. (1991). An analysis of changes in grandparent-grandchild visitation following an adult child's remarriage. *Canadian Journal on Aging, 10,* 113-126.

Hagestad, G. O., & Speicher, J. L. (1981, April). *Grandparents and family influence: Views of three generations.* Paper presented at the annual meeting of the Society for Research in Child Development, Boston, MA.

Hagestad, G. O. (1985). Continuity and connectedness. In V. Bengston & J. Robertson (Eds.), *Grandparenthood* (pp. 31-48). Beverly Hills, CA: Sage Pub.

Hanson, S. M. (1986). Father-child relationships: Beyond Kramer vs. Kramer. *Marriage & Family Review, 9,* 135-149.

Johnson, C. L. (1983). A cultural analysis of the grandmothers. *Research on Aging, 5,* 547-567.

Johnson, C. L. (1988). Active and latent functions of grandparenting during the divorce process. *The Gerontologist, 28,* 185-191.

Johnson, C. L., & Barer, B. M. (1987). Marital instability and the changing kinship networks of grandparents. *The Gerontologist, 27,* 330-335.

Kennedy, G. E. (1990). College students' expectations of grandparent and grandchild role behaviors. *The Gerontologist, 30,* 43-48.

Kennedy, G. E. (1992). Shared activities of grandparents and grandchildren. *Psychological Reports, 70,* 211-227.

Kennedy, G. E., & Kennedy, C. E. (1993). Grandparents: A special resource for children in stepfamilies. *Journal of Divorce & Remarriage, 19,* 45-68.

Kivett, V. R. (1985). Grandfathers and grandchildren: Patterns of association, helping, and psychological closeness. *Family Relations, 34,* 565-571.

Kivett, V. R. (1991). The grandparent-grandchild connection. In Susan Pfeifer and Marvin Sussman (Eds.), *Families: Intergenerational and generational connections* (pp. 267-289). New York: The Haworth Press, Inc.

Kivnick, H. Q. (1983). Dimensions of grandparenthood meaning: Deductive conceptualization and empirical derivation. *Journal of Personality and Social Psychology, 44,* 1056-1068.

Kornhaber, A., & Woodward, K. (1981). *Grandparents/grandchildren: The vital connection.* Garden City, NY: Anchor Press/Doubleday.

Kruk, E., & Hall, B. L. (1995). The disengagement of paternal grandparents subsequent to divorce. *Journal of Divorce & Remarriage, 23,* 131-147.

Matthews, S. H., & Sprey, J. (1984). The impact of divorce on grandparenthood: An exploratory study. *The Gerontologist, 24,* 41-47.

McCrimmon, C. A., & Howell, R. J. (1989). Grandparents' legal rights to visitation in the fifty states and the District of Columbia. *Bulletin of American Academic Psychiatry Law, 17,* 355-366.

Myers, J. E., & Perrin, N. (1993). Grandparents affected by parental divorce: A population at risk? *Journal of Counseling and Development, 72,* 62-66.

Nahemow, N. (1985). The changing nature of grandparenthood. *Medical Aspects of Human Sexuality, 19,* 81-92.

Neugarten, B.L., & Weinstein, K. K. (1964). The changing American grandparent. *Journal of Marriage and the Family, 26,* 199-204.

Robertson, J. F. (1976). Significance of grandparents: Perceptions of young adult grandchildren. *The Gerontologist, 16,* 137-140.

Sanders, G. F., & Trygstad, D. W. (1993). Strengths in the grandparent/grandchild relationship. *Activities Adaptation & Aging, 17* (4), 43-53.

Thomas, J. L., & Datan, N. (1982, November). *Grandparenting and change.* Paper presented at the 35th Annual Scientific Meeting of the Gerontological Society of America, Boston, MA.

Thomas, J. L. (1986). Age and sex differences in perceptions of grandparenting. *Journal of Gerontology, 41,* 417-423.

Thompson, R. A., Scalora, M. J., Limber, S. P., & Castrianno, L. (1991). Grandparent visitation rights: A psycholegal analysis. *Family and Conciliation Courts Review, 29,* 9-25.

U.S. Bureau of the Census. (1990). *General population characteristics, 1960-1990; Census of population and housing, summary population and housing characteristics, Nevada.* Washington, DC: U.S. Government Printing Office.

Wallerstein, J. S. (1986). Child of divorce: An overview. *Behavioral Science and the Law, 4,* 105-118.

Wilcoxon, S. A. (1987). Grandparents and grandchildren: An often neglected relationship between significant others. *Journal of Counseling and Development, 65,* 289-290.

Williams, F. S. (1986). A father's post-divorce struggle for parental identity. In J. W. Jacobs (Ed.), *Divorce and fatherhood.* Los Angeles: American Psychiatric Press.

Index

Note: Page numbers followed by *f* indicate figures; page numbers followed by *t* indicate tables.

Access denial
 analysis of, 49-60. *See also under*
  Non-custodial parents
 "parentectomization" of, 51
Adaptability, lack of, anger effects
  on, 158,162
Adolescence, acceptance of lesbian
  family identity during,
  190-194,192t-193t
Age, as factor in changes in child
  custody arrangement, 26
Ahrons, C.R., 80,91
Ainsworth, M.D., 122
Allen, K.R., 180-181
Amata, P.R., 132
Anger, in divorced women, 157-168.
  See also Custodial parents,
  mothers, state-anger in
Apartments, children living in,
  following divorce, 28
Arditti, J.A., 82-83
Arendell, T., 91

Babcock, G., 140
Behavioral problems, in boys *versus*
  girls, judges' beliefs
  regarding, 12
Bender, W.N., 123
*Beyond the Best Interests of the
 Child,* 5
Blumer, H., 79-80

Bottoms v. Bottoms, 173
Bowlby, J., 121,122
Bowlby's (1969) theory of
  attachment, 121
Bozett, F.W., 195
Brennan, K.A., 132
Broken loop, 152
Buchanan, C.M., 30
Burke, P., 152,153
Burton, L.M., 82

Careau, L., 21
Chauncy, J., 84
Cherlin, A., 90-91
Child adjustment, parental conflict
  and various behavioral,
  psychological and social
  indicators of, correlation
  between, 50
Child custody
 decisions related to, 3-14. *See
  also under* Judge(s), beliefs
  related to child custody
  decisions
 as factor in satisfaction in
  relationship, 119-133
 to fathers, 119-133
 to gay fathers, stigma related to,
  171-181. *See also* Lesbian
  mothers, in custody cases,
  stigma related to
 joint custody, 17, 18

225

early experience with, 5
judges' beliefs regarding, 13
mobility of, factors affecting,
    29-30
study of, 24t,25,25t,27-28
laws related to, changes in, 4
to lesbian mothers, stigma related
    to, 171-181. *See also*
    Lesbian mothers, in custody
    cases, stigma related to
living arrangements related to, types
    of, 17. *See also* Residential
    custody arrangements, in
    separated families
maternal. *See under* Mother(s)
mother *versus* father
    discussion of, 123
    problem statement related to,
        123-124
    study of
        discussion, 131-133
        instruments in, 125-126
        method, 124-126,124t
        participants in, 124-125,
            124t
        procedure, 126
        results, 126-131,128t-130t
mother's ability to nurture child
    effect on, 4
non-custodial parents, access
    denied to, 49-60. *See also*
    under Non-custodial
    parents
same sex, judges' beliefs
    regarding, 11-12
sole custody by father, 17,18
sole custody by mother, 17,18
stability of, study of, 29-30
Child support
    and access to children,
        relationship between, 51-52
    monies paid for, 78
Child support guidelines
    legislation for, 65-67
    in New Hampshire, 63-74

adherence to, 68-69,69t
alternatives to, 72-73
amending of, attorneys'
    opinions concerning,
    70-71,71t
deviation from
    divorcing parties' request to
        attorneys for, 70,
        70t
    empirical studies related to,
        67
    reasons for, 69-70
initiative for, 64
legislation for, 66-67
outcome of, 73
research on, objective of,
    64-65
Senate Bill 648, 64
study of
    discussion, 71-72
    implications for future
        initiatives, 73-74
    methods, 67-68
    results, 68-71,69t-71t
Child support payment, visitation by
    non-custodial parent and,
    judges' beliefs regarding,
    14
Children Cope With Divorce
    (CCWD), 35-47
    aim of, 36
    described, 36-37
    effectiveness of, judges' views of,
        45-47,45t
    National Survey of Judges, 39t
    1996 survey of referring judges
        of, 40-45
        judge sample in, 41,42t
        judges' views of, 45-47,45t
        methods, 40
        representativeness of sample
            in, 41-45,43t,44t
    non-profit agencies running, 37
    number of persons yearly who
        attend, 36

Children Cope With Divorce
(CCWD) model, 37-38,37t
Children Cope With Divorce
(CCWD) provider network,
38-40,39t
Cloutier, R., 19,21,23,29
Coalition for Children's Access to
Parents (C-CAP), 52
Collins, N.L., 122
Comprehensive Child Development
Project (1996), 83-84
Constant comparative method, 144
Continuity hypothesis, 91-92
Custodial parents
fathers
effect on nonresidential
mother, 139-154. *See also*
Mother(s), nonresidential
prevalence of, 140
gender of, as factor in grandparent
contact following divorce,
208,210-211
mothers
attributions of responsibility
for divorce in, 162
state-anger in, 157-168
adaptability affected by,
158-159
attribution of responsibility
to ex-spouse due
to, 159
causes of, 158
child's adjustment affected
by, 158
effects of, 158-168
and postdivorce adjustment,
165-166
self-esteem affected by,
158,162
study of, 160-163
discussion, 165-168
interventive
implications, 168
measures in, 161-162
method, 160-163

procedure, 163
research implications,
167-168
results, 163-165
sample in, 160-161
theoretical implications,
166-167
time spent with children, 120-121

Datan, N., 209
Davis, K.E., 133
Day care, for children of employed
mothers, judges' beliefs
regarding, 11
Demo, D.H., 180-181
Depner, C.E., 21
Depression, among non-custodial
parents, 140
Discontinuity hypothesis, 92
described, 89
Divorce
anger following, in women,
157-168. *See also* Custodial
parents, mothers,
state-anger in
children coping with, judges'
views of, 45-47,45t
effects on children, 49-50,
120-122
"emotional," described, 160
family disruption due to,
described, 120
grandparent involvement
following, 203-221. *See
also under* Grandparent(s),
involvement following
divorce
in Greece, maternal and paternal
accounts of, 89-110. *See
also* Non-custodial parents,
fathers, disengagement
from children's lives, Greek
study
negative effects of, 36

parent-child interactions
    following, 120
prevalence of, 36,120
quality of relationship between
    ex-spouses following, as
    predictor of father's role,
    91
sexual misconduct prior to,
    judges' beliefs regarding,
    13-14
Divorcing parents, educational
    seminar for, impact of,
    35-47. *See also Children
    Cope With Divorce
    (CCWD)*
Dornbusch, S.M., 30
Drolet, J., 19,21,23,29
Duffy, M.E., 120

Education, of child, non-custodial
    father's impact on, 83-84
Educational seminar, for divorcing
    parents, impact of, 35-47. *See
    also Children Cope With
    Divorce (CCWD)*
Electronic Fund Transfer (EFT)
    program, 52-53
Emery, R.E., 132
"Emotional divorce," described, 160
Emotional support, by non-custodial
    fathers, 83-84
    factors affecting, 78-79

Families First, in *Children Cope With
    Divorce,* 36-37
Family Adaptability and Cohesion
    Evaluation Scale (FACES),
    162
Family disruption, divorce and,
    described, 120
Family Support Act of 1988, 65-66
Family systems theory, 80

Father(s)
    child custody to, 119-133
    child's obedience to, judges'
        beliefs regarding, 13
    custodial
        prevalence of, 140
        study of, 23,24t,25t,27
    non-custodial, 77-87. *See also*
        Non-custodial parents,
        fathers access denied to,
        49-60. *See also under*
        Non-custodial parents,
        access denied to
    sole custody by, 17,18
Ferguson, R., 55
Financial support, by non-custodial
    fathers, factors affecting,
    78-79
Fisher, D.C., 154
Fisher's Exact Test, 102,106
Forehand, R., 131-132,133
Freud, A., 5
Furstenberg, F.F., Jr., 90,91,92

Gays, in custody cases, stigma
    related to, 171-181. *See
    also* Lesbian mothers, in
    custody cases, stigma
    related to
Gender
    anger and, 166
    as factor in changes in child
        custody arrangement, 26
    of grandparents, as factor in
        contact following divorce,
        205-206,209-210
Geographic location, as factor in
    grandparent contact
    following divorce, 205,
    209
Glenn, E., 141
Goffman, E., 171,172
Goldstein, J., 5
Golombok, S., 189

Grandparent(s)
  gender of, as factor in contact
    following divorce,
    205-206,209-210
  and grandchildren, relationship
    between, 204
  involvement following divorce,
    203-221
    factors influencing amount of
      contact with grandchildren,
      205-208
    gender as factor in, 205-206,
      209-210
    gender of custodial parent as
      factor in, 208, 210-211
    geographic proximity and,
      205,209
    influence of, 204
    kin position of parents and
      grandparents as factor in,
      206-207,210
    study of
      analyses, 213-214
      description of instrument,
        212-213,213t
      discussion, 217-221
      methods, 211-214
      results, 214-217,216t,217t
      sample in, 211-212
    support offered by, 204
Greece, divorce in, maternal and
    paternal accounts of,
    89-110. *See also*
    Non-custodial parents,
    fathers, disengagement
    from children's lives, Greek
    study

Hall, B.L., 207
Hazan, C., 122,126
Hendricks, L.E., 84
Herek, G.M., 175
Hetherington, E.M., 92,120-121

House Judiciary and Family Law
    Committee, in New
    Hampshire, 64-65
Huggins, S.L., 198

Identity salience, described, 149
Identity standard, described,
    149-153,151f
Identity theory formula, 149-153,
    151f

Johnson, E.H., 166
Johnston, J.R., 19
Joint custody, 17,18
  early experience with, 5
  judges' beliefs regarding, 13
  mobility of, factors affecting,
    29-30
  study of, 24t,25,25t,27-28
Judge(s), beliefs related to child
    custody decisions, 3-14
  behavioral problems in boys
    versus girls, 12
  "best interests of child" standard
    in, 4
  changes in, 4-5
  day care for children, 11
  effects of, 14
  joint custody, 13
    early experience with, 5
  latitude in, 6
  in Louisiana study, 6-7
    discussion, 10-14
    materials in, 8
    methods, 7-9
    procedure, 8-9
    results, 9-10
    subjects in, 7-8
  maternal custody, 5-6
  maternal employment, 11
  mother's ability to nurture child
    in, 4
  obedience of children to mothers
    versus fathers, 13

remarriage, 12
same sex custody, 11-12
sexual misconduct prior to
    divorce, 13-14

Keith, B., 132
Kelly, J.B., 92,121
Kelly, M., 82-83
Kennedy, G.E., 209,212
Kin position, as factor in grandparent
    contact following divorce,
    206-207,210
Kirkpatrick, L.A., 133
Kivett, V.R., 205
Kline, M., 19, 29
Kornhauser, L., 14
Kruk, E., 89-110,207
Kunen, S., 6,9

Lawyer, R., 6,9
Legislation, child support, federal,
    65-67
Lesbian family, living in, young
    people's attitudes toward,
    183-200. *See also* Lesbian
    mothers, post-divorce,
    children raised by, study of
Lesbian mothers
    in custody cases, stigma related
        to, 171-181
    study of, 175-177
        discussion, 178-180
        measurement in, 176-177
        procedure, 176
        recommendations, 180-181
        results, 177-178
        sample in, 175-176
    post-divorce
        acceptance of, study of, during
            adolescence,
            190-194,192t-193t
        children raised by, study of,
            183-200

discussion, 194-200
follow-up study, 188-190
initial study, 188
measures in, 188-190
methods, 186-190
results, 190-194,192t-193t
subjects in, 186-188
family identity in, acceptance
    of, 190
in adulthood, 194,196t-197t
well-being of, study of, 185-186
Lewis, K.G., 185,189
Loneliness, of non-custodial parents,
    140
Louisiana, judges' beliefs dealing
    with custody issues in,
    3-14. *See also* Judge(s),
    beliefs related to child
    custody decisions, in
    Louisiana study

Maccoby, E.E., 21,30
Majchrzak, A., 74
Maternal. *See under* Mother(s)
Matthews, S.H., 207
McAdoo, 84
Miller, R.B., 80
Milton, C., 82
Mnookin, R.H., 14,21
Mother(s)
    child's obedience to, judges'
        beliefs regarding, 13
    custodial
        judges' beliefs regarding, 5-6
        study of, 23,24t,25,25t,27
        time spent with children,
            120-121
    employed, judges' beliefs
        regarding, 11
    "natural superiority" of, in child
        custody decision-making, 4
    nonresidential, 139-154
        distress among, 141
        identity dissonance in,
            139-154

motherhood in, 141
role altering behaviors of,
    148-149
study of
    discussion, 147-149
    identity model in, 149-153,
        151f
    measurement in, 143-144
    method, 141-144
    recommendations related
        to, 153-154
    results, 144-147
    sample in, 142-143
    unacceptance of, 140
nurturing ability of, in child
    custody decision-making, 4
sole custody by, 17,18
Motherhood, societal expectations
    and ideological trappings
    associated with, 140-141

National Center on Fathers and
    Fathering (1996), 83
National Jobs for All Coalition
    (1996), 84
National Survey of Children, 90
National Survey of Families and
    Households, 90
New Hampshire, child support
    guidelines in, 63-74. *See
    also* Child support
    guidelines, in New
    Hampshire
New Hampshire Child Support Study
    Committee (1995), 64
New Hampshire Revised Statutes
    Annotated (RSA), 66-67
Newman, K.S., 84
1989 New Hampshire Child Support
    Guidelines, 66-67
Non-custodial parents
    access denied to, 49-60
        effects on children, 50

social/psychological effects of,
    51
study of
    findings, 55-59,58t
    methods, 52-53
    sample in, 53-55,56t
fathers, 77-87
contact with children, 90
described, 78
disengagement from children's
    lives, Greek study, 89-110
assessment of paternal
    relationship with children
    pre- and post-divorce by
    current contact, 114t-117t
data collection and
        measures in, 95,
        101
demographic
        characteristics,
        95-96
demographic
        characteristics,
        101-102,103t
discussion, 100,103t,
    107-110
factors after divorce, 99,
    103t,106-107
factors during divorce,
    98-99,103t,106
fathers' emotional
        attachment to
        children before
        separation, 103t,
        105
father's influence on their
        children's
        development
        before separation,
        103t,105
involvement in domestic
        activities, 103t,
        104
involvement in infant care,
        102,103t,104

method, 93-95,100-101
paternal role ideologies,
        105-106
pre-divorce factors, 96-98,
        97t,102-106,103t
results, 95-99,97t,101-107
sample in, 93-95,100-101
statistical design, 95-96,
        101-102,103t
weekly hours of contact
        between father
        and child before
        divorce, 103t,
        104-105
disengagement of, 90-93
effect on educational
        well-being of child, 83-84
effect on psychological
        well-being of child, 83-84
emotional support by, factors
        affecting, 78-79
financial support by, factors
        affecting, 78-79
guilt and self-blame effects on,
        81
impediments experienced by,
        78
involvement of, impact on
        minor children, 83-84
lack of involvement of, 78
models of, development of,
        79-81
new family formation effects
        on, 80
and one-parent family, 81-83
percentage of, 89
perceptions of roles and
        responsibilities by, 79-80
provider/caretaker role of,
        79-80
theoretical frameworks in,
        79-81
unemployment effects on, 79
financial responsibilities of, 50

financial support provided by, and
        access to children,
        relationship between, 51-52
growing interest in, 78
relationships of, nature of, 141
suffering, loneliness, and
        depression among, 140
visitation by, as factor in child
        support payment, judges'
        beliefs regarding, 14
Non-traditional postdivorce
        heterosexual families,
        family identity in,
        acceptance of, 190

Obedience, to mothers *versus*
        fathers, judges' beliefs
        regarding, 13
One-parent family
        non-custodial fathers and, 81-83
        percentage of, 90
One-parent family(ies). *See also
        under* Father(s); Joint
        custody; Mother(s);
        Non-custodial parents
        children in, prevalence of, 78
Open coding, 144

Parent Satisfaction Scale, 146
Parent-child relationship
        following divorce, 120
        same-sex custody as factor in, 19
"Parentectomize," described, 51
Pasley, K., 82
Personal Assessment of Intimacy in
        Relationships Inventory
        (PAIR), 125,126
Peters, M., 84
Post-divorce adjustment, anger and,
        165-166
Psychological well-being, of child,
        non-custodial father's
        impact on, 83-84

Ray, M., 69
Read, S.J., 122
Rein, M., 64
Reitzes, D., 153
Relationship Beliefs Inventory
    (RBI), 125,126
Remarriage, judges' beliefs
    regarding, 12
Residential custody arrangements
    in separated families
    apartment living, 28
    changes in, direction of, 27-28
    changes in over time, 19
    evolution of, 17-31
    importance of regular contact
        with both parents, 18-19
    stability of custody, 29-30
    study of
        apartment living, 28
        changes as function of
            original custody
            arrangement,
            22-27,24t,25t
        changes by younger
            children and girls,
            30-31
        changes in custody
            arrangements,
            direction of, 27-28
        custodial father, 23,24t,
            25t,27
        custodial mothers, 23,24t,
            25,25t,27
        discussion, 28-31
        distribution of children
            according to
            custody
            arrangement at T1
            and T2, 22,24t,25t
        gender as factor in changes
            in, 26
        joint custody, 24t,25,25t,
            27-28
        method, 20-22
        questionnaire in, 22

results, 22-28,24t,25t
stability of custody, 29-30
subjects in, 21
types of, 17,18
Responsibility, parental attributions
    of, following divorce, 162
Role identity(ies), 149-153,151f
Romantic relationships, attachment
    style in, 122
Rosen, K.S., 132
Rothbaum, F., 132

Same sex custody
    as factor in quality of parent-child
        relationship, 19
    judges' beliefs regarding, 11-12
Santrock, J.W., 30
Self-esteem, in divorced women,
    anger effects on, 158,162
Seltzer, J., 55
Senate Bill (SB) 648, in New
        Hampshire Legislature, 64
    voting history of, 64
Sexual misconduct, prior to divorce,
        judges' beliefs regarding,
        13-14
"Shared meaning," 50
Shaver, P.A., 122,126,132
Simpson, J.A., 122
Solnit, A., 5
Sprey, J., 207
Stamps, L.E., 6,9
Stanford Child Custody Project, 55
State-anger
    described, 159
    in divorced women, 157-168. *See
        also* Custodial parents,
        mothers, state-anger in
State-Trait Anger Expression
        Inventory (STAXI),
        161-162
Stigma
    in custody cases, described,
        172-175
    defined, 172

"Strange Situation" Test, 122

Tasker, F., 189
"Tender years doctrine," in child
        custody decision-making, 4
"The best interests of child"
        standard, in child custody
        decision-making, 4
Thomas, J.L., 209
Tschann, J.M., 19

Unemployment, as factor in father's
        role as non-custodial
        parent, 79

Visitation rights, of non-custodial
        parent, as factor in child
        support payment, judges'
        beliefs regarding, 14

Wallerstein, J.S., 19,92,121
Warshak, R.A., 30,123
Weitzman, L.J., 19

Zaslow, M.J., 123

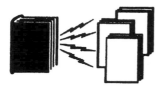 Haworth
DOCUMENT DELIVERY
SERVICE

This valuable service provides a single-article order form for any article from a Haworth journal.

- *Time Saving:* No running around from library to library to find a specific article.
- *Cost Effective:* All costs are kept down to a minimum.
- *Fast Delivery:* Choose from several options, including same-day FAX.
- *No Copyright Hassles:* You will be supplied by the original publisher.
- *Easy Payment:* Choose from several easy payment methods.

Open Accounts Welcome for . . .
- Library Interlibrary Loan Departments
- Library Network/Consortia Wishing to Provide Single-Article Services
- Indexing/Abstracting Services with Single Article Provision Services
- Document Provision Brokers and Freelance Information Service Providers

---

MAIL or *FAX* THIS ENTIRE ORDER FORM TO:

Haworth Document Delivery Service | **or FAX:** 1-800-895-0582
The Haworth Press, Inc. | **or CALL:** 1-800-342-9678
10 Alice Street | 9am-5pm EST
Binghamton, NY 13904-1580 |

PLEASE SEND ME PHOTOCOPIES OF THE FOLLOWING SINGLE ARTICLES:

1) Journal Title: _____
   Vol/Issue/Year:_____ Starting & Ending Pages:_____
   Article Title:_____

2) Journal Title: _____
   Vol/Issue/Year:_____ Starting & Ending Pages:_____
   Article Title:_____

3) Journal Title: _____
   Vol/Issue/Year:_____ Starting & Ending Pages:_____
   Article Title:_____

4) Journal Title: _____
   Vol/Issue/Year:_____ Starting & Ending Pages:_____
   Article Title:_____

(See other side for Costs and Payment Information)

COSTS: Please figure your cost to order quality copies of an article.

1. Set-up charge per article: $8.00
   ($8.00 × number of separate articles) _____

2. Photocopying charge for each article:
   1-10 pages: $1.00 _____

   11-19 pages: $3.00 _____

   20-29 pages: $5.00 _____

   30+ pages: $2.00/10 pages _____

3. Flexicover (optional): $2.00/article _____

4. Postage & Handling: US: $1.00 for the first article/
   $.50 each additional article _____

   Federal Express: $25.00 _____

   Outside US: $2.00 for first article/
   $.50 each additional article _____

5. Same-day FAX service: $.35 per page _____

GRAND TOTAL: _____

METHOD OF PAYMENT: (please check one)

❑ Check enclosed ❑ Please ship and bill. PO # _____
   (sorry we can ship and bill to bookstores only! All others must pre-pay)

❑ Charge to my credit card: ❑ Visa; ❑ MasterCard; ❑ Discover;
   ❑ American Express;

Account Number: _____ Expiration date: _____

Signature: ✗ _____

Name: _____ Institution: _____

Address: _____

_____

City: _____ State: _____ Zip: _____

Phone Number: _____ FAX Number: _____

MAIL or *FAX* THIS ENTIRE ORDER FORM TO:

Haworth Document Delivery Service	**or FAX:** 1-800-895-0582
The Haworth Press, Inc.	**or CALL:** 1-800-342-9678
10 Alice Street	9am-5pm EST)
Binghamton, NY 13904-1580	